First edition; first printing in 2024

Copyright © 2024 Martina & Hans Thörn Durefelt Helförlag

ISBN 978-91-86889-16-6

www.hansmartinatwinflames.com

INTRODUCTION P. 5

PART 1

Chapter 1
THE STRUCTURE OF THE ZODIAC P. 13

PART 2

Chapter 2
THE ASCENDANT & THE SUN
IN THE BIRTH CHART P. 31

Chapter 3
THE ASCENDANT & ITS DEEPER
MEANING FOR OUR SOUL P. 35

PART 3

Chapter 4
ARIES IN THE ASCENDANT P. 51

Chapter 5
TAURUS IN THE ASCENDANT P. 74

Chapter 6
GEMINI IN THE ASCENDANT P. 97

Chapter 7
CANCER IN THE ASCENDANT P. 121

Chapter 8
LEO IN THE ASCENDANT P. 146

Chapter 9
VIRGO IN THE ASCENDANT P. 170

Chapter 10
LIBRA IN THE ASCENDANT P. 195

Chapter 11
SCORPIO IN THE ASCENDANT P. 220

Chapter 12
SAGITTARIUS IN THE ASCENDANT P. 245

Chapter 13
CAPRICORN IN THE ASCENDANT P. 269

Chapter 14
AQUARIUS IN THE ASCENDANT P. 293

Chapter 15
PISCES IN THE ASCENDANT P. 317

PART 4

Chapter 16
ASPECTS FROM THE ASCENDANT P. 344

Chapter 17
YOUR CHART RULER IN THE BIRTH CHART P. 381

THE ASCENDANT

WHERE YOUR SOUL MEETS THE EARTH

SOME WORDS ABOUT ASTROLOGY

Astrology describes your connection with the Starry Sky and the energies that were around you, the moment you were born. So, the energies that were prominent at our birth thus became part of our energetic constitution – part of our body, our consciousness and our emotions. It is precisely these star combinations at that moment that form our unique Birth Chart. There is enormous power and infinite potential in our Birth Chart! It shows us our past but also our potential future. Above all, it shows our potential for this incarnation and more around strong life themes for us. We can think of our birth chart as a life map – designed to guide us through challenges and through the processes of life.

Through our Birth Chart we can see our deep spiritual needs but also where we need to increase our awareness and evolve to expand and heal. For example, if we have the Sun in the sign of Aries, we are here to take the lead in our life, dare to throw ourselves out and face the unknown from time to time. If we have the Sun in the sign Gemini, our life is about communication - how we communicate and how we can develop that part of ourselves and move towards increased awareness.

This book takes you on an astrological journey where we delve into the ascendant sign. We look at what your ascendant tells you about you and your journey in this life. We also show how you can interpret your ascendant sign in combination with your Sun and what the combination means. In addition to that, we look at aspects from the ascendant and other themes that can guide you.

INTRODUCTION
ASTROLOGY & SPIRITUALITY

Astrology as a subject has its roots long before our reckoning, and the interest in the stars and space has probably existed since man began to walk here on Earth. Through the centuries that have passed, the subject has been rewritten and changed an infinite number of times, although a large part of the basics remain. Our work is based on Western modern Astrology, but we choose to weave in the importance of the soul to a greater extent than many Astrologers do. We have seen how Astrology and spirituality together can create profound transformation for people but also open new avenues for expansion.

Energies from our Solar System

Our solar system consists of the Sun and the planets that move around the Sun in their specific orbits. In addition to orbiting planets, we have other celestial bodies such as asteroids and dwarf planets. The planets lie close to the ecliptic, that is, the path the Sun moves along during the year.

There are seven planets in the Solar System, and they are the ones we work with in Astrology. They are Mercury, Venus, Mars, Jupiter, Saturn, Uranus, Neptune and Pluto. Pluto is actually a dwarf planet but counts within Astrology as one of the main planets. In addition to the planets, we also have the Moon, which revolves around the Earth in its fixed orbit.

Just as in the expression as above so below, there is a constant interaction between us humans here on Earth and the celestial bodies around the Earth. Everything affects each other and we are all part of this great cosmic puzzle. Each planet has its own unique energy and when we live here on Earth we feel the movements of the planets - whether we are aware of it or not. We know with all certainty how much the Sun affects us as it keeps us alive and gives us vital energy. Similarly, we gain access to Mercury's energy when the planet has a prominent position in the starry sky or in our birth chart. The energy finds its way down into our energy system and becomes part of our personality and our chakra system.

The planets that are closest to Earth usually affect us more in everyday life than the planets that are very far away. In Astrology, they are called personal planets, precisely because of their proximity to us.

Planets that have a longer distance from the Sun and thus also from the Earth are called generation planets. They usually affect more entire generations as they are in the same zodiac sign for a long time. Pluto can be in the same sign for 20 years, which means that everyone born within this time span has the planet in the same sign. However, the more distant planets can have a strong influence in our life, when they come into contact with our personal planets or other important points in the Birth Chart.

Astrology & Spirituality

For us, Astrology and Spirituality go hand in hand and the Birth Chart is a unique tool that we can use to understand ourselves, heal and move more into our full potential. We can also use it to do deep healing work and to find our spiritual gifts and our life mission.

By studying placement of planets, signs, houses and aspects, we get an opportunity to find subconscious and dormant aspects of ourselves, something that gives us the opportunity to activate them. The chart helps us understand what we carry with us and how our energy is distributed within us.

For example, if we have a lot of fire in the chart, we have a great need for movement, power, action and passion. If we had to suppress our energy and our fire in childhood, we may have to make room for these themes in our life as an adult. In this way, the birth chart is very valuable! It shows us what we need to feel good in everyday life but also what we need to develop spiritually. Many times, we can see blockages and challenges in the chart and through that awareness begin our inner work of change.

The birth chart does not show anything fixed or static, but rather opportunities and potential blockages. We can take the planet Mars as an example. Mars has an explosive energy and represents our willpower and our ability to stand up for ourselves – to fight for what we believe in. We now imagine that the planet Mars is in the twelfth house or in a more challenging placement in the birth chart. Here we often see challenges around our willpower and around our ability to express ourselves. We may have difficulty standing up for ourselves and we don't know what we want. If we do not get the opportunity to develop these qualities during childhood, they can become underdeveloped, and this is often seen in one way or another in our Birth Chart.

If we have the Moon in a tough placement or in tough aspects, it can indicate a blockage in our emotions. Perhaps we had to suppress our emotions or suppress our sensitivity as children, which led to us as adults needing to unlock this part of ourselves.

An important key to healing during our spiritual journey involves becoming aware of and understanding our emotions. Above all, we need to accept and let them become part of our person and our consciousness. Our Birth Chart can help us become aware of patterns that help us evolve to the next level.

The birth chart & our Spiritual Ascension

Today we live in a time where more and more people are waking up and entering into their spiritual awakening. It is a turbulent and exciting time where we search more and more for ourselves - who we are on a deep spiritual level and what we do here on Earth. We encounter situations, people and energies where we are more or less forced into transformation - all in order for our soul to get what it seeks.

In our work, we often meet individuals who have felt different and outside here on Earth for as long as they can remember. Many of them also have a strong attraction to other galactic locations and they are what we refer to as starseeds or star travelers. Whatever our spiritual journey looks like, we can break it down into a few specific parts, parts that make up the very essence of awakening and that most people recognize.

The first part is about liberation, that is, we free ourselves from old things that hold us back or limit us in various ways. Here it is usually about breaking patterns and templates that we got with us from early childhood and that gradually became part of our personality. By breaking these patterns and beliefs, we can create new patterns that better match us and our unique energy. We can transform beliefs that hold us in fear into awareness and power that help us move forward and achieve our goals.

The second part is about deep healing and transformation. This can be a long and, in many ways, painful journey, where we really need to turn our gaze inward and look at our inner self. By becoming aware of blockages and limitations we carry, we can change energy states and raise our general frequency. Here we have seen time and time again that childhood has an extremely important role. The vast majority of us carry pain and unresolved trauma from childhood, stored trauma that remains as energy memories in our body. They create blockages and limit our life energy but also our physical body in different ways. Old, trapped anger settles in our joints and muscles and creates tension but also various forms of illness in the short term. Unprocessed grief can manifest as ulcers, stomach problems and food sensitivities, etc.

Healing our childhood is not something we do overnight but it requires great effort and determination on our part. We need to be willing to reevaluate what we have been through, ask questions and above all be prepared to face the pain that comes up when we heal deep blockages.

As small children, we are completely open to what is happening in our immediate surroundings and we are constantly picking up signals, energies and vibrations. These then become part of our chakra system and also part of our defense – how we face and resolve stress during life. This becomes extra prominent for individuals who are highly sensitive. Here we have seen large connections between highly sensitive children and various forms of dysfunctional patterns as adults. Highly sensitive children have a strong tendency to internalize their emotions early in life, which means that they direct their energy, expression and feelings inward rather than outward. This leads to a great strain on the body and energy system, which can later manifest as lack of energy and various pain conditions, but also confusion about who one is.

The third part during our spiritual awakening is about finding our energy back – expanding and moving into our full potential. By freeing ourselves from old baggage and healing our inner self, we make room for deep spiritual development. We realize that we are so much more than the limitations we have carried during life.

You who are reading this book are most likely an old soul with many lives behind you. From these lives you carry with you imprints and energy memories in your cells and in your DNA, something that can be activated during this life through encounters with people or through special situations. That is a big reason why many old souls find it challenging here on Earth.

By understanding and working with our Astrological Birth Chart we can get powerful tools, insights but also Healing during our Spiritual journey. The chart gives us clues about what we carry with us from past lives, strong themes from childhood and where there may be blockages in our energy system but also in our physical body.

The fourth house shows what we have received through inheritance and through our upbringing. Planets there provide important information about experiences, themes or feelings connected with childhood.

The eighth house is the house of transformation, healing and crises. The sign, any planets and aspects connected to the eighth house provide valuable information about our spirituality and our intuitive abilities.

By studying the twelfth house, we gain access to what lies deeply hidden within us, in the subconscious. Planets here often show qualities and skills that we were "forced" to suppress or repress during childhood, due to various circumstances. The twelfth house also shows what we carry with us from past lives and what we may need to dissolve karmically to heal past lifetimes.

The nodes of the Moon show very valuable information about what we carry with us from past lifetimes but also what we are here to master and achieve in this lifetime.

The placement of the moon shows where we may be carrying emotional blockages from past lives and where there is a great sensitivity within us. It can also show the relationship with our mother and how it affected us during the first part of life.

The ascendant shows how we meet the outside world and how we protect ourselves and vice versa - how we take in other people's energies.

We can see the birth chart as a spiritual chart where everything we see has significance for our life. By learning to understand the codes that the chart conveys to us, we gain access to the codes for our own life, the life path we have chosen to walk here on Earth.

PART 1
ENERGIES OF THE ZODIAC

CHAPTER 1
THE STRUCTURE OF THE ZODIAC

The zodiac is a division of the paths of the Sun, the Moon and the planets in the starry sky. It consists of 12 zodiac signs and 12 houses as well as all planets, asteroids, aspects and other points that can be interpreted. The entire zodiac consists of 360°, which means that each sign is 30°. In Western Astrology, the vernal equinox in March is usually used as the first starting point of the Zodiac. This means that Aries is the first sign in the chart, as the sun is in Aries at that time (around March 23rd). After Aries comes Taurus, then Gemini followed by Cancer, etc. The zodiac consists of the following basic elements:

- 12 Zodiac signs
- 12 Houses
- Planets & Asteroids
- Power Points (AC, DC, MC & IC)
- 4 Elements
- 3 Modalities
- The lunar nodes
- Aspects

There are several different directions in Astrology and two of them are Western (tropical) Astrology and Eastern (sidereal) Astrology. The majority of Astrologers in the Western world work based on the tropical model and so do we. There are a number of developed house systems in Astrology, and this means that the houses will have different places in the Birth Chart if we compare different systems with each other. We use the Whole Sign house system, as we find it most useful in our work. It is also one of the very oldest and most proven house systems in Astrology. Whole Sign means that every house is the same size. A house is 30°, which means that a house and sign have the same size. Practically in the chart we will see that each zodiac sign occupies exactly one specific house.

The twelve zodiac signs

The zodiac consists of 12 zodiac signs, and they have their basis in 12 different star constellations in the sky. Each sign has its own unique characteristics and energetic qualities as well as challenging parts. Most individuals we meet usually know which zodiac sign they were born in, that is, which sign the Sun was in when they were born. So, if the Sun is in Cancer when we are born, we are born in the zodiac sign Cancer. This means that we can be sensitive, empathetic or have other qualities that Cancer stands for.

   Below you can see all the zodiac signs with associated keywords. More in-depth information about each zodiac sign comes later in the book.

Aries: Leader, Pioneer, Initiator, Inspirer

Taurus: Stability, Creator, Builder, Manifest

Gemini: Communication, Writer, Flexibility, Curiosity

Cancer: Emotional, Understanding, Caring

Leo: Creativity, Leader, Artist, Children, Youth

Virgo: Perfection, Improving, Service, Health, Healer

Libra: Relationships, Therapist, Mediator, Balance, Beauty

Scorpio: The unknown, Profound, Exploratory, Black or white

Sagittarius: Discovery, Traveling, Moving, Knowledge, Teacher

Capricorn: Structure, Discipline, Project Manager, Power

Aquarius: Rebel, Innovator, Breaker of Norms, Technology

Pisces: Intuition, Imagination, Dreams, Creativity

The Twelve Divine Houses

The zodiac is divided into 12 parts, each of which corresponds to 30°
on the chart. These parts are called houses and represent different
parts of our life. The houses symbolize areas of life where different
energies, themes and events are played out during our life here on
earth. As we mentioned earlier, we use the Whole Sign house system,
which means that each house will be as big as a Zodiac sign, that is
30°. When using other house systems, the houses may have different
sizes, depending on which part of the world we were born in.

The twelve houses are calculated based on the zodiac sign that rose
over the eastern horizon at the moment we were born. The exact
number of degrees thus marks what we refer to as the Ascendant. In
order to find out which ascendant sign we have and thus be able to
know how our houses stand in the Zodiac, we therefore need to know
our exact time and place of birth.

Each house is made up of energy themes and represents different stages of our development – from being born, starting to communicate, creating our identity, building relationships and manifesting things out into the world.

The sign in which the house is located shows how we act and do things, connected with that particular area of life. If we have planets in a house, they show predetermined energies and themes that we will most likely experience during this incarnation. Below is a brief description of each house with its current themes.

The First House
The first house is always the same as the ascendant sign and it represents our appearance, how we act in meeting other people and strong life themes during this lifetime.

The Second House
The second house is connected to our self-worth, how we value ourselves and what we carry with us in form of natural resources. The house also has a connection to money, finances and abundance (or lack of money).

The Third House
The third house represents our communication style, i.e. how we communicate with other people in everyday life but also how we think and reason. The house also has a connection to our immediate environment during growing up, such as siblings and neighbors.

The Fourth House

The fourth house represents our roots and what we carry with us in terms of genetic inheritance but also behavioral and emotional inheritance. The house also has a connection to our inner world and the private, things that we carry inside us.

The Fifth House

The fifth house represents creation, expression, play and children. Furthermore, it is connected with how we express our creative ability in the outside world, for example art, dance, song or something else.

The Sixth House

The sixth house represents our health, our everyday life and the routines we need in everyday life to feel good. It is also connected with our daily work and service.

The Seventh House

The seventh house represents relationships, relationship dynamics and the type of relationships we seek and attract into our lives. It also shows how we are in relationships, what we need to develop and what can be challenging.

The Eighth House

The eighth house represents depth, healing, crises and transformation. It also has a strong connection to common resources such as our partner's money. The house is also connected with intimacy and transformation through deep closeness.

The Ninth House

The ninth house represents discovery, travel of various kinds but also the search for our inner truth. In this house we also find themes such as learning, mentorship and knowledge.

The Tenth House

The tenth house represents our public imprint in this life, such as our profession or what we do to contribute to the world around us. The house has a strong connection with our life mission and how we can manifest it here on Earth in a powerful way.

The Eleventh House

The eleventh house represents society and what we can do to contribute to the greater whole. The house also connects with friends, groups, media, internet and platforms to reach a lot of people.

The Twelfth House

The twelfth house is the last house of the Zodiac, and it represents our innermost aspects, such as our subconscious and our dreams. It also has a connection to spirituality and past lives as well as qualities and energies we could not or were not allowed to fully express while growing up.

The four Elements

There are four elements in the Zodiac, and these are fire, water, air and earth. Each zodiac sign carries one of the elements and since there are twelve zodiac signs this means that there are 3 signs within each element i.e. 3 fire signs, 3 water signs, 3 air signs and 3 earth signs.

Below we see all the elements, which characters they are connected with and important keywords.

Fire in the Birth Chart

The fire signs of the zodiac are Aries, Leo & Sagittarius. Keywords for this element are power, instinct, courage, passion, motivation, warmth, inspiration, physical activity and spontaneity. Fire as an element is connected with our life energy and inner power.

Water in the Birth Chart

The water signs of the zodiac are Cancer, Scorpio & Pisces. Keywords for this element are feelings, intuition, flow, knowing, intimacy, connectedness, relationships, empathy and creativity. Water as an element is connected with our emotions and our general flow in the body.

Air in the Birth Chart

The air signs of the zodiac are Gemini, Libra & Aquarius. Key words for this element are thoughts, communication, collaboration, mental processes, learning, the abstract and ideas. Air as an element is connected with our thoughts and our social processes.

Earth in the Birth Chart

The earth signs of the zodiac are Taurus, Virgo & Capricorn. Keywords for this element are stability, details, structure, organization, grounded, focus, building, money and the material. Earth as an element is connected to our physical body.

The three Modalities of the chart

There are 3 modalities in Astrology, and they are termed as cardinal, fixed & mutable. The modalities describe how we handle the various processes of life, that is, how we initiate, maintain and change something. If we have a lot of cardinal energy in our chart, we are generally good at initiating and starting ongoing projects. If, on the other hand, we have predominantly fixed energy, it is easier for us to retain something over time, for example building a company. If we have a lot of mutable energy in our chart, we are flexible and we usually find it easy to make different kinds of changes. The division of Modalities looks like this:

Cardinal signs: Aries, Cancer, Libra & Capricorn
Keywords: leadership, introduction, beginning, fresh start, initiation, start project

Fixed signs: Taurus, Leo, Scorpio & Aquarius
Keywords: keep, stabilize, long-lasting, firm foundation, push through

Mutable signs: Gemini, Virgo, Sagittarius & Pisces
Keywords: flexibility, adaptation, changeable, change, compliant

Birth chart polarities – Yin & Yang

There are two polarities or opposing energies in the Birth Chart and they consist of the feminine and masculine aspects – or yin and yang.

Half of the zodiac signs have a masculine energy while the remaining six signs carry a more feminine energy. This division is valuable to know as the masculine and feminine energy represent different qualities. If we have a lot of masculine energy in our chart, it is possible that we have an easier time expressing and using these qualities, and on the contrary, with a lot of feminine energy, we often see how it dominates the chart.

Masculine energy is more outgoing and stands for qualities and attributes such as outward, action, doing, acting, thinking, analyzing, intellect and physical manifestation. Feminine energy is more receptive in nature and stands for the following qualities and attributes, taking in, feeling, being, feelings, flow, intuition and dreams. Below is a short guide to see which of the Zodiac signs are feminine and which are masculine.

Aries – masculine energy
Gemini – masculine energy
Leo – masculine energy
Libra – masculine energy
Sagittarius – masculine energy
Aquarius – masculine energy

Taurus – feminine energy
Cancer – feminine energy
Virgo - feminine energy
Scorpio – feminine energy
Capricorn - feminine energy
Pisces - feminine energy

The four Angles of the Zodiac

There are four angles in the Birth Chart that are significant and all of which carry a magnetic force. These points are also called Power Points. Depending on which house system we use in Astrology, the Zodiac and the angles will vary slightly in position. In Whole Sign house system, the Ac & Dc will always end up in houses 1 and 7 respectively. However, the Ic & Mc can end up anywhere in houses 2–6 and houses 8–12 respectively. This phenomenon is governed by our geographic position and where we are in the world.

What the angles have in common is that they carry a very concentrated and strong energy. This means that everything around the angles in the Birth Chart is manifested in our life, in one way or another. In this book, we do not focus so much on the other angles, but mainly focus most on the Ascendant and its significance. Below, you will see some key words for each angle.

The Ascendant (As)

The Ascendant is located in the first house of the Birth Chart and arises through our time of birth. The ascendant is a powerful point in the chart that represents you, how you relate to the environment but also how you were shaped during your upbringing. The Ascendant also shows strong life themes that you are meant to develop and expand through in this lifetime. A more in-depth description of the Ascendant comes later in the book.

The Descendant (Dc)

The Descendant is a power point that is exactly opposite the Ascendant. Located in the seventh house, this point represents strong relationship themes, how you perceive other people and also what you attract into your life in terms of encounters and relationships. This often happens on an unconscious level until you become aware of your patterns and behaviors here.

Immune coeli (Ic)

Imum Coeli corresponds to the lowest part of the Birth Chart and this point represents your origin, that is, where you come from and your roots. Here we can see patterns connected with family and childhood but also themes that have been passed down in the family. Furthermore, this point shows what you carry deep inside you, things that you got with you through inheritance and DNA.

Midheaven (Mc)

The Midheaven is exactly opposite the Imum Coeli and thus constitutes the highest point in the Birth Chart. So, while the Imum Coeli shows what you've got and more about your background, your Midheaven shows your highest potential. The point shows where you have great opportunities to manifest and make an impression in this lifetime. Many times, this is related to your career, great job opportunities or your life mission.

The 10 Planets in the Zodiac

There are 10 planets in Astrology, and this also includes the Sun and the Moon, although they are not actually real planets. Of these 10, the Sun, Moon, Mercury, Venus and Mars are counted as Personal Planets, while Jupiter, Saturn, Uranus, Neptune and Pluto fall under the term Generational Planets. Below you will see a brief description of each planet and important keywords they are connected to.

The Sun: A Key to our Soul's Manifestation
Characteristics: Light, Power, Life Energy, Vitality, Joy, Center, Purpose, Manifestation, Masculine, Father

The Moon: A Key to Deep Emotional Satisfaction
Characteristics: Receptive, Intaking, Feminine, Mother, Intuition, Emotions, Subconscious, Memories, Reactions, Deeper Soul needs

Mercury: A Key to our Divine Expression
Characteristics: Communication, Speech, Writing, Thoughts, Mental Processes, Intuition, Perception, Perception, Expression, Receiving Information

Venus: A Key to Love & Balance
Characteristics: Attraction, Beauty, Balance, Relationships, Money, Values, Self-worth, Material, The physical, Creativity, Resources

Mars: A Key to Courage & Strength

Characteristics: Life Energy, Power, Courage, Strength, Will, Passion, Sexuality, Masculinity, Warrior, Protector, Inspiration

Jupiter: A Key to our Soul Expansion

Characteristics: Expansion, Wisdom, Higher Learning, Higher Communication, Travel, Spirituality, Faith, Flow, Luck, Opportunities, Other Cultures

Saturn: A Key to Success & Manifestation

Characteristics: Limitation, Mastery, Discipline, Hard work, Master of something, Long-term, Patience

Uranus: A Key to Liberation & Freedom

Characteristics: Freedom, Liberation, Chaos, Awakening, Higher Thoughts, Rebellious, Innovative, Intelligent, Genius, Innovation, Higher Purpose, Technology

Neptune: A Key to Forgiveness & Divine Love

Characteristics: Dreams, Creativity, Higher Dimensions, Higher Self, Empathy, Boundless, Unconditional Love, Forgiveness, Escape, Imagination, Illusion

Pluto: A Key to Spiritual & Deep Transformation

Characteristics: Soul Transformation, Kundalini, Rebirth, Healing, Shared Resources, Intimacy, Contrasts, Black or White, Deep Emotions, Crisis

Other important points in the Birth chart

In addition to the planets, there are other aspects that are valuable to interpret in the Birth Chart. Some of them are the asteroid Chiron and the Moon's nodes, that is, the South Node and the North Node. They are not planets, but all have an important meaning in our life journey. More detailed information about these points and about all the planets can be found in our previous book *Astrology for the Soul*.

The asteroid Chiron

The asteroid Chiron symbolizes the spiritual archetype "The Wounded Healer" and we can see Chiron as our inner Healer. By looking at Chiron we can see where we are carrying deep spiritual blocks and fears from the past. These may be fears from early childhood, but these fears often have their origins in previous lives. The deepest wounds within us rarely come from this life but are a direct continuation of the patterns and themes we started a long time ago. For that reason, Chiron is often one of our great challenges in the same way that it is our great guide. When we heal this part of ourselves, we become powerful healers, and we gain the ability to help people on a profound level.

The South Node

The South Node is a mathematically calculated point in the Birth Chart similar to the North Node and they are opposite each other. The South Node symbolizes what we carry with us from past lives, in the form of gifts, energy and karmic patterns. Depending on where we have the South Node in our chart, we can see part of our history and our soul's journey through time. The South Node shows which characteristics, behaviors and qualities we developed in the past, both in a positive and negative sense.

The North Node

The North Node symbolizes the direction we are meant to go in this lifetime. The North Node shows characteristics and qualities that can be a little uncomfortable for us, as we simply haven't been in this energy much before. We can see the North Node as a guiding star for the Soul, a point of destiny that shows where we will go in the course of life. During our work, we have seen fantastic examples of individuals who achieved several of their goals and life dreams, by following the energy of their North Node. When we become aware of this point in our Birth Chart, we can strategically work towards developing what we need, to find deep spiritual satisfaction.

Example of a birth chart

The image below shows an example of a Birth chart, although it may differ slightly depending on which program we use when creating a chart. In the picture we see the symbols for all the zodiac signs in the outermost circle. The chart is divided into 12 houses, and we see the houses by looking at the numbers that are further towards the middle.

The first house is in the sign Aries, and this means that the ascendant sign is precisely Aries. We also see that it says As in the first house, which is also short for the Ascendant.

The second house is in the sign of Taurus and here is also the planet Neptune. The third house is in the sign of Gemini and here there are no planets, but it is empty. The fourth house is in the sign of Cancer and here is also the power point Ic. The fifth house is in the sign of Leo and here we also see the planet Uranus. We jump on to the sixth house which is in the sign of Virgo. Here we see the asteroid Chiron together with the South Node.

The seventh house is in the sign of Libra and here is also the planet Venus, quite close to the power point Ds. The eighth house is in the sign of Scorpio and here we see the planets Sun, Mercury and Saturn. The ninth house is in Sagittarius and the planet Mars is here. The tenth house is in the sign of Capricorn and here we see the power point Mc and the planet Jupiter. The eleventh house is in the sign of Aquarius and here is also the Moon. Finally, we have the twelfth house which is in the sign of Pisces. Here in lies the planet Pluto and the North Node.

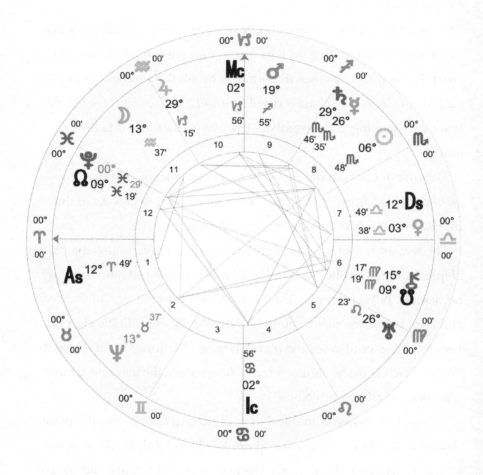

PART 2
THE ASCENDANT & THE SUN
IN ASTROLOGY

CHAPTER 2
THE ASCENDANT & THE SUN
IN THE BIRTH CHART

Further on in the book, we will delve deeper into the ascendant and what significance it has for our lives - from an energy perspective but also from a health perspective. But before we do that, we need to understand the connection between the ascendant and the Sun. We need to know how they complement each other but also how they differ.

Just as the Sun in our solar system is the very center of the system, it has a large and important role in our birth chart. Without the Sun we cannot exist here on Earth and if we translate that to Astrology, we have seen that people who do not follow and live according to their Sun Sign can have great challenges in life. We can experience a great lack of energy, feelings of meaninglessness but also emotions and low mood or depression. The Sun is a strong and important source of energy, a place in the Birth Chart where we can collect and fill up with new life energy. The Sun shows where we are meant to shine in this life and where we have great potential to make a physical impression. The Sun also shows what we need to get into our life to feel alive and at our most vital.

Some of us are born into an environment that supports us and helps us express the energy of our Sun Sign. If, on the other hand, we are born into a restricted environment where our parents find it difficult to support us or where there are major stressors, we can suppress much of the energy in our Sun Sign but also in our other chart. By studying the Birth Chart and seeing what energy we carry and how we are meant to live it out, we can get invaluable help on our life journey. We can look at the placement of the Sun to see how we can reclaim our power and live in accordance with our higher purpose here on Earth.

To look at the Sun's meaning and what role it has for us, we need to look at both the sign and the house it is in. The sign the Sun is in shows the energy itself and the qualities the Sun is connected to in our chart, while the house shows which area is central – that is, where we are meant to shine.

The difference between the Sun & the Ascendant

Our Sun Sign is a part of our chart that we usually grow into during life, while the Ascendant sign is something we are shaped into while growing up. This means that we can often recognize ourselves more in our ascendant sign than in our Sun sign.

Imagine being born with the Sun in Cancer! You have a great sensitivity, and you carry a strong intuition and an empathic ability. But you grow up in a family where sensitivity is not accepted, which causes you to shut down and suppress this part of yourself. The family you grow up in is forward-thinking and social with a large network. They socialize a lot with people and there is a lot of physical activity such as sports and theater in the picture. As a child, you are appreciated and seen when you express yourself jokingly or when you manage things on your own.

So, you have the Sun in Cancer BUT you have the ascendant in Leo. You have been shaped into a Leo and by taking on the characteristics that belong to Leo you feel safe and seen. Of course, this is not something we do consciously, but it happens in the interaction with our surroundings as small children. We are shaped by the patterns and energy around us.

In the example above, it may be that during the course of life you need to develop and bring out your Cancer, that is, your sensitivity that has been hidden within you. By affirming your sensitivity but also your abilities that you learned through Leo, you can find a balance where you express both parts.

How well we can express our Sun Sign and how prominent our Ascendant becomes depends on how we are as people, our sensitivity to our surroundings and what our growing up environment actually looks like.

There are many parts in the Birth Chart that are important and to get a complete picture of us with all the layers we need to interpret everything that is happening. But by looking at the Ascendant sign and the Sun sign, we can get a fantastic picture of our purpose here on Earth, where we have great potential and how we were shaped and how we can develop spiritually.

The combination we have with the Sun and the ascendant in our Birth chart is unique. There are a total of 144 combinations of the ascendant and the Sun in a birth chart. This means that our particular combination will be 1 in 144.

Example of combination of the Ascendant & the Sun
The image below shows a simplified birth chart with only the combination of ascendant and Sun sign. In the picture, the ascendant is in the sign of Libra, while the Sun is in the sign of Cancer, in the

tenth house. Based on that, this person is meant to shine with their sensitivity, their intuition and their empathetic ability - in the field of career and work.

Since the ascendant is in Libra, it is possible that this person grew up in a family where relationships and mediation were a central theme. In order for the person to find balance between his Sun and ascendant, a balance between both these parts of the chart is needed. So, in this case, the person needs to affirm their sensitivity and find a job that matches the Sun in the tenth house, but also work on finding balance in their closest relationships to enter the higher energy of the ascendant sign. This is a simple example to show what the combination might look like.

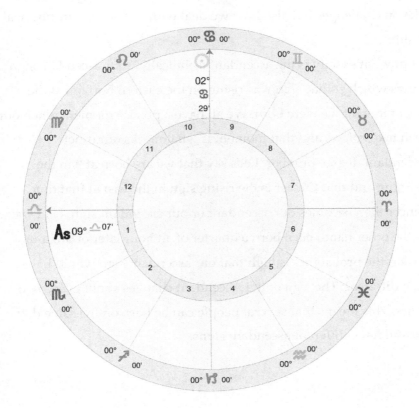

CHAPTER 3
THE ASCENDANT & ITS DEEPER SIGNIFICANCE FOR OUR SOUL

As we previously described, the ascendant has a great importance when it comes to the construction of the Birth chart, as the ascendant sign determines the first house and thus the rest of the houses in the chart. But the meaning and significance of our ascendant sign goes far much deeper than that. By studying the ascendant, we can gain deep insights into who we are, how we have been shaped into life, how we take on challenges but also how we deal with stress and our physical health.

But what exactly is the ascendant technically? Our ascendant sign shows which zodiac sign was rising on the eastern horizon at the exact moment we were born. We all have a precise moment when our birth takes place, and that moment is what marks our exact Ascendant degree number. Let's say that we are born at 9 in the morning and that Cancer is the rising sign in the east at that time. Cancer then becomes our ascendant or our ascendant sign. Had we, on the other hand, been born a quarter of an hour later or an hour earlier, the probability is high that our ascendant sign would have been different. The sign of the Ascendant changes about every two hours. This means that several people can be born on the same day but still have different ascendant signs.

While the ascendant shows the sign that rose on the eastern horizon at our birth, the descendent (in the seventh house) shows the zodiac sign that set in the west.

Since the ascendant is always connected with the first house in the Birth chart, we can see it as the composer for the rest of the chart. We can also see our ascendant as a gateway to the rest of the chart and all that takes place there. Based on that, everything that happens in our chart is filtered through our ascendant sign. If we have a water sign as ascendant, we may be extremely open, receptive and empathetic in meeting other people, even if we have our Sun in a fire sign and our Moon in an air sign. We filter information and experiences through the sign that makes up our ascendant (plus any planets in the first house, more on that later).

The Ascendant – A bridge between our soul and the outside world
We strongly believe that our life here on Earth is predetermined and that we choose major and important life themes before we incarnate in this body. Before we come here, we determine the family we will be born into based on experiences from past lives, matching of energy and vibration as well as based on old karma and potential for great learning. We've seen it over and over in our spiritual work, how we step into families and lineages that match the energy and inner challenges we've been carrying from before - so that we have the opportunity to heal, grow and expand over the course of life. We also choose which time we will incarnate here on Earth based on the conditions that exist as well as our parents and details about our birth. So, our birth is carefully planned and predetermined, which means that we are all born exactly when we are supposed to.

In other words, our Birth chart with placement of planets, points, nodes and Ascendant is predetermined. We are born at just the right moment where all the planets and universal energies are in the right way – the right way to create and build our soul constitution. This is what makes Astrology and our Birth Chart so interesting to study, as it shows us information about things we carry with us from the past but also what we have the potential to achieve in this life.

So, we are born at a certain time and that time becomes the starting point of our ascendant. In a way, we can see the ascendant as a bridge between our soul and our outside world here on Earth. It represents our first encounter with the Earth and what is going on here - not only emotionally but also physically. So, by looking at our ascendant sign we can see how we experienced our birth. The sign here and any planets near the ascendant can give us information about how we experienced the moment of birth and if something traumatic happened. If we have Uranus near or on the ascendant, there is a high probability that something unexpected happened at our birth, for example that we or our mother was dying. Also, Pluto here can indicate that something earth-shattering and profoundly transformative happened right at or shortly after our moment of birth. The challenge here is that we rarely (or never) remember these events, but we can get information by looking at the birth chart and sensing intuitively or taking help from someone.

When we are born, a certain energy is created, based on how we feel and experience the moments immediately after our birth. If we have, for example, Cancer as an ascendant sign, it can mean that we already created strong family ties with our mother during the time in the womb and immediately after birth. This is because Cancer represents our feelings, security and family.

If we have Aries as the ascendant, we may have experienced that our mother was there and gave birth to us but did not really meet us emotionally, because Aries is by nature independent and does well on its own.

The text above shows a few different examples of what it might have looked like, but there are an infinite number of scenarios here. The important thing is not knowing exactly what happened, although that can be helpful and healing. The most important thing is to become aware that we actually chose our ascendant sign even before we were born and that we are meant to have certain experiences connected with this.

In a way, we can see our ascendant as part of our soul contract in this life and the sign shows what we are here to master and learn in meeting other people.

The Ascendant and our upbringing

Our upbringing lays the foundation for how we develop and are shaped as individuals. If we grow up in a family that supports us and gives us unconditional love, we take the positive energy into our energy system, our chakras and our cells. We create patterns within ourselves where we value ourselves and we get the opportunity to build up a basic inner security. If, as children, we have parents who see us and who teach us to manage our emotions, it has great positive consequences for our whole life. We may still carry heavy baggage from past lives with us and we will very likely experience tough experiences and traumas while growing up anyway - but we get a great deal of protection through our parents and thus in ourselves.

If, on the other hand, we grow up in an environment with strong stress, a lot of conflict, abuse or other things going on, it is the negative energy we capture and take into our energy system. We learn that we are not sufficient, and we learn to shut down our inner selves, due to lack of support from our surroundings. Above all, we do not learn to manage our emotions, but we unconsciously suppress them, which creates conditions for physical and emotional problems later in life. In our work, we have seen large connections between experiences of strong stress and trauma in childhood and autoimmune diseases and pain conditions in adulthood.

So, our upbringing is important on many different levels. The patterns we create in childhood are the patterns we then navigate from as adults, until we consciously choose to heal and change them into something better for us.

Our ascendant sign plays a big role when it comes to our upbringing and by studying our ascendant, we can get important clues about our upbringing and how we were shaped in our early years. There are of course many parts of the Birth Chart that are important to look at to get the whole picture, but only through the ascendant can we see important parts that can help us in our inner growth.

Our ascendant sign shows what qualities were appreciated by our parents when we were growing up. During our work, both within Astrology and other spiritual work, we often see individuals who have developed certain personality traits and characteristics very strongly - based on how they were shaped by their upbringing. If we have a father who values or even insists that we achieve in everything we do, we can build our personality around achievement and demands.

If our mother is ill and has difficulty dealing with life and her emotions, it is possible that we as small children step in and take on the responsibility for our mother.

We overdevelop qualities related to caring, responsibility and many times also various forms of co-dependency.

Our ascendant sign shows us which characteristics, behaviors and patterns were appreciated or accepted during growing up, in the meeting with our parents (or other guardians). This does not mean that we will always develop extremely dysfunctional traits linked to our ascendant, but there is a large spectrum here. Someone with Capricorn here may have learned to take on a lot of responsibility at home, due to many younger siblings, while another individual with the same ascendant sign may have grown up orphaned and forced to fend for themselves at a young age. So, we cannot assume that individuals with the same ascendant sign have had the same or an identical background, but on the other hand, we can almost always see common themes and a certain basic energy that is included in the picture.

Through childhood and through meeting our parents, we learn how to go out and meet people ourselves. If we grow up in a home where our parents have strong networks and a lot of socializing, we will most likely have an easier time with this part as adults, than if we grow up with two parents who live in isolation and who themselves struggle with the social part. The patterns we get with us from childhood often sit on a deep subconscious level, which means we don't think about them. They are in the way we act, greet, run and walk. Based on that, it is valuable to examine how our patterns actually look and thus create patterns that move us forward in life. In a way, our childhood lays the foundation for our personality, but nothing is static. Through conscious work, we can recreate parts and aspects within us.

When we look at our ascendant sign, we can see what we brought with us from home, in terms of attributes and characteristics but also when it comes to pure survival strategies and protection.

The Ascendant and our Health

Our ascendant represents our external personality and how we learned to be in the meeting with other people and it also has a strong connection to our body, both physically and energetically. By studying our ascendant, the current sign and any planets (more on that later), we can see important themes connected to our health over the course of life. We can also experience physical or inner transformation processes when we have planets transiting our first house in transits. Generally speaking, the sixth house in the Birth Chart represents themes such as health, routines and everyday life. When it comes to the ascendant and its connection to our health, there is a strong correlation to our physical body, how we move physically, how we process what happens in the environment but also how we take in things in terms of energy.

To get a complete picture of the theme of health we need to look at the whole chart, but by looking at the ascendant and the sixth house in the chart we get a lot of information we can use to take care of our body and our energy and to create good routines in everyday life.

41

Our physical Body & our Defenses

When we meet people out on the town or in a group, there is a fairly high probability that we can guess their ascendant sign, both based on how the person behaves and acts but also based on the person's appearance. This will not always be the case as some people have a greater similarity with their Sun or with their Moon, but it is common for our ascendant sign to shine through strongly, as part of our overall expression. If a person has Aries as ascendant, it can be seen in the form of a clear structure in the face, prominent jawbones and a slightly athletic body shape. If, on the other hand, the ascendant is in Leo, it can show itself in the form of playfulness, a startling appearance or a lot of creative energy. Sometimes it is more obvious and sometimes less so.

Our ascendant sign shows more about our body constitution and what we need to feel good physically. It also shows which parts of our body are extra prominent, both positively and negatively. Each Zodiac Sign in the Zodiac represents specific body parts, systems and organs in the body. The body parts that are connected with our ascendant sign are parts of our body that we should pay extra attention to and take good care of. So, let's say we have Sagittarius as ascendant! Sagittarius is connected to our hips, thighs and nervous system. This means that precisely these parts can be extra strong with us, but they can also be more exposed.

Our defense in Stressed situations

In the same way that we can understand part of our personality and our body through our ascendant, we can also learn more about our defenses, that is, how we deal with stress and challenging situations in everyday life. Because our ascendant sign is strongly shaped by our childhood and through the patterns we learned there, we can often see how these patterns and strategies follow us through life. We keep rehearsing them as long as they work well and as long as they help protect us in threatening situations. So, if we have Leo here, we might protect ourselves physically by going into "attack". It does not mean that we need to attack someone, but rather that we do something, we act. If we have Cancer as ascendant, it is more likely that we withdraw and "crawl" into our shell where we feel safe, because that is what we learned growing up.

When it comes to protection and defense, these can be used both when it comes to more practical threats or threats linked to our emotions. It may also be that we use these protections if we experience general stress in a situation or in our everyday life.

In general, we can see that water signs in the ascendant carry with them a great vulnerability in meeting other people. If we have a water sign as ascendant, we often learned to be extremely empathetic as children and learned to scan everything that happens in the environment. This applies most of all to Cancer and Pisces here, as they are both very receptive and empathetic to everything that is going on around them. This means that we may have to protect ourselves a little extra if we have one of these in the first house. We will also see that individuals with water as the ascendant sign automatically protect themselves more and they can be harder to get close to and really get to know. There is a shell that we need to get behind to get to the core.

Fire signs are generally good at protecting themselves as they have a strong inner strength and usually a lot of life energy to draw from.

This can change if there are planets in the first house or if there are challenging aspects to the first house and the ascendant.

When it comes to earth signs as ascendant signs, we can often see an individual with a grounded energy. The contact with the Earth, the land and the material surrounding means that there is generally good protection in these individuals.

With air signs here, there can be a tendency to pick up and capture a lot through their thoughts. An individual with, for example, Gemini in the ascendant can be so much in his thoughts that he or she becomes ungrounded, which opens up a vulnerability.

Regardless of which zodiac sign is our ascendant sign, it shows traits and strategies we have learned to protect ourselves when we experience stress or chaos around us. Here we can become aware of how we act in that type of situation and use the higher energy and quality of the sign, something we look at later on in a deeper review of all ascendant signs.

Our Aura & related Chakras

Our ascendant sign thus shows a lot about our appearance, our body and how we deal with stress. It also provides valuable information about our energy system, i.e. how we pick up and sense energy in the environment and how we store it within us.

Each zodiac sign has a connection with a chakra, which allows us to see which chakra is prominent for us and how we can take care of it in the best way.

Our chakra system consists of seven major chakras: the root chakra, the sacral chakra, the solar plexus chakra, the heart chakra, the throat chakra, the third eye and finally the crown chakra. We also have smaller chakras above and below the rest of our energy body, but we put less focus on them in this book. Another word for chakra is Energy Center, i.e. center in our body that handles our life energy. Each chakra has its own vibration and represents different characteristics and stages during our spiritual development. All the chakras are located in line with our spine and brain except for the crown chakra which is located about 10 centimeters above our head. Together they form a chakra system, and this system is extremely important. Our life energy flows in and out through these chakras and is then transported to the respective organs and glands in the body. Our three lowest chakras (root chakra, sacral chakra & solar plexus) are strongly connected with the practical and earthly in our lives as well as our security and our basic needs. Our three upper chakras (crown chakra, third eye and throat chakra) regulate our higher development, our divine expression and our soul expansion. In between is the heart chakra, which connects our higher and lower chakras – or Earth and Heaven if we choose to see it that way.

Our chakras are shaped and developed to a large extent during our upbringing. If we experience a safe existence with a lot of stability and love, we have better conditions to build up balanced chakras and an energetic flow in the body. If, on the other hand, we experience a lot of stress, conflicts or conditional love, it can become challenging for our chakras and the life energy starts to be stopped - that is, we create blockages in the body.

The sign Leo is strongly connected with the heart chakra, which makes that particular chakra and its energy an important part of our inner development. Here we need to look over the heart a little extra and make sure that we follow our heart but also do things that fill the heart with energy. It can also be about healing old pain and sadness that has been stored precisely in the heart, in this or previous lives.

The sign of Gemini has a strong connection with the throat chakra, which means that it is critical to express our voice and review our expression when we have this sign as ascendant. Here, our task is about creating balance right in the throat so that we say yes to what we want and no to what we don't want in life.

Our Aura can be seen as an extension of our energy system, and it surrounds us like an invisible cocoon. Its function is to protect us and sort incoming energies from the outside, so that we can choose what we want to take in and not take into our energy system. If we have many blockages in our energy body, difficulty standing up for ourselves and weak boundaries towards others, it is common for us to get damage in our aura. Our ascendant does not show any exact information about our aura, but it does show how we receive and deal with external energies in general.

Let's say we have Pisces as ascendant. Pisces is a feminine mutable water sign, which in itself means that there is a great sensitivity and an openness to our surroundings. The feminine energy is, just as we previously described, more receptive and empathetic, while the masculine energy is more outgoing and extroverted. The element of water is connected with emotions and flow. The mutability of the sign Pisces means that there is a certain tendency to move - to be flexible and sometimes even volatile. All this means that individuals with the ascendant in Pisces are extremely receptive and open to energies in their environment. They pick up everything, both positive and negative, which in the long run can create problems in the flow in terms of energy but also physically. So, for individuals with this ascendant sign, it can be very valuable to work with their energy, learn to set healthy boundaries and protect their integrity.

Spirituality in the Birth Chart & the Contribution of the Ascendant
Our Birth Chart is truly a map for our soul and the more we study a chart we discover new layers and more nuances, things we didn't even notice at first. We also have the more physical part of the chart, that is, how we can interpret parts that relate to our appearance, our health and our physical body. We can also focus on psychological and mental processes in the chart, by studying where the planet Mercury is located, which sign our third house is in, and important aspects connected with these parts of the chart. The Moon tells us a lot about our feelings, how we express them but also what we need emotionally to feel fulfilled and at peace.

In addition to the physical, psychological and emotional, we can also interpret a lot about our spirituality, our great lessons and about the development of our soul in this life. With the help of the chart, we can see more about how we can develop our highest potential and understand important areas for our spiritual ascent. Furthermore, there are many parts of the chart that help us understand how to heal ourselves, find energy blockages and transform fear into expansion.

There are above all three houses in the Zodiac that have a strong connection with themes such as spirituality, healing and past lives. They are houses 4, 8 & 12. By looking at the associated signs and any planets connected with these particular houses, we can see more about our spiritual nature and what we need to access to se the inner depths of our soul - both in the form of blockages and gifts.

The fourth house shows what we carry within us in the form of energetic heritage but also what gifts we naturally have within us. Through the sign here, we can become aware of what we have received in the form of family patterns from family and lineage, which can be both positive and negative things.

The eighth house is the house of spirituality, healing and transformation. Signs and planets here show how we can transform and bring out our healing power during our journey.

The twelfth house is the house of spirituality, our subconscious, and here there is also a strong connection with past lives, that is, things that we carry with us from previous lifetimes.

As we learn more about our Birth Chart, we will notice that everything that unfolds has something to say about our spiritual development. The planet Pluto shows where we need to undergo major transformation during life, in order to really get out the energy and the qualities found in the sign and the house.

The planet Neptune shows where we have a great sensitivity and also where we have a direct connection to our spiritual ability. If we learn to master the lower part of Neptune, which can be different forms of escape, chaos and illusion, we can open up great inner abilities that have been hidden from us.

So, what about the ascendant sign when it comes to spirituality, spiritual awakening and inner transformation?

As we mentioned earlier, our time of birth is predetermined and thus our ascendant sign and any planets around the ascendant. This means that we are born into a moment that gives us exactly the energetic composition we need in this particular life. We grow up in an existence that helps shape our personality, our ascendant sign.

The sign here symbolizes great lessons for our current life, which qualities we must learn to balance as well as which energy we need to learn to master.

With a water sign here, we have a big task when it comes to our emotions and our inner self. We need to learn more about our emotions, how they work in our body and thus develop a strong emotional awareness.

If our ascendant is an air sign, our thoughts and the mental are important aspects to understand, develop and work with during this life.

Usually, we have developed the abilities and qualities that our ascendant sign represents, but they can still be out of balance. Based on that, an important part of our spiritual work involves looking at our ascendant sign and seeing what it represents, both in its lower and higher form – and then striving to reach the highest energy of the sign. The same applies if we have planets near the ascendant. They show us which energies and areas are extra prominent in our lives, but also what we need to consciously work on developing and healing within us.

When it comes to our inner healing, our ascendant shows several things – partly how we go through major transformational processes, partly how we deal with challenges that come along the way. Depending on what we received as children (and from previous lives) in the form of security and inner capacity, this will differ. If we had a tough upbringing where we entered into a lot of adaptation and co-dependence or where we were not given the opportunity to develop our personality, we can struggle in the sign's lower energy. Here we need to become aware of what happened in our past and free ourselves from old patterns, which can be a long process.

The Ascendant is not separate from the rest of the chart, rather it is the point that somehow ties the rest of the chart together. Much of what we experience will be filtered through our ascendant, as it forms the basis of our way of looking at things, moving forward and finding solutions.

PART 3

THE ASCENDANT THROUGH THE

12 SIGNS OF THE ZODIAC

CHAPTER 4
ARIES IN THE ASCENDANT

Aries

Qualities: Fire, Cardinal, Masculine

Ruled by the planet: Mars

Connected to house: 1

Soul Archetypes: Warrior, Pioneer, Leader

Connection to chakra: Solar plexus

Aries Characteristics & Energy

Aries is the first sign out of the Zodiac and specifically symbolizes themes such as new beginnings, initiation, initiating and trying new terrain. Other qualities associated with Aries are courage, strength, vital energy, and curiosity. The sign carries a fiery cardinal masculine energy, which means there is a lot of leadership and executive power. Soul archetypes associated with Aries are the Warrior, the Pioneer and the Leader.

Aries as ascendant

Aries is one of the most, if not the most energetic sign in the entire Zodiac. Since Aries is the first sign in the Zodiac, we can also see it as the very beginning of everything, that is, our birth and the life energy we receive with us when we are born. When we are born, we usually have a lot of life energy at our disposal, and we rarely see small babies without a large portion of life force and energy. It is only when we grow up and are molded into different templates, forced to follow rules and adapt to the environment we live in, that we inhibit our energy and our power.

With Aries in the ascendant, we have a strong and tangible life energy, unless there are other parts of the chart that oppose or block this energy within us. As a rule, we find it easy to take on new challenges in life and there can be some kind of restlessness that makes us almost drawn to experiences and phenomena that make us feel alive. Maybe we have an attraction to physical events where we get to use the body in some way.

Aries is an independent sign and does not like to follow other people too much. There is a strong will and a stubbornness here that needs to come out in a balanced way, where there is consideration both for oneself and others.

Since the ascendant shows how we act in meeting other people and how we navigate through life, Aries energy becomes prominent when it comes to these very parts. People who meet us meet an energetic, initiative-taking and independent individual. That doesn't mean that's all we are, but it's the role we've taken on through upbringing and through past experiences.

We have a strong warrior energy in our personality, which means that we are prepared to fight for what we believe in. It can be things in political matters, something related to spirituality or just things related to our inner emotional life. Sometimes we have a tendency to see warrior energy as something negative in society, because of the charge of the word. But it is precisely this direct and penetrating energy which is our essence - and which can ensure that changes take place, both within ourselves but also in society.

Soul contract/Soul plan

With Aries as the ascendant sign, we are here on Earth to learn to be independent and to make our own decisions, based on our own needs. We are also here to understand our impulses and our life energy and how we can use it in a balanced way. By developing the qualities of Aries and healing the parts that are dysfunctional or unbalanced, we can enter more into the highest energy of the sign. It leads us towards development on a deep spiritual level. It also helps us use our life energy in a powerful way, manifesting positive things for ourselves and others.

Childhood & patterns from growing up

When we step into a body here on Earth, we choose a family and an environment that matches our current energy and vibration as well as the lessons we want to learn and deal with during this life. We thus choose a family that helps shape our ascendant.

Individuals with the ascendant in Aries have usually had an upbringing where they learned to be independent and where their parents valued this very ability. They are shaped into a context where they are seen or appreciated when they are able to complete things and projects on their own or when they focus on physical things, rather than emotional ones.

In our work, we have seen examples of individuals with Aries in the ascendant, who grew up on a farm or who grew up with parents who were very focused on physical performance. A man grew up with his parents on a farm. He otherwise had a lot of water in his birth chart and a great sensitivity within him, but because of the practical environment he grew up in, he had the ascendant precisely in Aries. He learned early on to temper his sensitivity and focus his energy more on external and physical things. As an adult, this caused some health problems, as he shut down his own energy and emotions for many years.

It doesn't always have to be like in the example above, but it's important to also look at the rest of the chart to see how things play out there.

Here it is valuable to look at our upbringing to see which patterns and characteristics we developed, based on how our everyday life looked. Some valuable parts to look at are what qualities and behaviors were valued, i.e., what we felt safe doing and expressing.

If we have Aries in the ascendant, it can also mean that we experienced our childhood as so challenging and stressful that we completely gave up trusting other people - we have learned that we need to cope with life and solve everything on our own. As small children, we need help in dealing with our inner self and what is happening in our lives. If we don't get that help, we learn that the only one we can trust is ourselves. For this reason, it is quite common for people with this ascendant to have difficulty with trust, at least when it comes to deep closeness and intimacy. It's easier to be on our own so we don't have to face the fear of rejection when we show our inner vulnerability.

Common Challenges

It is common for individuals with Aries in the ascendant to feel that they need to prove something and that they need to perform in order to feel appreciated. If we experience this in our lives, it is valuable to create an awareness of where it comes from and see how we can lower the demands on ourselves. We need to allow ourselves to enjoy life more and to slow down and experience stillness once in a while. Because we have a strong and direct energy, we need to learn to direct our energy where it should go. For example, if we experience frustration or impatience, we need to learn to deal with this within ourselves, rather than projecting it onto people around us.

Strengths & Gifts

Aries' great gifts lie in its direct and passionate energy, something that can inspire other people on an infinite number of different levels. There is an ease and an ability to throw yourself into new projects, although this can vary from individual to individual. Aries gifts are often visible and prominent as they are strongly connected with the masculine more extroverted energy.

Our great gifts with Aries ascendant lie in our ability to act quickly, solve things independently and to dare to try new things. There is a courage within us that gets us through life, and we can use that quality to get ahead purely practically but also in terms of healing. By daring to explore new terrain and what we carry within us, we can bring out additional qualities and gifts but also become more balanced in general.

Health & energy flow

There are many important parts to look at in the Birth Chart when it comes to health and two of them are the ascendant sign and the sixth house. The ascendant has a strong connection to our physical body, how we move physically but also how we protect ourselves and absorb energy. The sixth house is the house for health, daily routines and shows what we need in everyday life to get flow in a general way.

When Aries is in the Ascendant, we usually have a good physique and great access to our life energy. In general, we have seen that individuals with fire signs as ascendant have a strong physical body, a lot of energy to take off and a good strategy to cope with various challenges, both emotional and physical. Due to the masculine and outgoing energy found in Aries, individuals here find it somewhat easier to "shake off" problems around them or protect themselves in a powerful way.

Aries has a quick energy which can be positive as it helps to initiate processes, make things happen and expand energy. The challenge here, when it comes to health, lies in not forcing things and thus running over important signals in the body. With Aries as ascendant, it is important that we learn to stop sometimes and tune into the body and our emotions, to see what is going on there. Otherwise, we may miss important information that our body is trying to convey.

One of Aries' strengths lies in its ability to defend itself! Individuals with Aries here have learned to stand up for themselves and also defend themselves from various dangers around. The defense helps to protect from danger but can also become a defense or a barrier to the inner, that is, emotions we need to face in order to heal on a deep spiritual level.

Due to the strong basic energy found in Aries, there is a great need for movement, both physically and energetically. There needs to be room for physical expression and an opportunity to express spontaneous needs and feelings. If that possibility is not present, it can create energy blockages and stagnation in the body. With Aries, it is therefore of great importance that we work with this flow, through something that we are passionate about or feel passionate about. In general, Aries here find it difficult to do anything that creates boredom and there needs to be a motivation in the picture.

With Aries as the ascendant sign, this means that our sixth house is in the sign of Virgo. The sixth house is also related to our general health and shows what we need in our everyday life to feel good but also to build healthy routines and have flow in our energy. Virgo as a sign stands for themes such as health, routines, details, accuracy, service and perfection.

There is a grounding and practical energy to this sign, something very different from the energy of Aries.

With this combination, it is valuable for us to find a balance here, in terms of our health and our everyday life. We can use the spontaneous and passionate energy of Aries in what we do, but make sure that we get the qualities of Virgo in our everyday life, with some form of routine and structure. All people need something to hold onto during everyday life, some kind of framework that we can fall back on. Precisely because of the fire that Aries has, this can be very valuable. It helps us to ground ourselves and to incorporate important health routines.

With Virgo in the sixth house, it is also important that we review our food and diet so that we get good energy and the nutrition our body needs. It's not about getting stuck in strict rules, but finding a balance between movement, healthy food and routines that benefit us in the long term.

Related Chakra

Aries has a strong connection to the solar plexus chakra. The solar plexus chakra sits below the heart at the upper abdomen. The chakra represents our ability to stand up for ourselves, our identity and our inner pride. It also has to do with our integrity and how much we are prepared to fight for ourselves and what we believe in.

When the solar plexus chakra is out of balance, it often manifests itself in the form of low self-esteem, difficulty getting ahead and we have difficulty setting healthy boundaries for ourselves, both in terms of other people and in terms of physical activity. In balance, we know who we are, and we stand up for ourselves when needed. There is a pride within us that drives us forward and helps us deal with challenges.

With Aries in the ascendant, the solar plexus is a very central area of our body and for that reason we need to take extra care of it. We need to look at whether we were given the opportunity to develop these qualities while growing up or whether it is something we can work on here and now. By becoming aware of how we relate to people around us, we can begin to build relationships with more balance and a positive flow.

The solar plexus chakra also has a connection to our inner child and many of the traits we mentioned above are ones that develop during our first years of life together with our parents. We learn to stand up for ourselves, show our own will and through the age of defiance we begin to build our own identity and a sense of pride within us.

The Career Houses

When it comes to job, career and life path in the birth chart, there are many parts to look at, such as our composition of the chart with all the planets and where our power point MC (Midheaven) is located. But there are some important parts we can look at already here. By looking at the qualities and the energy that our ascendant represents, we can see what we need jobwise, to develop. When we know what our ascendant sign is, we can also see what our career houses are, that is, what signs and elements they are in. The career houses are 2, 6 & 10.

With the ascendant in Aries, the three career houses are in the signs Taurus, Virgo & Capricorn, all of which are earth signs. Earth represents the practical and material things around us, what we can touch. Having the career houses in earth signs means that we have great resources within us when it comes to creation and building, something we can use to build our career and manifest what we dream of. This is further enhanced if we have the Sun, Moon or other planets in these three houses.

So, what does it mean to have Aries in the ascendant and the three career houses in earth signs?

With this combination, we can use the fire and passion of Aries and at the same time build something big for the long term, using the earth found in our career houses. Just fire and earth together have a strong ability to start up and then complete different ideas and projects. Both fire and earth have a physical character, which means that we can be drawn to jobs where we have to do something physical or practical. Some examples of jobs that can fit with this combination are inspirer, project manager, health coach or something in training.

The tenth house is one of the workhouses and perhaps the most important to look at, in terms of career but also in terms of our life mission – what we are here to manifest in this life. In this constellation, the tenth house is in Capricorn in the Birth Chart, which means several different things. Capricorns are good at pushing projects through, structuring and following through on their goals – even climbing mountains if necessary. This means that we have great opportunities to build a strong career or follow our life's mission, if we use these qualities. Capricorn is well suited as a boss, leader or entrepreneur and with the independent energy of Aries in the Ascendant, that energy is amplified.

If we grew up in an environment where we were restricted or where we were forced to lock up much of our power, due to parents or circumstances, it is important that we become aware and heal this. When we do that, we can use the enormous power and potential associated with our career houses and associated qualities.

Spirituality, Transformation & Deep Healing

With the ascendant in Aries, important and great lessons, which we need to become aware of, come through and master within ourselves. These lessons lie in understanding ourselves, our energy and thus also understanding our surroundings. Aries is the sign of independence and of courage. It is also the sign of spontaneous actions and through the energy of the sign we follow our impulses and our instinct. We were born into this life to learn more about these parts of our inner self and to understand what it is that motivates us forward. There is an activation that shines through the energy of Aries, which ignites and lights the way for other people.

But many times, we need to do a lot of inner work to reach the highest potential of the sign, before we feel secure in ourselves and who we are. Here lies the challenge in getting to know ourselves but also understanding the people around us. Opposite Aries is the sign Libra, which represents the opposite of Aries – namely relationships, balance, duality and mediation. An important part for Aries is to follow their impulses and follow their instincts, without doing so at the expense of other people or by being overly self-focused. When we learn to follow our inner self but also take into account the Libra opposite, i.e. relationships and those we meet - then we find the balance.

The lowest energy of Aries is associated with self-absorption, excessive focus on the ego and the need to always get one's way.

In order to heal these lower parts and raise our energy, we will come across situations that give us the opportunity to face this very thing within us. We will also encounter themes connected with relationships where we will have the opportunity to see what still needs to be adjusted and healed within us.

There are three houses in the birth chart that relate to our inner depth, our transformation and our spirituality. It is houses 4, 8 & 12. House four shows what we carry with us from family and lineage. House eight shows how we undergo transformation during life but also what healing abilities we have. House twelve shows what we carry in our subconscious and what energy we need to lift up and make conscious. If we have planets in one of these houses, the energy and focus there becomes even stronger.

With the ascendant in Aries, we have our spiritual houses in Cancer, Scorpio & Pisces. This means that the spiritual houses are in water signs. When these houses are in water, we get a great depth and a great sensitivity. Many individuals with water in these houses have great abilities in mediumship and healing. There is an ability to sense what lies beneath the surface, both for ourselves and for other people.

Here we can use our direct energy, and the courage found in Aries, to dive deep into our spiritual houses and thus find things that have been hidden from us. There is tremendous opportunity for expansion here if we dare to be in our feelings and allow ourselves to be vulnerable.

Combination with the Sun

Now follows a review of Aries in the ascendant in combination with all Sun signs. Look at your ascendant sign in the Birth Chart and then where your Sun is. Combining these two energies gives you a strong indication of what you are here to delve into and manifest in this life. It also gives you guidance for spiritual themes you can develop and understand within yourself and in your life.

The ascendant shows how you have been shaped, how you meet your surroundings as well as important life themes and lessons for you in the course of life. The sun shows where you are meant to shine in this life and where you have a great opportunity to make an impression with your energy.

Ascendant in Aries & Sun in Aries
With both the ascendant and the Sun in Aries, they are in the same sign and house, the first house. The first house represents new beginnings, initiation, leadership and our personality.

When both the ascendant and the Sun are in the same sign and house, the energy mixes and they create a strong unity. Our inner core goes hand in hand with our personality and how we were shaped during our upbringing. The energy of Aries becomes extra prominent here and we have strong qualities such as courage, strength, drive and a lot of life energy. With this placement, we are here to strengthen our inner leadership and follow what awakens our inner drive – what we are prepared to fight for. With the Sun here, many of our great lessons come when we ourselves take the initiative and lead ourselves forward in a courageous way. We have a great power within us and by using it we can achieve our highest goals in life. We can also use that power to dare to face our inner self and receive the healing we need during our spiritual ascent.

Ascendant in Aries & Sun in Taurus
With the ascendant in Aries and the Sun in Taurus, this means that the Sun is in the second house - the house of material resources, self-worth, money, abundance and scarcity.

With the Sun in the second house, you are here to develop your inner sense of worth and to build up your resources, both internally and materially. Inner resources can be, for example, your intuition, education or your capacity to cope with things. Material resources can be money or physical things in general. This lifetime is about your soul's relationship to resources and how you value yourself. Through experiences of failure or lack, you are forced to go deep within yourself to find new ways. When you realize your divine value as the soul that you are, you can create all that you need in life. The Sun is in Taurus, the sign of material resources, creativity and stability. So, to develop your Sun here you need to develop these areas over the course of life.

Through the courage and drive of Aries together with the patience and stability of Taurus, you can work towards abundance in the various areas of life. Aries dares to try new directions and once you find your direction, the Sun in Taurus can help keep it there.

Ascendant in Aries & Sun in Gemini
With the ascendant in Aries and the Sun in Gemini, this means that the Sun is in the third house - the house of communication, perspective, learning and mental processes.

With the Sun in the third house, you are here to learn all about communication and finding your own true expression. This lifetime is about your soul's relationship to communication and how you let your soul express itself here on Earth. To find your unique expression and what you want to convey, you may need to experience the lower energy of this theme first, i.e. difficulty making your voice heard or getting your messages across. The Sun is in Gemini, the sign of communication, curiosity and learning. This means that these are qualities that you can use to develop your Sun and to fill up with Life Energy.

To develop in this area, you can use the courage and drive of Aries together with the curiosity and flexibility of Gemini. Through flexibility and curiosity, you find new perspectives and paths to follow. Be sure to ground yourself a little extra with this combination.

Ascendant in Aries & Sun in Cancer

With the ascendant in Aries and the Sun in Cancer, this means that the Sun is in the fourth house - the house of home, family, security, roots and origins.

With the Sun in the fourth house, you are here to understand your roots and what you carry with you from there. Family is a big theme in this life. You may find that you have an attraction to your family, either the family you grew up in or the family you yourself choose to create as an adult. This lifetime is about finding a home within yourself and understanding who you are deep down. There may also be some kind of karma in your family that you need to free yourself from on a deep spiritual level. The sun is in Cancer, the sign of home, security and family. This reinforces the theme of the fourth house.

You are very sensitive, and your feelings can change quickly. With the Sun in Cancer, it is very valuable that you get to know your emotional life and that you learn to master your various emotions, both positive and negative. Your challenging emotions can be the key to your greatest healing and release.

Through this combination, you can use the sensitivity you carry with you in Cancer and, together with the courage of Aries, overcome challenges that come your way. Dare to try new terrain every now and then, so you don't get stuck in security and stagnation.

Ascendant in Aries & Sun in Leo
With the ascendant in Aries and the Sun in Leo, this means that the Sun is in the fifth house - the house of creativity, sports, creation, expression, children and playfulness.

With the Sun in the fifth house, you are here to develop your creativity and to affirm your playfulness. This lifetime is about allowing your creative expression to emerge and flow in the different areas of life, and you may be drawn to create. There are many ways to create and since the fifth house is in Leo, creative energy is doubled. You have an ability to spread joy in people around you and people in your environment can be drawn to your passionate energy.

With Aries in the ascendant and the Sun in Leo, you have a fiery, imaginative and passionate energy that you need to live out. One piece of advice is to find some form of expression where you can contribute with inspiration or help people in some way. You can choose to create something for yourself, but the power becomes infinite when you create for other people.

Ascendant in Aries & Sun in Virgo

With the ascendant in Aries and the Sun in Virgo, this means that the Sun is in the sixth house - the house of health, routines, service, mastery and work.

With the Sun in the sixth house, you are here to learn all about health and everyday routines. You are here to build an everyday life that resonates with you and your soul. This lifetime is about your soul's relationship to health and service. When you understand your body and its needs, you can create an everyday life that gives you energy and flow. Service is also an important keyword with this placement. By developing knowledge and skills around health and energy, you can teach other people to take care of themselves. The Sun is in Virgo, the sign of precisely service, health and routines. This means you need to look at these themes and see how you can manifest them in your life in a positive way. With the Sun in Virgo, you are meant to contribute some form of service to other people. Be sure that you help people in a balanced way, without codependency or at the expense of your own energy.

Here you can use the energy in Aries to dare to try new paths and to dare to throw yourself into unknown terrain when necessary. Aries can help you activate and reboot while Virgo has the ability to create routines that are healthy and positive for you.

Ascendant in Aries & Sun in Libra

With the ascendant in Aries and the Sun in Libra, this means that the Sun is in the seventh house - the house of relationships, balance, relating and other people. This placement also means that the ascendant and the Sun are opposite each other in the chart.

With the Sun in the seventh house, you're here to learn all about relationships. This means that you are here to build the relationship with yourself but also your other relationships in life. To become an expert in this area, you need to face some challenges first. This may mean that during the course of your life you struggle with dysfunctionality in relationships, for example in the form of codependency or adaptation. The seventh house is in Libra, the sign of relationships. This means that the theme of relationships becomes extra prominent for you. Many of your great and profound lessons in this lifetime come through your relationships and through partnerships. Strive to develop your relationships to the highest good for you, both the relationship with yourself and with others. Heal what isn't working for you and surround yourself with relationships that raise your energy.

To bring balance to your Sun in the seventh house, you can use the courage and power found in Aries to create change and try new things. With this combination, you need to ensure that you affirm your own energy but also the needs that exist in your closest relationships. Balance here leads to great expansion for your soul. You heal patterns from past lives and create new ones for future lives.

Ascendant in Aries & Sun in Scorpio

With the ascendant in Aries and the Sun in Scorpio, this means that the Sun is in the eighth house - the house of transformation, transformation, shared resources, intimacy and deep aspects of ourselves.

With the Sun in the eighth house, you are here to understand yourself on a deep spiritual level. This lifetime gives you the opportunity for deep conversion and transformation, something that is amplified when the Sun is in Scorpio. With this placement, you are very likely to experience periods of crisis or even trauma. All to lead your soul towards the transformation you decided on before you stepped down on Earth. An important task for you in this life involves learning to master all shades of emotions and energies. You need to dare to face the very lowest within you, what no one else dares to look at. By daring to face what is going on inside you, you can transform it. You become a powerful healer with great gifts to help other people on their journey. With the Sun in Scorpio, it is important that you constantly work with your flow, so that you don't get stuck in stagnation emotionally.

To cope with this and to face the challenges that come along the way, you can use the power and courage found in Aries, your ascendant. Scorpio is your sensitivity and your intuition while Aries leads you forward with its stubborn and fiery energy.

Ascendant in Aries & Sun in Sagittarius
With the ascendant in Aries and the Sun in Sagittarius, this means that the Sun is in the ninth house - the house of exploration, travel, adventure, wisdom and belief.

With the Sun in the ninth house, you are here to explore life's big questions but also to expand as a soul. You may feel drawn to understand yourself better but also to different forms of knowledge and travel – all that give you new insights and growth. With this placement, you have great potential to become a teacher or inspirer of other people, especially when you find home within yourself. The Sun is in Sagittarius, the sign of learning, expansion and beliefs. This means that these themes become extra prominent for you in this life. With the Sun in Sagittarius, it is very important that you strive to find your inner truth, that is, what resonates with you and your soul. It could be about your view of spirituality, knowledge or any other area.

With the Sun in Sagittarius and the ascendant in Aries, we get double fire. This means that you may sometimes need to stop in the course of life, to really look at where you are going, so that you do not run through life without direction. Be sure to ground yourself, so that you maintain your contact with the body and the earth.

Ascendant in Aries & Sun in Capricorn
With the ascendant in Aries and the Sun in Capricorn, this means that the Sun is in the tenth house - the house of work, career, life task, manifestation and greater impact.

With the Sun in the tenth house, you are here to make a mark in work, career or through your life's task. You are also here too free yourself from family patterns and build your life on your terms, based on your own longing. When the Sun is here, you may feel a pull to do something that has a greater meaning for people. The Sun is in Capricorn, the sign of drive, discipline and hard work. This means that these are qualities you should strive for in order to reach your goals and make it all the way to the top. With the Sun here, you have great possibilities to get far in the field you choose to focus on.

You can also take help from the courage and fire of Aries in the ascendant, to defeat any challenges but also to bring inspiration and creativity into what you do. When you mix the energy of fire and earth, you get a mix of creativity and physical manifestation.

Ascendant in Aries & Sun in Aquarius

With the ascendant in Aries and the Sun in Aquarius, this means that the Sun is in the eleventh house - the house of groups, networks, visions of the future, community involvement and innovation.

With the Sun in the eleventh house, you are here to contribute something to the great mass, based on a higher purpose. It can be about conveying information, creating a network, writing books or finding innovative ways of working. With this placement, you may feel drawn to create something outside the box and you may experience that you are different from the people around you. Affirm your unique energy with this placement and you will be able to make a big difference to the world. The Sun is in Aquarius, the sign of innovation and new thinking. This means that there will be a doubling of these themes. To develop your Sun and fill up with life energy, you need to live life in your unique way, outside of given templates. You have great abilities when it comes to finding solutions to things and you see things from a higher perspective.

You can use the courage and fiery energy of Aries to dare to throw yourself out when needed and to bring a creative and passionate energy to what you do. When you mix Aries' ability to initiate and Aquarius' ability to create innovation - then you become a great asset to society.

Ascendant in Aries & Sun in Pisces

With the ascendant in Aries and the Sun in Pisces, this means that the Sun is in the twelfth house - the house of subconscious processes, spirituality, dreams and escape.

With the Sun in the twelfth house, you are here to explore your inner self and to affirm your sensitivity. With this placement, you may find that you need a lot of your own time to process things and to replenish your energy. When the Sun is in this house, you have deep spiritual abilities and a strong intuition, something that will be strengthened through inner work and by daring to face what is going on within yourself. By mastering the energy here, you become a powerful healer, and you can work with spirituality and help people. The Sun is in Pisces, the sign of spirituality and sensitivity but also of escape. This means that you are extremely sensitive, and you sense energies from people and from the collective. With the Sun here, it is very important that you ground yourself and that you dare to remain in lower states of emotion. When you dare to face yourself, you become a strong healer for others.

To find balance between the Sun and the ascendant, you can use the courage and spontaneous energy of Aries to develop within you. You can use your sensitivity in Pisces and together with Aries courage move forward and find new paths for development.

CHAPTER 5
TAURUS IN THE ASCENDANT

Taurus

Qualities: Earth, Solid, Feminine

Ruled by the planet: Venus

Connected to house: 2

Soul Archetypes: Builder, Artist

Connection to chakra: Root Chakra

Taurus Characteristics & Energy

Taurus is the second sign in the Zodiac and symbolizes themes such as stability, holding on and getting things and projects done. Other qualities associated with Taurus are creation, creativity, physical strength and material things - for example money. The sign carries a grounding firm feminine energy, which means there is a lot of determination and a strong ability to see projects through.

Soul archetypes associated with Taurus are the Builder, the Banker & the Artist.

Taurus as ascendant

With its earth element, Taurus as a sign has a strong connection to the material world. These are things we can see, touch and value. Taurus values the practical and many times there is an attraction to surround themselves with fine and also financially valuable things. It can be about money but can also be other things such as beautiful art, a nice garden or good food. Taurus carries a fixed energy, which means that there is a strong determination but also an unwavering loyalty.

With Taurus in the ascendant, we have an inherent stubbornness and need to do things our own way. It is difficult to influence the Taurus, if the Taurus themselves do not want or feel like it. With this ascendant sign, we are often very keen to have a stable everyday life, where we can build and create at our own pace. There is a simplicity here and unlike the sign Scorpio opposite, which is drawn to chaos and depth, we often seek precisely the simple and obvious in our everyday life. We thrive when we have peace and quiet and when we can focus on what we think is important.

Taurus is a physically strong sign and with this ascendant sign we often have a calmness within ourselves as well as an ability to attract people and various projects. People around us usually perceive us as secure in ourselves and they feel that we move forward with certainty, unless there is something else in the chart to the contrary.

Soul contract/Soul plan

With Taurus in the ascendant, we are here on Earth to learn to enjoy the good and beautiful in life, what we have around us and what we ourselves create. We are also here to master the physical over the course of life and through that learn to manifest things in physical form. A great lesson here lies in finding the balance between the material and the inner emotional – to master the physical but not get caught up in it.

Childhood & patterns from growing up

When we step into a body here on Earth, we choose a family and an environment that matches our current energy and vibration as well as the lessons we want to learn and deal with during this life. We thus choose a family that helps shape our ascendant.

With Taurus as the ascendant, we have usually been formed in an environment where our parents valued the practical and material over the emotional. It doesn't necessarily mean that emotions were completely absent during our upbringing but there was a focus on what we could see and touch. With this ascendant, it is also common for us to be praised or appreciated for being calm and patient. Depending on how balanced our parents were, there will be a spectrum here, where at the lowest end of this spectrum we are cut off from our emotions and our inner emotional life. But it can also be that we have access to our emotions but feel more at home in the physical and practical.

Since Taurus has strong resources within itself, we have learned during growing up to get ahead in a fairly determined and purposeful way. We have been taught to see the value in the things we have around us. We may also have grown up with one or two parents with a creative energy, something that we have taken with us in our way of living and looking at things.

With this ascendant, we've been taught that stability and loyalty are important themes, whether that means we got these attributes from our parents or more forced into them by circumstances. In our work, we have seen that most of us carry the lower energy of our Ascendant in some form, right up until we become aware and work with it.

Common Challenges

The Taurus's big challenge lies in finding flexibility, above all when it comes to everyday life. There is a fixed energy here that needs to be mixed with a more moving energy of the chart, in order for us to bring in more balance. Taurus is persistent and can push through large and long-term projects, but here a certain input or activation is often needed for it to happen. So, in that way, the Taurus can be sluggish and get stuck in the comfortable, what is already familiar and accustomed.

With Taurus as ascendant, we need to make sure that we break out of old habits and patterns every now and then, otherwise we easily get stuck in stagnation. This may involve changing workplaces when the time is right or building new routines when the old ones no longer work. The loyalty we have can be a great asset or a limitation, depending on how we use it. When we have this ascendant sign, it is valuable that we check in every once in a while, to see if we are on a favorable path or if we are stuck in old and dysfunctional patterns.

Strengths & Gifts

Our strength with Taurus in the ascendant definitely lies in our ability to create stability and security, in ourselves and in our surroundings. We have a gift for spreading calm and harmony when meeting people, and many see us as a safe rock to fall back against. There is a calmness and determination, which makes us trustworthy to those around us.

We live in a time where many of the qualities of Taurus are highly valued, especially in the Western world. We are programmed to fend for ourselves and to be able to build a pleasant and stable existence around us. These are qualities that Taurus usually find easy, which means that we have a lot of resources we can use to build and manifest the life we want. The harmony of Taurus spreads waves of trust and confidence where there is worry, chaos and stress.

Taurus is patient and hardworking! With this patience combined with a clearly defined goal, we can get through even the most challenging situations in the course of life. In addition to what we mentioned, Taurus has great creativity, which can be shown through a beautiful singing voice, an eye for art or a talent for crafts.

Health & energy flow

There are many important parts to look at in the Birth Chart when it comes to health and two of them are the ascendant sign and the sixth house. The ascendant has a strong connection to our physical body, how we move physically but also how we protect ourselves and absorb energy. The sixth house is the house of health, daily routines and shows what we need in everyday life to get flow in a general way.

With the ascendant in Taurus, we usually have good health as we have inner peace. That calm allows us to avoid strong stress and anxiety. What we may need to pay attention to is our diet and what we eat, as Taurus may have a slightly slower metabolism than average. Because of the fixed energy found in the sign, we can get too attached to things, both emotionally, practically, but also physically. There is a risk of ending up in stagnation during the course of life, if we do not take care to introduce flow and a certain flexibility in what we do.

Like all earth signs in the Zodiac, there is a strong ability to handle stress and to stay grounded. This means that we naturally remain in the body, even when we encounter tough emotions. If we are grounded and keep in touch with our body, we have a strong protection within ourselves.

In order to strengthen our energy with Taurus in the ascendant, it is important that we constantly maintain the connection with our physical body, to see how it is doing and what is going on. But at the same time, we need to strive for movement and some form of activity. It can be activity through physical movement or through something creative. We constantly need to get new life energy into the body. It helps us to strengthen our general energy and power but also to keep a good balance in our organs and internal systems.

With Taurus as the ascendant sign, it means that our sixth house is in the sign of Libra. Libra as a sign stands for themes such as balance, relationships and aesthetics. There is an airy and social energy in this sign, something that differs somewhat from the energy of Taurus.

This combination is unique in its own way as both Taurus and Libra are ruled by the planet Venus. This means that there is a common denominator here, although the energy of the signs also differ. What strongly links these signs here are themes such as aesthetics, creativity and a focus on the beautiful in life. So, with this combination, it is important that we build an existence where these themes are present in some form. It helps us feel alive and at peace with ourselves and with life. It can look many different ways. We may have a strong attraction to music or art, or to creating something through our imagination. So, we need to find a way to use our creative energy.

Libra as a sign has a more clear focus on relationships and how we balance and relate to other people. So, with Libra in the sixth house, it is extremely important that we surround ourselves with people who help us create this balance. This does not mean that we should only seek simple and casual relationships, but rather become aware of where we need to bring in more balance and flow. Balance comes from within and by setting boundaries that feel good to us and by being authentic we build healthy relationships.

Since the sixth house shows what we need in everyday life to feel good, we also need to find balance in what we do - in our habits and routines but also, for example, at work. It can be about setting limits at work when it becomes too much.

When it comes to our diet and what we put into us, it can be extra important to find a balance, as the planet Venus represents sugar and sweets. If we feel that we have an attraction to this, it can be good to look at how we can get in a more nutritious and energy-rich food. Both Libra and Taurus as signs can tend to put on weight easily, which we can prevent if we are aware of it.

Related Chakra

Taurus has a strong connection to the Root Chakra in our energy system. This means that it can be valuable to look over that chakra a little extra, through an awareness of what it stands for and how it affects us.

The Root chakra is our lowest chakra (at least of our seven main chakras) and is located at the bottom of the spine. The chakra is connected with our inner security, stability, our roots and our connection with the physical body. It is also related to our ability to feel grounded and to bring out energy in a physical manifestation - that is, manifesting things in our life.

When the Root Chakra is out of balance, we may experience that we are ungrounded and that we have difficulty finding inner peace. We can also find it difficult to build things in the material world and feel generally restless.

When the chakra is balanced, we have a natural calm within us, and we move forward in a systematic and grounded way. We have our basic security within us, something that is there regardless of the stress factors in our environment.

With Taurus in the ascendant, the Root Chakra is very central and depending on how we grew up, the chakra will be more or less in balance. If we have gained a strong foundation to stand on during childhood and security in the meeting with our parents, the probability is high that we have balance here. We know how to solve things, and we are good at solving things in a practical way.

During our work with Astrology, we have seen that individuals with Taurus sometimes have a tendency to become too "fixed" in their earth energy, which means that in a way they have overactivity precisely in the Root Chakra. There is an excessive focus on security and the material, something that can be good to be aware of. If we feel that we have a great need for control or that we find it difficult to break our routines or ingrained patterns, we may need to bring in more flexibility and mobility.

To get a good flow in the root chakra, it is positive if we can find our inner security, build up stability but also create and test new things from time to time. Balance comes through patterns of mobility and stability.

The career houses

When it comes to job, career and life path in the Birth Chart, there are many parts to look at, such as our composition of the chart with all the planets and where our power point MC (Midheaven) is located. But there are some important parts we can look at already here. By looking at the qualities and the energy that our Ascendant represents, we can see what we need jobwise to develop. When we know what our ascendant sign is, we can also see what our career houses are, that is, what signs and elements they are in. The career houses are 2, 6 & 10.

With the ascendant in Taurus, the three career houses are in the signs Gemini, Libra & Aquarius, all of which are air signs. Air represents communication, mental processes, knowledge and learning. Having the career houses in air signs means that we have great resources within us when it comes to communication and learning, something we can use to build our career and manifest what we dream of. This is further enhanced if we have the Sun, Moon or other planets in these three houses.

So, what does it mean to have Taurus in the ascendant and the career houses in the air sign?

With Taurus in the ascendant and the career houses in the air, we get an exciting mix of energies. Here we can use our strength and stability of Taurus and mix it with our communicative and analytical side. Earth and air together create abilities in areas such as structure, analysis, psychological work, journalistic and data. We can feel drawn to jobs where we get to use our physical body but also where we get the opportunity to express our ideas and thoughts.

The tenth house is one of the career houses and perhaps the most important to look at, in terms of career but also in terms of our life mission – what we are here to manifest in this life.

With this constellation, the tenth house is in Aquarius. Aquarius is good at going their own way and finding new innovative solutions. There is a pull to do things outside the box and with this sign in the tenth house we should find a way to bring this energy into what we do. It can be about building a career or carrying out our life's task in a way that awakens people or that opens up new paths.

Taurus and Aquarius have big differences in their energy and here we may have to let go a little of the security we have in our ascendant sign and give space to Aquarius, especially when it comes to choosing a profession and career. With the combination of these two signs, we can create great changes for society if we choose to use the strong will and determination found in both signs - for a higher purpose.

Spirituality, Transformation & Deep Healing

With Taurus in the ascendant, we have great lessons here on Earth and there are several aspects here. An important part is about learning to master the practical and material things around us, in a way that helps us in our growth. We have a strong practical energy and if we use this power in a positive way, we can create great changes within ourselves but also for other people. We can use our calmness and stability to build something long-term. Our ability to take things at our own pace combined with our physical focus gives us an opportunity to use these qualities to create the existence we want around us. It can, for example be to, deal with our finances, our housing, investments or some other project.

Our challenge here can be as we mentioned earlier - that we get stuck in the material, that we enter stagnation or that we move in our safety zone. If we feel that we are stuck in the old, it is valuable and healing to take help from the Energy of Scorpio which is opposite, in the seventh house. Scorpio is drawn to the hidden, the complex and searches for things that give deep meaning. There is an energy of chaos and crisis here, something we may need to let in at times with Taurus on the ascendant.

The lowest energy of Taurus is rigid, fixed and stagnant while the highest energy of the sign is expectant, creative, productive and trusting. Here we can look at how we were shaped while growing up and investigate whether there are negative patterns we are stuck in. By lifting up these patterns, we can consciously work to change them. During our spiritual ascent we can see two prominent tendencies in Taurus. One is that we hold ourselves back, by staying in the familiar and secure. The second is that we use our earth energy and our contact with the Earth, to take small steps forward towards development and expansion. If we can use the latter strategy, we can harness the amazing energy of Taurus and move ourselves forward in a powerful way.

There are three houses in the Birth Chart that relate to our inner depth, our transformation and our spirituality. It is houses 4, 8 & 12. House four shows what we carry with us from family and lineage. House eight shows how we undergo transformation during life but also what healing abilities we have. House twelve shows what we carry in our subconscious and what energy we need to lift up and make conscious. If we have planets in one of these houses, the energy there becomes even stronger.

With the ascendant in Taurus, we have our spiritual houses in Leo, Sagittarius & Aries. This means that the spiritual houses are in fire signs. When these houses are on fire, we get a strong penetrating and fiery energy. Many individuals with fire in these houses have great abilities in energy work and an ability to transform strong energy.

There is a great contrast between Taurus and the fire energy found in the deep houses, but this contrast we can use in our inner work and through transformational processes. Taurus is grounded and calm, while all three fire signs have a more explosive essence in their energy. We have seen that individuals who have their spiritual houses in fire signs often have a dynamic inner world. It can be in the form of strong emotions or an inner drive. It is important that we allow this fiery side of us to come forward and take the place it needs in our life, because otherwise we tend to suppress that energy. If we suppress explosive energy and strong emotions, we can eventually develop stagnation or various forms of pain symptoms in the body. All the energy we have within us needs to be allowed to move and be expressed in some form. The reason we highlight it here is because of the contrast between fire and the three deep houses. Houses 4, 8 & 12 are naturally linked with our 3 water signs, meaning they have a feminine, introspective and watery energy to them. The fire signs, on the other hand, are masculine and they have a strong outward energy. For this reason, we need to look at how we can express our innermost feelings and find a way to channel emotions and strong energy within us - for example through creativity or healing.

The eighth house represents our inner depth but also how we deal with crises and what we need to transform and transform things in our life. In this combination the eighth house is in Sagittarius, which is a mutable and freedom-seeking sign. This means that we need to have a certain form of freedom in order to heal ourselves and it is extremely important for us to find our inner truth and our convictions. By following the direction that feels true to us, we will constantly undergo the transformation we need. Through an inner journey and through exploration within ourselves, we can access what has been hidden from us, what needs to be made visible and transformed.

The twelfth house represents the subconscious, and the sign here often shows which energy and which qualities we more or less shut down during our upbringing. With Aries here, it is important to become aware of inner impulses and the spontaneous fiery energy that may need to be tapped.

Perhaps we have learned to be matter of fact and stick to the practical or material during childhood. Then it can be valuable to allow the power and spontaneity of Aries to emerge for us.

With Taurus in the ascendant and the three spiritual houses in fire signs, we can use our grounded energy that we carry and use the fire to transform a lot of energy and blockages within us. Taurus helps us stay grounded and purposeful, while the fire and power that exists otherwise helps us find new paths and explore our passion and strong life energy.

Combination with the Sun

Below follows a review of the ascendant in Taurus in combination with all Sun signs. Look at your ascendant sign in the Birth Chart and then where your Sun is. Combining these two energies gives you a strong indication of what you are here to delve into and manifest in this life. It also gives you guidance for spiritual themes you can develop and understand within yourself and in your life.

The ascendant shows how you have been shaped, how you meet your surroundings as well as important life themes and lessons for you in the course of life.

The sun shows where you are meant to shine in this life and where you have a great opportunity to make an impression with your energy.

Ascendant in Taurus & Sun in Aries

With the ascendant in Taurus and the Sun in Aries, this means that the Sun is in the twelfth house - the house of the subconscious, creativity, dreams, spirituality and escape.

With the Sun in the twelfth house, you are here to develop a deep understanding of your inner self but also of your spirituality. You are here to master what is going on in your subconscious mind and heal old things that are limiting you. With the Sun here, you may experience that you need a lot of your own time, to process and process what is happening around you. With this placement, you can experience that you have a lot going on inside you, but which can be difficult to bring out at times. Work a lot on expressing your energy in a conscious way. The Sun is in Aries, the sign of courage and spontaneity but also of activation. This means that these are qualities you need to strive to develop in the course of life. In order to develop your Sun and fill up with life energy, it is important that you dare to try new things and let your spontaneity guide you from time to time. Aries is brave and dares to venture into the unknown.

Here you can use the stability and earth you have in Taurus to slowly but surely reach your life goals. Through Aries, you get the initial energy you need to start new processes, processes in your inner self or in the outer world.

Ascendant in Taurus & Sun in Taurus

With both the ascendant and the Sun in Taurus, it means they are in the same sign and house. Both the ascendant and the Sun are in the first house which represents leadership, initiative, activation but also our outer personality.

When both the ascendant and the Sun are in the same sign and house, the energy mixes and they create a strong unity. Our inner core goes hand in hand with our personality and how we were shaped during our upbringing. Taurus' energy becomes extra prominent here and we have strong qualities when it comes to the material, creating and building things in the long term.

With the Sun in the first house, you are here to develop your leadership but also to follow your inner direction and what you stand for. The ascendant reinforces this, and it may be that you grew up in a family where you had the opportunity to develop some form of leadership. By using the stability and patience found in Taurus, you can build things in the long run. Taurus is also a creative sign, which means that you carry strong creative abilities, something that you can express in many different ways. With both the Sun and the ascendant in Taurus, it is very important that you get mobility and flow in different ways during life. Make sure the direction you go resonates with you, so you don't struggle too long in something that doesn't benefit you.

Ascendant in Taurus & Sun in Gemini

With the ascendant in Taurus and the Sun in Gemini, this means that the Sun is in the second house - the house of material resources, self-worth, money, abundance and scarcity.

With the Sun in the second house, you are here to build your resources and to build your sense of worth. Your soul is here on Earth to experience profound themes of scarcity and abundance. By realizing your true divine value, you open up new abilities and resources to take place within you. You go from lack to abundance in different areas of life. The Sun is in Gemini, the sign of communication and learning, but also curiosity. This means that you should strive to develop these qualities, to bring out your Sun and develop in this area. You need to find your unique expression and express what is important and true to you.

To master and get through challenges, you can use Taurus's patience, calmness and stability - and build a solid foundation within yourself in the long run. With the stability of Taurus combined with the mobility of Gemini, you get a dynamic and creative energy.

Ascendant in Taurus & Sun in Cancer

With the ascendant in Taurus and the Sun in Cancer, this means that the Sun is in the third house - the house of communication, learning, development and mental processes.

With the Sun in the third house, you are here to learn all about communication and to find your true expression. By exploring the topic of communication, you will eventually build up a sense of security and you will learn to convey your knowledge to other people. It is important that there is an emotional connection in your expression, as the Sun is in the sign of Cancer – the sign of emotions and intuition. So, an important aspect for you is about conveying your communication in an intuitive way, where your inner self permeates what you say.

Your calmness and stability that you possess through Taurus in the ascendant will help you to work in the long term and to cope with the challenges you may face along the way. Since both Taurus and Cancer strive for security in their own way, it is valuable to dare to step outside the comfort zone from time to time. It helps you on the path to expansion and development.

Ascendant in Taurus & Sun in Leo

With the ascendant in Taurus and the Sun in Leo, this means that the Sun is in the fourth house - the house of family, security, base, roots and our heritage.

With the Sun in the fourth house, you are here to build a solid foundation within yourself – in other words, find your home within yourself. You are also here too free yourself from dysfunctional family patterns that limit you. With the Sun here, it is common for you to have some kind of karma connected with family that you need to heal in this life. The Sun is in Leo, the sign of creation and leadership. So, these are also qualities that you should strive to develop in the course of life. With this placement of the Sun, it is important that you build your existence, and your safe base based on the norms and beliefs that suit you and that resonate with your soul.

To develop your Sun and heal your inner self, you can take help from Taurus and its grounding energy. Taurus has the patience and stability you need to get through life's toughest challenges.

Ascendant in Taurus & Sun in Virgo

With the ascendant in Taurus and the Sun in Virgo, this means that the Sun is in the fifth house - the house of creativity, sports, playfulness, children, expression and various forms of creation.

With the Sun in the fifth house, you are here to develop and express your creativity, something that can happen in many different ways. Your soul is infinite and there are really no limits to what you can create, if you yourself allow that life energy to emerge. Since the Sun is in Virgo, you may feel drawn to contribute some form of service here on Earth. Virgo also represents accuracy and perfection. An example of how you can express the Sun in this placement is to create something that can help or provide service to others. It can be a book, a work of art or a course.

To achieve your goals and to develop your solar energy to the maximum, you can use the earth and stability that Taurus in the ascendant gives you. Since both Taurus and Virgo are earth signs, you have a great ability to manifest things practically. Don't forget to bring your feelings into the picture, so that you combine earth with water - the practical with the intuitive.

Ascendant in Taurus & Sun in Libra

With the ascendant in Taurus and the Sun in Libra, this means that the Sun is in the sixth house - the house of health, routine, service, perfection, mastery and work.

With the Sun in the sixth house, you are here on Earth to learn everything about health and your body. You are also here to understand how your energy works and based on that, build an everyday life that resonates with you. Through inner healing and through insights into your own health, you become an expert for other people. The Sun is in the sign of Libra, the sign of relationships, balance and relating. Based on that, it is important that you strive for balance in everyday life, in terms of the body and your needs but also in terms of relationships. The sixth house is also connected with service and with the Sun here you can feel drawn to service and to contribute something to people.

By using your Taurus stability and patience, you can go far in whatever you set your mind to do. You can use your skills to help.

Ascendant in Taurus & Sun in Scorpio

With the ascendant in Taurus and the Sun in Scorpio, this means that the Sun is in the seventh house - the house of relationships, balance, social resources and relating. With this placement, it means that the ascendant and the Sun are opposite each other in the birth chart.

With the Sun in the seventh house, you're here to learn all about relationships. You are here to understand deep relationship themes in your life and to learn to transform dysfunctional patterns that hold you back. The Sun is in Scorpio, the sign of depth and transformation. This means that your major breakthroughs in relationships come precisely through crises and some form of transformation. With your Sun here, you also have strong gifts that make you a good psychologist or healer.

To manage and develop your Sun, it is valuable that you find a balance between Scorpio and Taurus. By giving yourself security while challenging yourself, you lead yourself towards inner development and towards your soul's purpose.

Ascendent in Taurus & Sun in Sagittarius

With the ascendant in Taurus and the Sun in Sagittarius, this means that the Sun is in the eighth house - the house of transformation, healing, intimacy, shared resources, depth.

With the Sun in the eighth house, you are here to learn the art of transforming energy. You are here to affirm your inner depth, even the very deepest parts within you. By daring to face heaviness and pain, you can learn to transform this into acceptance and balance. This placement makes you a powerful healer, especially if you work with your inner self and heal old baggage that limits you.

The Sun is in Sagittarius, which is the sign of exploration, belief and expansion. So, by having an exploratory approach to yourself and life, you will find what gives you expansion. With the Sun in Sagittarius, you also need a certain form of freedom to feel alive. You may feel drawn to various forms of learning and development.

In order to get through your inner processes and to be able to stand in everything you encounter, it is very valuable for you to take help of the stability, and the earth found in Taurus. Use the stability that Taurus has together with the curiosity and longing for development of Sagittarius, and you will end up where you need to go.

Ascendant in Taurus & Sun in Capricorn
With the ascendant in Taurus and the Sun in Capricorn, this means that the Sun is in the ninth house - the house of travel, expansion, exploration, belief and higher learning.

With the Sun in the ninth house, you are here to expand your soul and to find your inner truth about life. You are here to explore and experience life. Through contrasts and experiences come insights and wisdom. The Sun is in Capricorn, the sign of structure, discipline and leadership. This shows that you are a strong leader and by having clear goals and a structure in what you do, you can get far in what you choose to do. So, with this placement, you are meant to lead yourself forward and by spending time and commitment on what you think is developing, you create a great knowledge, something that you can pass on to others.

To develop your Sun and achieve your goals, you can use the calmness and patience that Taurus possesses in the ascendant. Both Taurus and Capricorn are earth signs, which means that you carry strong earth qualities. You can build and manifest in the physical. Don't forget to bring your feelings and your intuition into what you do.

Ascendant in Taurus & Sun in Aquarius
With the ascendant in Taurus and the Sun in Aquarius, this means that the Sun is in the tenth house - the house of work, career, life mission, manifestation and greater impact.

With the Sun in the 10th house, you are here to build something big and embody what you believe in. You are here to build your leadership and free yourself from expectations and norms that may have been with you from growing up. With the Sun here, you may feel a pull to invest in a career or to find your life's mission. You would like to leave some kind of imprint behind you here on Earth. The Sun is in Aquarius, the sign of innovation and new thinking. This placement gives you excellent conditions for contributing something new, something that can help people and society as a whole.

To achieve your goals here, you can use the stability and calmness that Taurus possesses in your ascendant sign. It helps you strive to get to the top - and manifest your goals.

Ascendant in Taurus & Sun in Pisces
With the ascendant in Taurus and the Sun in Pisces, this means that the Sun is in the eleventh house - the house of groups, community involvement, visions of the future, networks and innovation.

With the Sun in the eleventh house, you are here to contribute something to other people and to the great mass. It can be something grand or something smaller. You are here to live your life outside of the predetermined templates that exist in society. By finding your unique path, you show the way to others, and you become a strong role model and inspiration. The Sun is in Pisces, the sign of spirituality and creativity. This means that a big task for you in this life is about finding your unique touch of spirituality and bringing this out to other people. You have a great sensitivity, and you feel energies, both from people and from the collective.

You can take the help of Taurus and its stable power to move forward and to achieve your goals. By combining the grounding energy of Taurus and the mutable creative energy of Pisces, you can create something unique for your world around you.

CHAPTER 6
GEMINI IN THE ASCENDANT

Gemini

Qualities: Air, Mutable, Masculine

Ruled by the planet: Mercury

Connected to house: 3

Soul Archetypes: The student, the communicator, the writer

Connection to chakra: Throat chakra

Gemini Characteristics & Energy

Gemini is the third sign in the Zodiac and symbolizes themes such as communication, mental processes and learning. Other characteristics associated with Gemini are education and how we think and express ourselves in everyday life when meeting other people. The sign carries an airy mobile masculine energy, which means that there is a lot of flexibility and changeability here.

Soul archetypes associated with Gemini are the Student, the Communicator and the Writer.

Gemini as ascendant

When Gemini is in the ascendant, we usually carry an outgoing energy, due to the masculine energy that dominates the essence of the sign. If there is something else that pulls down or blocks this energy in the chart, it can be more subtle. Gemini as a sign has a strong connection to our thoughts and thus how we think about life but also how we take in and process information. It is also strongly connected to precise knowledge in various forms and individuals with this ascendant sign have a great curiosity and a constant longing to learn more and understand new things.

There is an objectivity in Gemini that makes it easy for us to talk about things and have conversations, as if we are part of the conversation but yet not. We are good at listening and gathering what people around us tell us. Our surroundings often perceive us as quite easy-going and easy to talk to. It depends on the mutability and flexibility that we have learned to act out in the meeting with others. It is easy for us to jump between different forms of conversation and thus adapt to the person we are talking to at the moment.

Gemini is probably the sign in the Zodiac that has the easiest time doing several things parallel and engages in multitasking. We can start a project here while starting something else over there, which means we have more balls in the air. This ability also allows us to get many things done. We get the ball rolling and make sure we're constantly moving forward.

Soul contract/Soul plan

With the ascendant in Gemini, we have a higher purpose and plan for our soul's development. We are here on Earth to find our Divine expression and to master this through our communication. By testing ourselves and through meetings with other people, we eventually find our way back to what is important to us on a deep level – what gives meaning to our soul and its development. The journey here is about moving from division to unity or as we can also put it; to collect our puzzle pieces into a complete puzzle.

Gemini manages to accumulate a lot of knowledge and insights during the course of life, something that can be used for development and to help other people along their journey.

When we have Gemini in the ascendant, we have a great need to find new things to immerse ourselves in, otherwise we can easily get bored.

Childhood & patterns from growing up

When we step into a body here on Earth, we choose a family and an environment that matches our current energy and vibration as well as the lessons we want to learn and deal with during this life. We thus choose a family that helps shape our ascendant.

With the ascendant in Gemini, we have usually grown up in a family where precise knowledge and communication were prominent or where we were appreciated for precisely these qualities. It could be that we had a well-educated parent who encouraged us to learn things or to make connections with people. So, the Gemini here can mean that we were formed in an environment where the intellectual was important and where emotions were more or less neglected.

The objectivity that Gemini carries is often formed while growing up, because we learn to use our thoughts and our social skills before our emotions and our heart. There is a large spectrum here and in a more positive situation we have had the opportunity to develop and express both parts. But if we have had a dysfunctional upbringing, this can sit deep within us and we can have a certain dissociation to our emotions - that is, we are not in full contact with them.

We have created a personality where we are flexible and where we can quickly change our way of being, based on how we think our surroundings want us to be. This means that it is easy for us to adapt to people, something that can be very positive in several contexts. We can move well in different contexts, and we can use our voice and our communication as a strong driving force. The challenge here becomes if we go into adaptation too much, at the expense of our well-being and energy.

Common Challenges

Gemini as a sign is, as we mentioned earlier, a mutable and flexible sign and in the same way that it can be a great gift, there can be some challenges here. With Gemini in the ascendant, we may find it easy to start and jump between different objects and phenomena but difficult to complete them. This can, for example, be shown by us starting a course without finishing it and then starting a new one. It can also be the case that, due to our curiosity and longing for new lessons, we seek out many different contexts with new knowledge, which is positive - if we can integrate the knowledge and do something with it.

During our work in Astrology, we have seen that individuals with this ascendant sign are extremely open and receptive to new information that can help them move forward on their journey. Sometimes this can lead to an excessive need to constantly find new projects or themes to get involved in. This can create a long-term feeling of division within us, and we can find it difficult to get deep enough into a subject, that we actually take it in as a deeper part of us. This can also be reinforced by the fact that, as children, we have often learned to create a certain emotional distance from what we do. We have learned to be rational and look at things from a logical perspective.

If we feel that we have cut off contact with our emotions or if we have difficulty bringing our emotions into what we do, it is valuable to try to reconnect with our heart and our feminine aspect. When we find a balance between the feminine and the masculine or between the heart and the brain, we can use the knowledge we have gathered in a holistic way.

We may also have a challenge where we find it difficult to know who we are, because we have been overly flexible and entered into roles and patterns that benefited those around us more than ourselves. We become divided and have difficulty seeing our essence and what is ours, in relation to others.

Strengths & Gifts

Geminis have great gifts and talents when it comes to communication. Not only in the form of being able to talk a lot and be social, but also in the form of a social intelligence. Individuals with Gemini in the ascendant can easily see what is needed in different contexts and they can move easily and smoothly between different topics and situations. This means that they have a lot to add to different workplaces and that they are often appreciated by other people.

When we have the ascendant in Gemini, it is precisely our ability to see things from different perspectives and angles that becomes one of our prominent qualities. By using these abilities, we can get ahead socially but also in the work we do spiritually. In a purely practical and social sense, we can use our social skills to create the right contacts and find networks that benefit us. On a more spiritual level, we can use these gifts to find important and rewarding information and knowledge for our soul.

Gemini is the sign of journalism and various forms of writing. Many authors have strong elements of Gemini and the planet Mercury in their birth chart. So, if we have this ascendant sign, we have great abilities in this particular area, something we can pick up and use if we feel drawn to it.

Health & energy flow

There are several important parts to look at in the Birth Chart when it comes to health and two of them are the ascendant sign and the sixth house. The ascendant has a strong connection to our physical body, how we move physically but also how we protect ourselves and absorb energy.

The sixth house is the house for health, daily routines and shows what we need in everyday life to have a good flow in a general way.

With the ascendant in Gemini, we usually have good predictions for a positive flow of energy in our body. The sign is masculine and, in general, the masculine signs of the Zodiac find it easier to shake off stress and heavy energy. Above all, there is a more outward energy, unlike feminine signs that direct the energy more inward.

However, we can experience a form of restlessness or stress with this ascendant sign, due to our difficulty staying in one place.

In order to have a positive flow, it is valuable that we find different ways to ground ourselves, to anchor our energy in the body. We need to ground ourselves and above all get some of the energy down in our thoughts, down into our physical body. It is easy for a Gemini to get stuck in the head and create a distance from what is happening in the body, which makes it very important to review that part. During our work, we have seen that individuals who have an excessive focus in the head and live through their thoughts often struggle with various physical symptoms. It can be ME, fibromyalgia and other pain conditions. Consciously working to bring down some of our focus and energy in the body is crucial for this ascendant sign, to create good and balanced health.

Another challenge for Gemini can be that we live in the future rather than stopping in the here and now. This is because our thoughts are faster than the rest of the body and we easily wander off with them. We can also experience stress when meeting people, as we feel that we need to meet them and be alert to what is happening.

Here it can be helpful to take a step back from time to time and observe rather than participate in everything that happens.

Since we learned from home that communication equals security, communication with others can also become part of our defense. We talk when we feel insecure, and we find silence difficult when meeting other people.

With Gemini as the ascendant sign, this means that our sixth house is in the sign of Scorpio. The sixth house is connected to our general health and shows what we need in our everyday life to feel good but also to build healthy routines and have flow in our energy. Scorpio as a sign stands for themes such as deep emotions, transformation and resources. There is a watery and solid energy to this sign, something very different from the Gemini energy.

When we have Gemini as ascendant and Scorpio in the sixth house, there is a need to bring in both of these energies, to build an everyday life with flow and balance. We need the flexibility and mobility of Gemini, but we also need to go deeper and access what is hidden. When we have Scorpio in the sixth house, it is important that we constantly work towards transformation in order to achieve good health in everyday life. We do this by digging within ourselves, freeing ourselves from old patterns and rebuilding ourselves from time to time. Since Scorpio is a deep-water sign, it shows the importance of getting in touch with our deepest feelings and what is going on inside.

When Scorpio covers our sixth house, it usually means that we will go through some transformational processes concerning our physical health and our body during the course of life. It does not mean that we will get sick, but that we may have to experience some kind of crisis or challenge here to find what is important to us - and how to live our life.

Both Gemini and Scorpio carry a strong longing for understanding and knowledge. The difference is that Gemini moves a little more on the surface, while Scorpio searches under the surface, in what may be hidden or subconscious. By using our Gemini curiosity and daring to look at what we carry within us, we can build a strong power, and we receive gifts that can contribute great help and healing to other people.

Related Chakra

Gemini has a strong connection with the Throat Chakra, which is located in our throat. The chakra represents our communication and our expression, that is, how we make ourselves heard during the course of life. It is also connected with our ability to make decisions and make choices based on our inner voice.

When the Throat Chakra is in balance, we find it easy to express ourselves and take space when we need it. We can speak up when something doesn't feel right, and we follow our own voice. We know when it's time to talk and when it's time to take a step back.

In the case of imbalance or a blocked Throat Chakra, we may have difficulty making our voice heard. We can feel a lump in our throat and like no one is really listening to what we say.

With Gemini in the ascendant, the Throat Chakra is prominent, and it is therefore valuable that we take care of that part of our energy system. If we had an upbringing where we had to suppress our expression or where we were silenced in some way, it is especially important to work with the Throat Chakra.

But we can also get an imbalance in the chakra when we focus on and communicate something that does not resonate with our inner voice and our intuition. When we grow up, it is common that on an unconscious level we pick up thoughts and reasoning that our parents have, and they become part of our programming. Since the Gemini quite often grows up in an environment where communication or intellect is prominent, it is important that we strive to find our own expression with this ascendant. This is even more critical if we know that we easily conform to others.

By finding what feels meaningful to us and communicating it to ourselves and our surroundings, we can maintain the balance in the Throat Chakra, and it also creates good conditions for the rest of our energy system.

With Gemini in the ascendant and a prominent Throat Chakra, we also carry a lot of healing in our voice. The more we heal imbalances and step into our authentic expression, the more power there is in the voice. We connect back with our true vibration and that vibration can help people heal – by speaking to them, singing or writing our message.

The career houses

When it comes to job, career and life task in the Birth Chart, there are many parts to look at, for example our composition of the chart with all the planets and where our power point MC (Midheaven) is located. But there are some important parts we can look at already here. By looking at the qualities and the energy that our ascendant represents, we can see what we need jobwise, to develop. When we know what our ascendant sign is, we can also see what our career houses are, that is, what signs and elements they are in. The career houses are 2, 6 & 10.

With the ascendant in Gemini, the three career houses are in the signs of Cancer, Scorpio & Pisces, all of which are water signs. Water represents intuition, flow, emotions and creativity. Having the career houses in water signs means that we have great resources within us when it comes to emotions and knowing what people need, something we can use to build our career and manifest what we dream of. This is further enhanced if we have the Sun, Moon or other planets in these three houses.

So, what does it mean that we have Gemini on the ascendant and the career houses in the water sign?

With this combination, we get access to an amazing energy that we can use in our work and to achieve our dreams in this field. While the air in the ascendant represents our thoughts and our communication, the water in the career houses represents our emotions, our creativity and our ability to reach people and their needs on a deep level. Thoughts and feelings are brought together and here we can become very skilled therapists, psychologists or healers. We are well suited to work with something where we come into contact with people, preferably on a deeper level. This can happen through conversations or direct meetings with others, but also through, for example, work as a teacher or lecturer.

With this combination, we need to have a job or career where we become emotionally involved. It needs to feel meaningful in order for us to have the motivation to work with it for less time - and even if it feels meaningful, we will most likely still want to try a number of different workplaces.

The tenth house is one of the career houses and perhaps the most important to look at, in terms of career but also in terms of our life mission – what we are here to manifest in this life.

In this constellation lies the tenth house of Pisces, the sign of dreams, intuition, imagination and emotions. Pisces is a mutable water sign and in combination with Gemini we get double the mobility. This means that we very likely need to change jobs or workplaces from time to time, in order to feel satisfied. We also need a job where there is a lot of flexibility and where we get to use our creativity in some way. Gemini is more logical while Pisces is more guided by intuition. Here we can sometimes experience an inner conflict between these. To achieve balance here, it is valuable that we allow both of these energies to emerge and take place, both in our private life and in our work.

The combination of Gemini and Pisces has the potential for an enormous amount of new ideas. With Pisces in the tenth house, we can achieve our dreams, if we are prepared to work for it. Due to the mutability found in both Pisces and Gemini, it is important that we watch out for different forms of escape. We need to make sure that we actually set goals, get through our milestones and complete things that we set out to do.

Pisces in the tenth house also lays a good foundation for various forms of intuitive work, such as healing and energy work.

Spirituality, Transformation & Deep Healing
There are many and profound lessons for us when we have the ascendant in Gemini. One of them is about discovering who we are, by exploring different perspectives and different points of view - to

finally discover what is true for us. At their lowest energy, the Gemini is divided and disconnected from themselves and their inner selves. There is a distance to the interior and an excessive focus on the exterior. In the worst case, we can experience it as a spiritual division within ourselves. We have difficulty knowing who we are and what is our inner core. If we have this problem, it is of the utmost importance that we find a way to reintegrate parts of ourselves into a unity. There are many different ways to do it and one of them is through intuitive energy work. By beginning to listen to what our body is conveying and allowing our emotions to be a part of our life, we open up to healing and transformation. In the same way, we help our body and soul to integrate parts that have been scattered within us.

In order to balance the energy in our ascendant sign, it is valuable to look straight across the Zodiac to the opposite sign, Sagittarius. Gemini represent knowledge, our thoughts in everyday life, how we communicate with our immediate environment and what we think about every day. This means that there is a closeness to the everyday and what we need to cope with in meetings with people in everyday life. Sagittarius also represents knowledge, thoughts and communication but on a higher level. While Gemini shows what we think about in everyday life, Sagittarius shows our larger beliefs - what we believe in spiritually or how we look at life. There is also a connection to higher communication and to expansion through a deep understanding of something.

So, with the Ascendant in Gemini, it can be positive and helpful to bring in some of the elements and qualities of Sagittarius from time to time, so that we find balance between everyday life and spirituality, between the logical and our inner truth. We integrate our everyday thoughts into a deeper spiritual meaning.

There are three houses in the Birth Chart that relate to our inner depth, our transformation and our spirituality. It is houses 4, 8 & 12. House four shows what we carry from family and lineage. House eight shows how we undergo transformation during life but also what healing abilities we have. House twelve shows what we carry in our subconscious and what energy we need to lift up and make conscious. If we have planets in one of these houses, the energy and focus there becomes even stronger.

With the ascendant in Gemini, we have our spiritual houses in Virgo, Capricorn & Taurus. This means that the spiritual houses are in earth signs. When these houses are in earth, we get an earthy energy here, something that allows us to work with our inner self and at the same time be grounded. Individuals with earth in these houses are good at combining development and spirituality with closeness to nature or to the physical body. There is an inner calm and stability, which we can use when we heal our inner self but also when we help other people.

When we have the ascendant in Gemini and our spiritual houses in earth signs, we get a mix of what goes on in our head and what happens purely physically in our body. This combination creates good conditions for maintaining a certain form of stability and calm, when we meet our inner self or when we work with healing work. Earth creates stability and security, which we need when we do transformative work within ourselves.

Sometimes we have seen that individuals with their deep houses in earth signs can have a hard time getting in touch with their feelings and their inner blockages. This is often because the practical side is a little in the way. Here we also have Gemini in the ascendant which is also logical in nature. Here we may have to work a little to get behind the practicalities and to get behind the body's defense mechanisms that we built up to protect our insides.

Combination with the Sun

Now follows a review of the ascendant in Gemini in combination with all Sun signs. Look at your ascendant sign in the Birth Chart and then where your Sun is. Combining these two energies gives you a strong indication of what you are here to delve into and manifest in this life. It also gives you guidance for spiritual themes you can develop and understand within yourself and in your life.

The ascendant shows how you have been shaped, how you meet your surroundings as well as important life themes and lessons for you in the course of life. The Sun shows where you are meant to shine in this life and where you have a great opportunity to make an impression with your energy.

Ascendant in Gemini & Sun in Aries
With the ascendant in Gemini and the Sun in Aries, this means that the Sun is in the eleventh house - the house of groups, networks, visions of the future, community involvement and innovation.

With the Sun in the eleventh house, you are here to contribute something to the great mass or to society as a whole. You do this by affirming your unique energy and by finding new innovative paths. It can be something outwardly grand but also something more subtle, like daring to be yourself fully. By breaking old norms and

111

preconceived notions, you can act as a role model for those around you and contribute to new approaches in the collective. The Sun is in Aries, the sign of courage, initiative and leadership. Here you may need to develop these qualities and characteristics in order to reach your goals and to get ahead in a powerful way.

To develop your Sun, you can also use the energy of your ascendant sign. Through Gemini's curiosity and through your social skills, you can go far in whatever you choose to do. Gemini and Aries together carry a strong masculine force, with the prerequisites to create motivation and inspiration for others. Be sure to bring in the feminine aspect every now and then, where you give space to your emotions, your imagination and your intuition.

Ascendant in Gemini & Sun in Taurus

With the ascendant in Gemini and the Sun in Taurus, this means that the Sun is in the twelfth house - the house of subconscious processes, spirituality, dreams and escape.

With the Sun in the twelfth house, you are here to develop your spirituality and to understand deeper parts of yourself. You may experience that you have a great sensitivity to energies and that you need a lot of your own time to process everything that is happening. With this placement, you are here to reconnect with your soul and express it through, for example, creativity or through spiritual work. You have a strong intuitive side and the more you work on transforming lower parts and states within you, the more you get in touch with your spiritual gifts. The Sun is in Taurus, the sign of stability, calm and creativity. This means that these are qualities that you need to develop in order to get your Sun to develop here.

Through patient work and determination, you can heal your inner self and become the healer you were born to be.

The Gemini ascendant helps you get ahead through curiosity and by constantly asking new questions that lead to development. The combination of Taurus earth and Gemini air gives you a fine balance between masculine and feminine, between body and intellect.

Ascendant in Gemini & Sun in Gemini

With both the ascendant and the Sun in Gemini, they are in the same sign and house, the first house. The first house represents new beginnings, initiation, leadership and our personality.

When both the ascendant and the Sun are in the same sign and house, the energy mixes and they create a strong unity. Our inner core goes hand in hand with our personality and how we were shaped during our upbringing. The Gemini's energy becomes extra prominent here and we have strong qualities such as communication, curiosity and an ability to be flexible and create contact with people.

With the Sun in the first house, you are here to affirm your own personality but also to develop strong leadership. The biggest development in your life comes when you take the initiative yourself and lead yourself forward in a conscious way. You will also experience that many of your great lessons come through meetings with other people and through communication. Since this combination gives you a lot of air, it is valuable to land in the body every now and then, to see what is going on there - and to communicate with your feelings.

Ascendant in Gemini & Sun in Cancer

With the ascendant in Gemini and the Sun in Cancer, this means that the Sun is in the second house - the house of material resources, self-worth, money, abundance and scarcity.

With the Sun in the second house, you are here to learn all about your own resources and about scarcity and abundance. You are here to understand your soul's relationship to the material and to resources. An important part for you in this lifetime is about realizing your divine value, the value that reflects your soul. Since the Sun is in Cancer, it is likely that your view of yourself was largely shaped by your upbringing and family. By healing yourself emotionally and by freeing yourself from beliefs and attitudes from your family that do not resonate with you, you build your self-worth. When you realize your worth on a deep level, you can create abundance in finances but also through other areas of life. Through inner emotional healing, you also build new resources and gifts within yourself.

Here you can take help of the curiosity and the longing for knowledge found in Gemini, your ascendant. With the Sun in Cancer and the ascendant in Gemini, you have a fine balance between thought and feeling. Be careful not to get too caught up in the safe but dare to broaden your horizons of life.

Ascendant in Gemini & Sun in Leo

With the ascendant in Gemini and the Sun in Leo, this means that the Sun is in the third house - the house of communication, perspective, learning and mental processes.

With the Sun in the third house, you are here to learn all about communication but also to reconnect with your divine expression.

When you find your true expression and when you express what comes directly from your soul and your inner wisdom, you can help people around you. Before you find your true expression, you will most likely experience a lower energy of this theme early in life. You may have been taught at home that communication is important, but communication is used in a superficial or dysfunctional way. The Sun is in Leo, the sign of creativity, pride and leadership. This means that there are qualities that you need to express to strengthen your Sun here. You are a strong soul with great resources within you. Use the power of Leo to spread joy and creativity in what you do.

Your ascendant in Gemini helps you work with your expression and with your communication - so that you can reach the highest energy of this. With the combination of Gemini and Leo, you have a strong masculine energy here, something that helps you create and manifest. Remember to bring in your feminine aspect from time to time, so that your feelings and your intuition are included in your expression.

Ascendant in Gemini & Sun in Virgo
With the ascendant in Gemini and the Sun in Virgo, this means that the Sun is in the fourth house - the house of home, family, security, our roots and our origins.

With the Sun in the fourth house, you are here to build a sense of security within yourself and thus find a home within yourself. You are also here too free yourself from limitations and from demands connected with family and upbringing. You may experience that you have a strong connection with family or that you have a strong desire to create a family of your own. Family patterns are important to look at to find balance and heal yourself. The Sun is in Virgo, the sign of perfection, health and accuracy. It could mean that you have brought with you a feeling of demands from home – that you have to be perfect or that you need to behave in a certain way. With the Sun in Virgo in the fourth house, you may feel drawn to work in service and helping people.

To heal yourself and free yourself from the old, you can use the curiosity and exploratory energy found in your ascendant sign, Gemini.

Ascendant in Gemini & Sun in Libra
With the ascendant in Gemini and the Sun in Libra, this means that the Sun is in the fifth house - the house of creativity, sports, creation, expression, children and playfulness.

With the Sun in the fifth house, you are here to find your creative expression and get it out into the World. You are here to affirm your playfulness and through that playfulness get in touch with your inner creation. Creating something from the heart and soul can help people raise their frequency and even heal. The Sun is in Libra, the sign of relationships and balance. This means that relationships are a big theme in your life, and it may also be that you can bring out your creativity precisely through your relationships. Many of your great lessons in this life come through meeting people and through your closest relationships.

To find your expression and to develop your Sun, it is valuable to take help from your ascendant sign Gemini. Use the curiosity and searching energy found here to achieve your goals. With the ascendant in Gemini and the Sun in Libra, you need to watch out for various forms of co-dependence and adaptation. Strive to heal your inner self where needed, so you can build strong and balanced relationships.

Ascendant in Gemini & Sun in Scorpio
With the ascendant in Aries and the Sun in Scorpio, this means that the Sun is in the sixth house - the house of health, routines, service, mastery and work.

With the Sun in the sixth house, you are here on Earth to learn all about health and to contribute some form of Service. You are also here to build a daily routine with routines that resonate with you and your unique energy. Through experiences and experiences, you learn what your body needs but also what it doesn't feel good about. The greatest lessons for you in this life come through transformation around your body and energy. When you understand yourself, you can contribute your expertise and knowledge to others, through service and healing. The Sun is in Scorpio, the sign of deep transformation and emotion. With this placement, you need to go deep within yourself to find what is best for you. It may also be that you go through some form of illness or crisis in health, in order to get the knowledge your soul seeks.

To reach your goals and to find what you are looking for, you can use the curiosity and searching that comes with Gemini, your ascendant. With the flexibility of Gemini and the depth of Scorpio, you can access even the most hidden aspects of yourself and your inner self.

Ascendant in Gemini & Sun in Sagittarius

With the ascendant in Gemini and the Sun in Sagittarius, this means that the Sun is in the seventh house - the house of relationships, balance, relating and other people. This placement also means that the ascendant and the Sun are opposite each other in the chart.

With the Sun in the seventh house, you are here to learn all about relationships and to understand the relationship with yourself. You are here to understand relationship patterns and through that understanding build healthy and energizing relationships. This placement is a relatively social placement so you may find yourself drawn to relationships and to other people. The Sun is in Sagittarius, the sign of higher learning, exploration and expansion. There is a searching side to you and many of your great lessons and insights come precisely through your relationships with other people – even through partnerships.

Your Gemini ascendant also has a searching energy and by combining the energies of Sagittarius and Gemini you will learn a lot about life and about what is true for you.

Ascendant in Gemini & Sun in Capricorn

With the Gemini ascendant and the Sun in Capricorn, this means that the Sun is in the eighth house - the house of transformation, transformation, shared resources, intimacy and deep aspects of ourselves.

With the Sun in the eighth house, you are here to experience a life of deep transformation. You are here to learn how to face states of sadness, pain and low energy. It may sound like an overwhelming and tough task, but it gives you the opportunity for deep spiritual expansion. You will probably experience more development than many other people around you and that makes you a powerful healer and light worker, especially when you have healed a part within yourself. The Sun is in Capricorn, the sign of leadership and authority. This means that you need to develop strong leadership within yourself and through that lead yourself through the challenges that come your way.

With the help of the ascendant in Gemini, you have a curious approach to life, something that makes you move on and forward, even when it feels heavy. You can use Gemini's mobility and social ability combined with Capricorn's discipline, to reach the top in life but also the lowest parts of yourself.

Ascendant in Gemini & Sun in Aquarius
With the ascendant in Gemini and the Sun in Aquarius, this means that the Sun is in the ninth house - the house of exploration, travel, adventure, wisdom and belief.

With the Sun in the ninth house, you are here to expand your knowledge and your soul. You are here to discover your meaning in life and what is true for you – that is, what resonates with your soul. With this placement, you may feel drawn to explore yourself and life through experiences and through travel, either internally or physically. The Sun is in Aquarius, the sign of innovation and new thinking. This means that you need to find your unique path, beyond what is considered normal for the environment and society. You are not here to fit into the norm, you are here to break it. When you dare to do things your way, you become a strong role model for people around you.

With Gemini in the ascendant, you have an exploratory and curious approach to life, something that will help you on your life's journey. With Gemini in the ascendant and the Sun in Aquarius, you have a strong intellect, and you are good at meeting people and solving challenging situations.

Ascendant in Gemini & Sun in Pisces

With the ascendant in Gemini and the Sun in Pisces, this means that the Sun is in the tenth house - the house of work, career, life mission, manifestation and greater impact.

With the Sun in the tenth house, you are here to make an impression on the World, through your job or through your life mission. It can be by writing a book, helping people or through some kind of service. With this placement, you may feel drawn to invest in something in work and career. There is a part of you that knows you are here to contribute something big. The Sun is in Pisces, the sign of spirituality, creativity and dreams. This means that you have great opportunities to work with something in spirituality or healing. You have a great sensitivity, and you can sense other people's energies, so it is important that you work on your integrity and boundaries, to maintain your power and energy.

With the Sun in Pisces and the ascendant in Gemini, you get a mix of spirituality and learning. Here you can use your curiosity and your search in the ascendant to find what you are looking for and to reach your goals. By combining logical thinking with emotions and intuition, you get the opportunity to contribute your unique perspective in this life.

CHAPTER 7
CANCER IN THE ASCENDANT

Cancer

Qualities: Water, Cardinal, Feminine

Ruled by the planet: The Moon

Connected to house: 4

Soul Archetypes: Mother, The Caregiver, Healer

Connection to chakra: The sacral chakra

Cancer Characteristics & Energy

Cancer is the fourth sign in the Zodiac and symbolizes themes such as home, family and security. Cancer also has a connection with our upbringing, what we need to feel at home and our emotions - how we feel and express our emotions. The sign carries a watery cardinal feminine energy, which means there is a lot of initial power as well as a great sensitivity.

Soul archetypes associated with Cancer are the Mother, the Caretaker, and the Healer.

Cancer as ascendant

Cancer is a feminine water sign and just like the other water signs in the ascendant there is a great and deep sensitivity. Cancer represents our feminine energy and nurturing energy. It is no coincidence that Cancer is associated with the archetype The Mother. We have seen that many individuals with Cancer in the ascendant have a natural ability to see and above all feel what people around them need to feel good. It is often instinctive and is part of the nature of the sign and therefore part of our personality with this ascendant sign.

With Cancer in the ascendant, we have a deep emotional life, and it is precisely this broad spectrum of emotions that is our great gift and at the same time our great challenge. We sense our surroundings wherever we are, and it is easy for us to see when something or someone around us changes shape. We can sense moods in a room, and we have a tendency to unconsciously scan what is happening around us before we start a conversation with someone.

Cancer has a watery and sensitive energy but there is also a cardinal energy, which means that the sign has strong leadership skills. Cancer can lead itself and other people forward and there is a great ability to start ongoing projects. There is a strong driving force and many times our motivation lies in creating security for ourselves or for our family, if we are parents.

With Cancer in the ascendant, we have a great need for security, to be in a context where we can relax and feel safe. When we feel safe, we can go as far as we want, and we have a strong creative side. If, on the other hand, we feel that our surroundings feel threatening, we can easily take a step back and crawl into our shell, until it feels a little calmer.

Cancer in the ascendant is looking for security and for its home during life. This home may consist of a love partner or a small group of close friends. Cancer usually does well without a large network, as long as it has its small group that it knows is there. Because of a deep longing for emotional bonds, Cancer is often drawn to deep relationships, sometimes with a positive energy and sometimes with a negative energy.

Because of the sensitivity that exists in us, we can easily go into defense, in a way to protect our inner self and our emotions. In the meeting, other people may perceive us as friendly, a little cautious and somewhat reserved. This can change if we have very communicative or otherwise outgoing signs in the chart, but overall, there is a more wait-and-see side here. If we've had a tough upbringing or experienced a lot of hardship in the course of life, we can be extremely protective and even come across as a bit harsh or withdrawn.

It is often because we put up a protection or a wall around us, to avoid showing our vulnerability or showing our feelings. Although we carry many emotions inside, it is not something we show outwardly, on the contrary, others can perceive us as quite neutral and good at keeping ourselves together emotionally.

When we have Cancer on the Ascendant, we are usually good at listening and picking up on other people's feelings. It is common for us to know people around us more than they know us, as it takes a lot for us to let someone in deeply and tell them about our own challenges. It makes us a good friend but can also lead us to never really allowing ourselves to develop with someone on a deep spiritual level. To evolve, we need to allow our vulnerability to emerge.

Soul contract/Soul plan

With Cancer in the ascendant, we are here on Earth to learn to master all the spectrum of emotions within us. This means that we need to face all emotions, from fear to love, in order to learn to understand them on a deep level. For that reason, we will encounter challenges, situations and relationships where we experience emotional opposites and contrasts.

Another aspect that is important here is about finding a home within ourselves. We search for our home on the outside, but it is only when we find our true essence and heart that we find our true home - the one that no one can take away from us. This is a deep spiritual journey that can take time and require some experiences and insights along the way. By living life and daring to face what comes our way, we learn to understand our emotional life and our reactions.

Childhood & patterns from growing up

When we step into a body here on Earth, we choose a family and an environment that matches our current energy and vibration as well as the lessons we want to learn and deal with during this life. We thus choose a family that helps shape our ascendant.

Individuals who have Cancer in the ascendant usually have a strong attachment or connection specifically to family and childhood. Not infrequently there are strong emotional ties with the mother, which can be more on the dysfunctional side or have a more positive energy. This connection can also be with the father or with another close person while growing up. During our work, we have worked with people who have the ascendant in Cancer. There we have seen clear patterns of dysfunctionality in childhood, although it can look different. It is common for there to be some form of co-dependency involved or an excessive responsibility for a parent already at an early age. An example is the woman who grew up with a mother who herself carried unprocessed trauma and who had difficulty bearing and taking care of her own feelings. In that case, the child will most likely step in and try to help her mother.

With Cancer in the ascendant, we can have a strong attraction to the familiar or to our roots, in the form of family or the environment we grew up in. We have learned during childhood that feelings are important and that we need to sense what is going on around us, by scanning what is going on. Through the atmosphere we grew up in, we have also gained appreciation when we have been empathetic, responsible and calm.

Depending on how our childhood looked more specifically, there will be a wide spectrum here, where some individuals have had to go into great adjustment and take responsibility for their parents while others have had it more functionally. Here it is valuable to look at how we grew up and try to identify patterns that hold us back. Many times, there is past life karma involved in the family when we have this ascendant sign. There are strong ties that we need to balance somehow.

An important task with Cancer in the ascendant is too free ourselves from the family patterns that are not good for us so that we can reach our highest potential in this life. This does not necessarily mean that we should distance ourselves from our family and our roots but find a healthy approach where we start from ourselves and our life. It is extremely important that we find our own identity and that we learn to build our life on our premises when we have Cancer in the ascendant.

When we have an ascendant sign in water, especially Cancer or Pisces, it is common for other parts of our chart to be suppressed. This applies above all if we had a childhood where we had to adapt a lot. For example, if we have a lot of fire in the chart, our life energy can be dampened when we have Cancer in the ascendant. This is because we had to shut down our instinctive behaviors and our power - to adapt and create peace for the environment. For that reason, we can have different states of pain or experience a lack of energy. If so, it is valuable to look at how we can live more authentically so that we access all of our elements, that is, our fire, our power and our spontaneity.

Common Challenges

With Cancer in the ascendant, it is quite common for us to have some kind of emotional dependency. This is due to the strong sensitivity we carry, but also to the fact that we have learned to create strong bonds or attachments to people or different things. So, a challenge here can be that we get drawn into relationships where we become too dependent on our partner or we go into some form of co-dependency, that is, we take care of our partner in a negative way. We may also have challenges with food, sugar or something else. It is often rooted in the fact that we try to suppress our strong emotions or that we carry deep emotional blocks. So, we look for security when we don't have security in ourselves. Our strong emotional nature in combination with the fact that we have learned to be sensitive and caring creates a "perfect" condition for co-dependency problems.

When we have Cancer as the ascendant sign, we also need to work with our boundaries and learn to protect our energy and integrity. This means that we learn to say no when necessary, something that helps us build up our natural protection. Sometimes Cancer has a tendency to run away completely or go on the defensive. It's a way to protect yourself, which can work to some extent. To find balance here, we can work on daring to face discomfort while learning to set the boundaries we need from time to time.

Cancer is very sensitive to energy and picks up the subtleties in its surroundings, such as the feelings of others but also the energy and frequencies from the collective. Because of this sensitivity, there is a tendency to pick up everything and absorb it into one's own energy – which in turn can lead to heaviness and pain.

Water signs are the most sensitive and open signs to have in the ascendant, which makes it extremely important to find ways to protect yourself and become aware of your attitude towards the outside world.

Strengths & Gifts

Cancer's strength lies in its deep emotional intelligence. With Cancer in the ascendant, we have the ability to see people with all their shades and spectrum. We can see and feel their pain the same way we can see their highest potential and power. This makes it easy for us to understand people and what they carry.

Cancer is an intuitive sign and with the ascendant here we have many times developed a strong intuition. We can sense what is going on around us and we can sense what lies unspoken in the air. It makes us emotionally intuitive, something we can use in healing work and to help people on a deep level. The more we heal our own emotional baggage the more we can help others in their emotional processes.

There is a helpfulness and a strong loyalty in Cancer, something that can be a great gift but also be our downfall. Our loyalty is one of our most prominent traits and this loyalty makes us a faithful partner, a helpful friend and a committed parent. Here it is important that we choose who and what we are loyal to. If we are loyal in the wrong situations, we can put ourselves in very negative situations, where we stay in relationships that hurt us or where we sacrifice ourselves for friends who take advantage of us.

Cancer has a deep understanding of life's various processes and contrasts, which makes them skilled therapists. Cancer is good at making people around them feel seen and understood.

Health & energy flow

There are many important parts to look at in the Birth Chart when it comes to the area of health and two of them are the ascendant sign and the sixth house. The ascendant has a strong connection to our physical body, how we move physically but also how we protect ourselves and absorb energy. The sixth house is the house for health, daily routines and shows what we need in everyday life to get flow in a general way.

In order to create good health and maintain our flow in the body, it is valuable to work with our emotions, especially if we have Cancer as ascendant. This is because our emotions are so active within us, and it is easy to become stagnant if we shut them down.

Cancer has a strong connection to the skin and to the stomach. When it comes to the skin, many times we can look at our skin to see how we experience the meeting with other people. If we have problems with our skin, such as acne or eczema, it may be that you feel uncomfortable or overwhelmed in the meeting. The skin is our barrier to the outside world and the more secure we feel in ourselves, the more balance we also get in the skin, along with other things in the body. The stomach is the organ that helps us process the food we put into us. But the stomach is also important from an energy perspective. The stomach and its function symbolize our ability to experience and process emotions. So, if we have major problems with the stomach or intestines, for example IBS or another type of inflammation, it is usually a sign that we are not comfortable with our emotions or that we experience them as overwhelming. Based on that, the stomach is a good part to look at to see how our emotions are doing. If we have the ascendant in Cancer, we can often experience uneasiness in the stomach or find it difficult to eat when we feel insecure or when we experience discomfort around us.

As we mentioned earlier, Cancer is exceptionally open and receptive to external energies and what is going on around them. That means we need to find a way to protect ourselves, not by putting up a wall but rather by being authentic and setting clear boundaries.

With Cancer as the ascendant sign, it means that our sixth house is in the sign of Sagittarius. The sixth house is connected to our general health and shows what we need in our everyday life to feel good but also to build healthy routines and have flow in our energy. Sagittarius as a sign stands for themes such as exploration, expansion, learning and travel. The sign can also have a connection with sports and physical activity, just like all three fire signs. There is a fiery and moving energy in this sign, something very different from the energy of Cancer.

By combining Cancer's energy with Sagittarius', we get valuable guidance about what we need to take care of our health. With Sagittarius in the sixth house, we have a great need for freedom and some form of movement in everyday life. It could be that we are doing some physical activity or that we are moving forward in terms of knowledge. Sagittarius is mobile and looking for expansion. If it gets too routine and casual, this sign gets bored easily. This energy differs in many ways from Cancer, which rather seeks security. But together they show that we need both parts to get balance in life.

We need to experience and meet our inner self in the form of our feelings but also give ourselves space to discover and explore new things in life. We can do that by doing things that arise our curiosity and that bring us closer to our soul.

Because Sagittarius seeks freedom, this placement can sometimes be too "free" and make it difficult for us to find any structure in everyday life. It can cause us to jump from thing to thing without having any routines in everyday life. It is positive if we can find a balance where we experience variety and freedom in everyday life and also in our work, but where we still have certain routines that we follow - and that benefit our energy and our health.

Related Chakra

Cancer has a strong connection to the Sacral Chakra, which is the second chakra from the bottom in our chakra system. The sacral chakra represents our emotions, relationship patterns and how we relate to other people and physical things. It is also related to intimacy, creativity and emotional attachment.

When we have balance in our sacral chakra, we usually have healthy relationships without negative emotional ties. We have learned to separate ourselves from others and we are not dependent on other people. We find it easy to be close to someone we like and find it easy to be in our creative energy.

With blockages or stagnation in the sacral chakra, we can experience imbalances in terms of relationships and the patterns we have there, especially in our close and intimate relationships. We may struggle with patterns of codependency or adaptation. Different forms of addiction also have their roots in this chakra, for example abuse of food, alcohol, sugar or exercise.

With Cancer in the ascendant, the Sacral Chakra is prominent and to maintain balance here it is important that we learn to relate to people, situations and things in a healthy way. It means that we enter into close relationships without taking excessive responsibility and that we eat food without numbing our pain and our feelings. We have a security in ourselves which makes us independent, even if we like to have other people close to us.

It is valuable to find an expression through, for example, creativity to strengthen this chakra. It can be singing, music or something else. The important thing is that we feel a passion for what we do, so that our feelings are included in the picture.

The career houses

When it comes to job, career and life path in the Birth Chart, there are many parts to look at, such as our composition of the chart with all the planets and where our power point MC (Midheaven) is located. But there are some important parts we can look at already here. By looking at the qualities and the energy that our ascendant represents, we can see what we need jobwise, to develop. When we know what our ascendant sign is, we can also see what our career houses are, that is, what signs and elements they are in. The career houses are 2, 6 & 10.

With the ascendant in Cancer, the three career houses are in the signs of Leo, Sagittarius & Aries, all of which are fire signs. Fire represents power, creativity, energy, passion and inspiration. Having the career houses in fire means that we have great resources within us when it comes to motivating and inspiring people. We also have the ability to start ongoing projects which we can use to build our career and manifest what we dream of. This is further enhanced if we have the Sun, Moon or other planets in these three houses.

So, what does it mean to have Cancer on the ascendant and career houses in fire signs?

With this combination, we have strong creative resources and abilities, and we need to have a job or a profession where we can use these qualities in some way. Water and fire together form an explosion of emotions, imagination and creative energy, something that we can use in what we do. Examples of areas that can fit well professionally with this mix are energy worker, creator, sport, physical activity, inspirer, motivator, mentor, coach and design.

The tenth house is one of the career houses and perhaps the most important to look at, in terms of career but also in terms of our life mission – what we are here to manifest in this life.

In this constellation, the tenth house is in Aries, the sign of motivation, fire, passion, power and courage. It is also a strong sign of entrepreneurship and leadership. Since both Cancer in the ascendant and Aries in the tenth house are cardinal signs, it can be beneficial to work with our own business or with a job where we get to be involved and have a great influence. With this combination, it is extremely important that we have a passion for what we do, because otherwise we will have a hard time maintaining our focus and motivation.

Spirituality, Transformation & Deep Healing

Cancer in the ascendant has several great lessons in this life. One of them is about learning to master one's emotions and to transform negative emotions and fear. So, with the ascendant in Cancer, we have a big task that involves facing discomfort and fear and then transforming it into a more neutral or high energy. This is not something we learn in school or through one-off courses. Rather, it is something we learn in the course of life, above all through various forms of crisis. This is a central part of this lifetime, and we will very likely face emotional crises during our spiritual ascent. It is for us to learn everything we need to about our emotions.

Cancer in its highest energy is a very powerful sign in the same way that in its lower energy it can be almost invisible. The only way for Cancer to truly build their true strength and power is through the courage to stay, even when it feels uncomfortable – to face resistance and fears to master it. To be able to do that, it is positive to have a safe environment or at least a safe person in your vicinity, who can act as a safe harbor.

Another important part when we have Cancer as ascendant is that we free ourselves from karma and negative family patterns that we grew up in, if that's how we can relate to this. If there are large and prominent negative events from childhood, we can work on healing ourselves by creating an awareness to begin with. If it had been calmer, we can still review the patterns we have brought with us that limit us, rather than move us forward towards expansion.

There are three houses in the birth chart that relate to our inner depth, our transformation and our spirituality. It is houses 4, 8 & 12. House four shows what we carry from family and lineage. House eight shows how we undergo transformation during life but also what healing abilities we have. House twelve shows what we carry in our subconscious and what energy we need to lift up and make conscious. If we have planets in one of these houses, the energy and focus there becomes even stronger.

With the ascendant in Cancer, we have our spiritual houses in Libra, Aquarius & Gemini. This means that the spiritual houses are in air signs. When these houses are in the air, there is a depth in our thoughts, and we analyze deeply about ourselves and our life. There are often great abilities in mediumship, and we can receive intuitive guidance, healing and information just through our thoughts or in writing.

With the combination of Cancer in the ascendant and our spiritual houses in air, we have our sensitivity through Cancer, but we also have a strong connection to our thoughts. We have seen that individuals with their spiritual houses in the air can have a tendency to get stuck in thought, which can hinder emotional and spiritual transformation. We think through our processes rather than feel them in the body. If we feel that our thoughts easily stop us, we can work on bringing our focus back to the body and thus grounding ourselves. We can do that by going from our thoughts down into the body and further from the body to the ground we walk on.

In this constellation, the sign Gemini is in the twelfth house. When we have Gemini here, it is quite common that growing up we had to silence our communication to make room for a parent or a sibling. In that case, it is beneficial that we practice expressing ourselves and that we find a way to channel our expression, for example through some creative project or through song.

Combination with the Sun

Now follows a review of the ascendant in Cancer in combination with all Sun signs. Look at your ascendant sign in the Birth Chart and then where your Sun is. Combining these two energies gives you a strong indication of what you are here to delve into and manifest in this life. It also gives you guidance for spiritual themes you can develop and understand within yourself and in your life.

The ascendant shows how you have been shaped, how you meet your surroundings as well as important life themes and lessons for you in the course of life.

The Sun shows where you are meant to shine in this life and where you have a great opportunity to make an impression with your energy.

Ascendant in Cancer & Sun in Aries
With the ascendant in Cancer and the Sun in Aries, this means that the Sun is in the tenth house - the house of work, career, life task, manifestation and greater impact.

With the Sun in the tenth house, you are here to make a mark in work and career or through your life's mission. You are also here too free yourself from family patterns that can limit you and thereby build your inner leadership. With this placement, you may feel drawn to invest in a job or career. You may have the feeling that you are here to contribute something special. The Sun is in Aries, the sign of leadership, courage and passion. This means that these are qualities that you are here to develop and use in the course of life and in your calling. When you live in the energy of spontaneity, courage and activation, you replenish life energy in your life.

With the Sun in Aries and the ascendant in Cancer, you have an intuitive and empathetic side, something you can use to get ahead and help people. By combining your sensitivity in Cancer with your passionate power in Aries, you can create something great for people, in whatever you choose to do.

Ascendant in Cancer & Sun in Taurus
With the ascendant in Cancer and the Sun in Taurus, this means that the Sun is in the eleventh house - the house of groups, networks, visions of the future, community engagement and innovation.

With the Sun in the eleventh house, you are here to contribute something to the collective or to society as a whole. You are also here to find your unique and innovative expression, the one that emerges when you dare to go against the flow. You may have a feeling that you don't fit into groups and that you need to do things your way. With this placement, you are not here to follow the norm in what you do, but to break it. The Sun is in Taurus, the sign of stability, methodical work and creativity. This means that you must develop these qualities over the course of your life. Through Taurus' stubborn and determined energy, you can achieve your goals in what you do.

With Cancer in the ascendant, it is important that you find security in yourself, rather than in your surroundings - so that you can follow your inner calling and develop your unique energy. With the combination of Cancer and Taurus, you need to strive to bring flow into life, both emotionally and practically. Otherwise, you can get stuck in your zone of safety and build up stagnation within you.

Ascendant in Cancer & Sun in Gemini

With the ascendant in Cancer and the Sun in Gemini, this means that the Sun is in the twelfth house - the house of subconscious processes, spirituality, dreams and escape.

With the Sun in the twelfth house, you are here to develop your spirituality and explore deeper parts of yourself. You have great sensitivity and can very likely sense energies and emotions tangibly in your surroundings. With this placement, you may experience that you need some time for yourself, to process everything that is happening in your life. You carry strong healing abilities, something that develops the more you heal trauma and lower aspects of your inner self. The Sun is in Gemini, the sign of mental processes and communication. This means that you have deep thoughts and if you had a dysfunctional childhood, it is important that you do not get stuck in low thoughts about yourself or about life. Work consciously to free yourself from thoughts and patterns that keep you in limitation. When you dare to be authentic in yourself and in your expression, you can make a big difference to people.

Your placement of the Sun combined with Cancer in the ascendant creates a great sensitivity and it is important that you learn to manage this part, so that you become master of your energy.

The Ascendant in Cancer & the Sun in Cancer

With both the ascendant and the Sun in Cancer, they are in the same sign and house, the first house. The first house represents new beginnings, initiation, leadership and our personality.

When both the ascendant and the Sun are in the same house and sign, the energy mixes and they create a strong unity. Our inner core goes hand in hand with our personality and how we were shaped during our upbringing. Cancer's energy becomes extra prominent here and we have strong qualities when it comes to our emotions, to empathize and to know what other people around us need.

With the Sun in the first house, you are here to develop strong leadership and to express your personality. Your great lessons and insights come when you take the initiative yourself and lead yourself forward. Cancer is a leadership sign so there is a built-in leadership within you. Together with your sensitivity and your ability to empathize with people, you can find a balance between your own creativity and humility in meeting others. With the Sun and the ascendant in Cancer, it is very important that you learn to set healthy boundaries and that you learn to understand your energy. Then your sensitivity can become your greatest gift.

Ascendant in Cancer & Sun in Leo

With the ascendant in Cancer and the Sun in Leo, this means that the Sun is in the second house - the house of material resources, self-worth, money, abundance and scarcity.

With the Sun in the second house, you are here to learn all about your own resources. You are also here to experience the contrast between scarcity and abundance and how to create what you need for yourself. An important task with this placement is about your sense of worth, how you value yourself. When you see and know your inner value on a deep level, you have the opportunity to create abundance in different areas of life, including the economy. The Sun is in Leo, the sign of leadership and creativity as well as pride.

This means that these are qualities you need to develop and affirm in order for your Sun to shine brightly with this placement.

With Cancer in the ascendant, you are empathetic and close to your feelings. You have an intuitive ability, something that you can use to develop your inner self. By using Cancer's sensitivity in combination with Leo's creative energy, you can contribute joy and inspiration to people around you.

Ascendant in Cancer & Sun in Virgo
With the ascendant in Cancer and the Sun in Virgo, this means that the Sun is in the third house - the house of communication, perspective, learning and mental processes.

With the Sun in the third house, you are here to learn all about communication and to find your true divine expression. You are here to transform lower thoughts and forms of communication into something higher – something creative that can benefit you and, by extension, people around you. The Sun is in Virgo, the sign of perfection, accuracy and service. This means that you have an ability to express yourself in communication in a concrete and precise way, something that you can use to write books or get your messages across. You are also here to contribute some form of service in this life, and you may feel yourself drawn to this before you find what specifically suits you.

The ascendant in Cancer makes you an empathetic and sensitive person, with a great understanding of other people. Cancer is a leadership sign, and you can use its power to move forward in life. Through the combination of Cancer and Virgo, you are here to guide yourself and other people through challenges.

Ascendant in Cancer & Sun in Libra

With the ascendant in Cancer and the Sun in Libra, it means that the Sun is lying in the fourth house - the house of home, family, security, our roots and our origins.

With the Sun in the fourth house, you are here to find security within yourself and thus find home within yourself. You are also here too free yourself from dysfunctional family patterns, that is, things that hold you back in limitation. It could be emotional blocks, co-dependency or some form of adaptation you brought with you from home. With this placement, you may feel drawn to the family and there may also be a longing to create a family of your own, whether it is in the form of your own children, animals or close friends. The Sun is in Libra, the sign of relationships and balance. This means that family and relationships as a whole are a major life theme for you in this life.

With Cancer in the ascendant, which also represents family, security and home, that theme returns again. Based on that, it is extremely important that you build up a sense of security in yourself and that you build up your existence according to your needs and based on what resonates with you energetically. It is of the utmost importance that you create balance in your relationships and learn to build dynamic relationships that raise your energy.

Ascendant in Cancer & Sun in Scorpio

With the ascendant in Cancer and the Sun in Scorpio, this means that the Sun is in the fifth house - the house of creativity, sports, creation, expression, children and playfulness.

With the Sun in the fifth house, you are here to reconnect with your soul's creativity and express it here on Earth. You are here to affirm your creative energy but also your inner child, the part of you that is spontaneous and alive. This placement means you have great creative gifts, something you should express in some way – in the form of art, music, writing, dance or through your job. The Sun is in Scorpio, the sign of deep resources and transformation. This means that you carry deep resources within you, but you may need to work a little to develop them. Scorpio always requires us to make some kind of transformation within ourselves in order to blossom fully.

With the ascendant in Cancer, you have great sensitivity, and you can tune in to what people around you need to feel good. By using that energy along with the depth and creativity that comes with the placement of the Sun, you can create something grand for yourself and for others.

Ascendant in Cancer & Sun in Sagittarius
With the ascendant in Cancer and the Sun in Sagittarius, this means that the Sun is in the sixth house - the house of health, routines, service, mastery and work.

With the Sun in the sixth house, you are here to learn all about health and your physical body. You are here to understand what your body needs, how your energy works and what you need in everyday life to get a flow. This means that you may be drawn to areas of health or experience some kind of challenges yourself, in order for you to receive the lessons that your soul seeks. The Sun is in Sagittarius, the sign of exploration, freedom and expansion. This means that these qualities are important for your Sun to develop and

142

shine in this placement. As you heal yourself physically and emotionally, you become a skilled and powerful healer. You understand what people need and can thereby contribute with service.

With Cancer in the ascendant, you have a great understanding of people's needs and through this combination you can help people develop and heal.

Ascendant in Cancer & Sun in Capricorn

With the ascendant in Cancer and the Sun in Capricorn, this means that the Sun is in the seventh house - the house of relationships, balance, relating and other people. This placement also means that the ascendant and the Sun are opposite each other in the chart.

With the Sun in the seventh house, you are here to understand yourself through relationships with other people. This means that many of your great insights and learnings come through relationships and partnerships. With this placement, you can feel drawn to relationships and there is a lot of development, especially in your closest relationships. The Sun is in Capricorn, the sign of leadership, discipline and structure. This means that these are qualities that you need to develop in the course of life in order to strengthen your Sun.

With Cancer in the ascendant, you have learned early on to be empathetic to the needs of others and you are very receptive to other people's energies. One piece of advice here is to work on building up your inner security, so that you are not drawn into any form of adaptation or co-dependency. Use the sensitivity of Cancer combined with the determination and discipline of Capricorn to create power and achieve your goals.

Ascendant in Cancer & Sun in Aquarius

With the ascendant in Cancer and the Sun in Aquarius, this means that the Sun is in the eighth house - the house of transformation, shared resources, intimacy and deep aspects of ourselves.

With the Sun in the eighth house, you are here to undergo a profound transformation in this lifetime. Based on that, your soul will lead you towards challenges and emotional crises, in order for you to develop and gain the insights you need. You may experience that you carry a lot of pain and that you feel other people's feelings. With this placement, it is extremely important that you learn to transform and transmute energy - so that you can heal and become the powerful healer you were born to be. The Sun is in Aquarius, the sign of innovation and new thinking. You are here to find new innovative ways to understand and use healing. You are not here to fit into the norm, but you should go your own way to develop your Sun here.

In combination with the ascendant in Cancer, you have a strong empathic ability, and you see what people around you need. If you dare to face lower parts of yourself and heal emotional blocks, you can go far in spirituality here.

Ascendant in Cancer & Sun in Pisces

With the ascendant in Cancer and the Sun in Pisces, this means that the Sun is in the ninth house - the house of exploration, travel, adventure, wisdom and belief.

With the Sun in the ninth house, you are here to explore the higher meaning of life, through experiences and through learning. You are here to understand yourself and expand your soul and through this journey you become a strong mentor or teacher to other people. With this placement, you may feel drawn to explore and travel, either through physical journeys in the World or through journeys within yourself. The Sun is in Pisces, the sign of spirituality, dreams and creativity. This means that there are strong elements of spirituality here. You have great possibilities to work in healing or function as a spiritual teacher with this placement. Pisces is the sign of dreams but also of illusions. This allows you to be extra sensitive to other people's opinions and beliefs. Be selective and careful in what you choose to do, so that it resonates with you and your inner being.

With Cancer in the ascendant, you have a great ability to sense what people around you need. You feel vibrations and you are responsive. With Cancer in the ascendant and the Sun in Pisces, you are extremely empathetic, and it is of the utmost importance that you learn to understand your inner emotional life and to set clear boundaries in life. When you master this, you have great gifts in healing work.

CHAPTER 8
LEO IN THE ASCENDANT

Leo

Qualities: Fire, Fixed, Masculine

Ruled by the planet: The Sun

Connected to house: 5

Soul Archetypes: Actor, Leader, Clown, Child

Connection to chakra: The heart chakra

Leo Characteristics & Energy

Leo is the fifth sign of the Zodiac and symbolizes themes such as playfulness, passion and creativity. Other qualities associated with Leo are leadership, strength, and physical activity. The sign carries a fiery firm masculine energy, which means there is a lot of explosive creativity and strong expression.

Soul archetypes associated with Leo are the Actor, the Leader and the Child.

Leo as Ascendant

All fire ascendant signs have a common denominator and that is their strong life energy and ability to spread warmth around them. Leo as an ascendant is powerful and carries strong resources within it, something that allows it to handle big changes and a lot of drama in the course of life. There is a playful and exuberant energy in Leo and with this ascendant sign we are good at creating joy and inspiration for those around us, unless there are other things preventing this in the chart. People around us see us as strong, stubborn and generally cool. There is a pride and a majestic energy that drives us forward and almost makes us seem unmoved by the things around us.

Leo is the sign of drama and with the ascendant here we have a colorful personality with strong emotions. This means that we can be very happy when we are happy and, conversely, very angry when we feel unfairly treated. There is generally a great variety in our feelings and in our expression, which makes us noticed by other people.

With Leo in the ascendant, we often have a natural attraction to express ourselves, in some creative form or through our being in the encounter with another person. Our expression can also be through our clothes or through our ability to be seen among other people.

It is no coincidence that Leo is usually seen as the classic theater monkey or the one who thrives in the limelight. We have seen that individuals with Leo here can have an attraction to the stage although this is not always the case.

With Leo in the ascendant, we have a great need to feel appreciated, seen and confirmed for who we are. We long to feel special and we find it difficult to live casually. We need to have some kind of excitement and passion in our life. In other words, we need to feel alive.

Leo is a fixed sign, which means it can be unyielding in its ways. Leo is loyal to those closest to him and comes with protection when needed – both for himself and those closest around him. Because of this fixed energy, there is also a meticulousness and a form of perfectionism, which can emerge through self-criticism. We have a hard time doing things half-heartedly but want to do it as well as possible. It is precisely this perfection that can make us extremely skilled in whatever we choose to do, whether it is sports, artistry or personal development.

Soul contract/Soul plan

With Leo in the ascendant, we have a big plan for ourselves in this life. There are also great and profound lessons that we can become aware of and discern in our lives.

Leo as a sign is ruled by the Sun, which represents our identity and who we are on a deep level. The Sun in the Birth Chart shows who we are meant to be and where we have a great opportunity to make a mark. This means that a big task with this ascendant sign is about finding exactly who we are - finding our core and our true identity. Through different experiences and through meetings with others, we finally find ourselves. Through creation in different forms, we learn to make our way and to find the path that suits us best, even if it may take a while.

For individuals with Leo ascendant, it is extremely important to learn to see the value in oneself and one's being, rather than through confirmation from other people. It can be a long way to go and many Leos here struggle with feeling inadequate until they see and feel their divine worth on a deep level. This happens through the heart and through self-love.

Childhood & patterns from growing up

When we step into a body here on Earth, we choose a family and an environment that matches our current energy and vibration as well as the lessons we want to learn and deal with during this life. We thus choose a family that helps shape your ascendant.

Leo is known for being the theater monkey or the one who likes to stand on a stage. The sign is also connected with archetypes such as the Clown or the Actor. This is true to some extent and the fact is that Leo is an expert at playing a role. But which role is played depends a lot on how we were shaped as children. If we have received appreciation when we were funny or when we made our parents laugh, then that is the role we play. If, on the other hand, we have received appreciation when we have performed or been good, it may as well be the role we play.

In our work, we have seen that there is a strong pattern from childhood in individuals who have the ascendant in Leo. This pattern means that we received a lot of confirmation when we were assertive or forward in some way. Leo has a masculine creative energy, something that may have been appreciated when we were children. Either we ourselves may have had one or two parents who were very in their Leo energy or the opposite - that we need to step in and be a Leo to lift or facilitate our parents. It is not entirely unusual for individuals with this ascendant to unconsciously enter the role of the "funny" or positive one, because it was otherwise difficult in the family.

Here it is valuable to look at what our upbringing looked like and whether we have entered into any particular role. Being able to step into different roles can be positive and many actors have the ascendant precisely in Leo. However, we should look at any dysfunctional parts here, so that we can be ourselves first and foremost and feel safe in that.

Common Challenges

With Leo on the Ascendant, we are usually experts at giving what people around us want or what we think they want from us. We can say the right comment, make the best joke, or act in a way that impresses or pleases others. Based on that we get stuck in behaviors where we constantly search for external confirmation. We do what it takes to maintain our mask and play the role that those around us are used to seeing us in.

It is not entirely unusual for people with this ascendant sign to be perceived as strong and confident, but behind the surface there may be a strong fear of not being enough. In order to feel loved, appreciated and seen, Leo can seek out situations or relationships where there is constant external confirmation, in order to confirm himself - his own value.

Because we have learned to be something or do something for other people, we have learned to protect ourselves and our inner vulnerability. This means that we can be perceived as somewhat insensitive or as if we do not care, when in fact we care extremely much.

Strengths & Gifts

In our opinion, Leo is one of the most resourceful signs in the Zodiac, and this means that people with the ascendant here usually have strong qualities within them. It can be resources in the form of physical strength and endurance, resources in creation or resources that are about building something big from a small core. The Leo is usually able to deal with strong setbacks in life because of his stubbornness and ability to single-mindedly move towards his goal.

With Leo on the Ascendant, we usually have great creative resources that we can use to build our lives the way we want them to be. We can also use creativity to help people and to spread joy. There is a generosity and a big heart that we are happy to open up to those who are closest to us. If, on the other hand, we are let down or abandoned, we can take it hard and become somewhat overprotective of ourselves and those around us.

This ascendant sign also makes us a strong leader and people around us perceive us as confident and proud. If we use this leadership in a positive way, we have great opportunities to go very far and make a big difference.

One of Leo's great gifts is their social skills and talent. They have learned the social interaction early and either they are often very social themselves and if they are not, it is easy for them to act as if they are confident. There is an ability to be able to read social interaction and then step into the role or what fits in that context.

Health & energy flow

There are many important parts to look at in the Birth Chart when it comes to health and two of them are the ascendant sign and the sixth house. The ascendant has a strong connection to our physical body, how we move physically but also how we protect ourselves and absorb energy. The sixth house is the house for health, daily routines and shows what we need in everyday life to get flow in a general way.

With Leo in the ascendant, we usually have a lot of energy and good health. The sign is ruled by the Sun and there is a strong vitality that permeates the physical body but also its energy flow. Just like the other masculine signs and above all when it comes to the fire signs in the Zodiac, there is an ability to protect oneself in a powerful way. This protection lies in the ability to set boundaries and to put up a shield, a form of protection for the environment.

In terms of the physical body, Leo has a strong connection with the heart and circulatory system, along with the opposite sign Aquarius. However, Leo has a stronger connection with the heart than Aquarius. Based on this, it is valuable to take care of and look over these parts of the body a little extra, when we have Leo in the ascendant. Physically, it is our heart that keeps our body alive, in the same way that our heart chakra is the center of our chakra system.

To take care of our heart, it is valuable and important that we allow ourselves to be vulnerable and perhaps even more important, that we allow ourselves to experience and feel sadness when we need it. Feelings of sadness have a tendency to get stuck right in the heart if we don't learn to experience and process these feelings. Because of the protection that Leo can put up against the outside world, in order to protect itself, it can sometimes lead to a closed or blocked heart. This applies even more if we had a tough upbringing or if we are involved in something very traumatic or painful in the meeting with other people.

If we have Leo as the ascendant, we need to make sure that we create and move forward in a creative way, no matter in which field it applies. Leo is creative by nature, but it is also a fixed sign, which means that it can sometimes get stuck in things a little too long, also because of its loyal side. If we feel that we are stuck in some area or if we feel that we feel stagnated, it is valuable to look at how we can move forward through some form of movement and creation. It also helps create flow in our circulatory system.

With Leo as the ascendant sign, it means that our sixth house is in the sign of Capricorn. The sixth house is connected to our general health and shows what we need in our everyday life to feel good but also to build healthy routines and have flow in our energy. Capricorn as a sign stands for themes such as discipline, structure and determination. There is a grounding energy to this sign, something very different from the Leo energy.

As we mentioned earlier, there are traits of perfectionism in Leo, and we have seen individuals with this ascendant sign who have been extremely meticulous in what they do. With Capricorn in the sixth house, we get a mix of Leo's perfectionist side and Capricorn's determination and discipline. This means that people with this combination are often very good at taking care of their health and setting up clear routines in everyday life. Capricorns are generally good at creating structure and sticking to it, even if it means sacrificing something else. What is important here is that we create routines and an everyday life where we follow our heart in what we do, that is, we have routines that make us feel good and that help us in the long term. Otherwise, our routines and our purposeful side can rather keep us stuck in patterns that drain our energy or burn us out.

Related Chakra

Leo has a strong connection with the Heart Chakra, which makes it extra important to maintain balance here.

The heart chakra is the chakra that lies in the middle and thus forms the area around our heart in the body. The heart chakra is our strongest and most powerful energy center in the body, as it is a direct link to our soul and thus our purpose here on Earth. When we create through and from our heart, we get flow in this chakra and there is tremendous power in what we do from the heart. If, on the other hand, we have blockages or a closed heart, we may experience that we are generally closed and that we feel disconnected from life and our true essence. We can also find it difficult to be close to a person and experience the depth that we need to get close to someone purely spiritually.

Since the Heart Chakra is prominent in Leo, it is important with this ascendant sign that we constantly strive for a higher form of creation. When we create from our inner power and from what feels true to us, then we get a higher form of creation. If we create only to please others, we get less flow and we lose the power of what we do. We also need to make sure to fill our lives with what brings us joy and what awakens our inner passion. A Leo who acts without a sense of passion can easily become depressed and feel that life feels meaningless.

Our Heart Chakra symbolizes the relationship with ourselves but also the relationship with others and with life. This means that relationships are a strong theme when we have Leo in the ascendant. We are here to experience love, drama and passion in relationships to ultimately find a higher form of love within us. To get to the higher form of love and ultimately pure self-love, we may have to experience the opposite first in the form of tough and draining relationships.

The career houses

When it comes to job, career and life path in the birth chart, there are many parts to look at, such as our composition of the chart with all the planets and where our power point MC (Midheaven) is located. But there are some important parts we can look at here. By looking at the qualities and the energy that our ascendant represents, we can see what we need jobwise, to develop. When we know what our ascendant sign is, we can also see what our career houses are, that is, what signs and elements they are in. The career houses are 2, 6 & 10. With the ascendant in Leo, the three career houses are in the signs Virgo, Capricorn & Taurus, which are all earth signs. Earth represents the practical and material things around us, what we can touch. Having the career houses in earth signs means that we have great resources within us when it comes to creation and building, something we can use to build our career and manifest what we dream of. This is further enhanced if we have the Sun, Moon or other planets in these three houses.

So, what does it mean to have Leo in the ascendant and career houses in earth signs?

With the social and creative energy of Leo together with the strong earth found in the career houses, we can create and build something big in career, if that's what we want. We have previously described that Leo carries strong resources both socially and physically. This means that it is a sign that is often prepared to fight for its cause and work hard to achieve its goals. The houses located in earth in our birth chart often show where we are prepared to spend time on something and to build something in the long term. Here, the career houses are in earth, which creates good conditions for really building something in career, job and life task. Earth is also connected to money and material possessions, which means that we can have a strong ability to create money and to manifest physical things around us, for example a nice house or something on a larger scale like a restaurant.

With Leo in the ascendant and the career houses in earth, we can fit well in professions where we get to use our social skills while at the same time using our practical abilities in what we do. Examples of occupations or keywords that may fit here are manager, sport, health, service, trainer, leader, actor, coach, investor and self-employed.

The tenth house is one of the career houses and perhaps the most important to look at, in terms of career but also in terms of our life mission – what we are here to manifest in this life.

In this combination, the tenth house is in the sign Taurus, the sign of long-termism, endurance, creativity and material things. Both Leo and Taurus have strong creative sides that come out in slightly different ways. Leo is generally more forward in his energy, while Taurus can create but at the same time take a step back to calmness. With the Ascendant in Leo and Taurus in the tenth house, our great gift lies in creating something through our creativity, whether it is in the form of theatre, song, food or something in communication. There needs to be enjoyment in what we do. If we only maintain working with a set of rules to please others, we will lose our inner spark and the creativity that needs to be included. For that reason, this combination makes us a very good entrepreneur and self-employed person, where we can set our own game rules.

Spirituality, Transformation & Deep Healing

Leo is the sign of great energy and great processes, which allows us to experience transformative phenomena with this ascendant sign. Leo as a sign rarely goes completely unnoticed and the same applies to the inner processes that come with transformation and ascension. We can experience drama, strong events and challenges that lead us closer and closer to our inner self and our soul.

At its lowest energy, Leo is overly focused on himself and there is an extreme need for validation from others. There is a drama that constantly permeates the meeting with other people, and we need the attention of others to feel special and sufficient.

In its highest energy, Leo is creative and does things from the heart, for himself but also for other people. There is an inner security and with that security we know that we are okay as we are, regardless of what those around us think. We feel special in our being without having to prove anything to others. In this energy we are good at protecting ourselves when needed but we have an open heart, an openness that makes us vulnerable and generous to those around us. Our courage and our strength become an inspiration to those we meet along our path.

So, the journey we need to make within ourselves with this ascendant sign is about moving from drama to creation. It is also about finding ourselves and our identity in the course of life, not the identity we were molded into but the identity we ourselves build up through experiences and through contact with the heart.

To create balance with our Leo, it can be valuable to bring in the energy from the opposite sign, that is, Aquarius. While Leo represents our identity, ego and creativity, Aquarius represents the big group and doing something for a higher purpose. Aquarius is also rebellious in their energy and does things outside the box, even if it is not always appreciated by others. If we get caught up in drama or in the search for other people's confirmation, we can focus on the Aquarius energy and focus on how we can contribute something to other people. We can also use that energy to get around the need for external confirmation by making actions and choices that break the norm and then work with the feelings of discomfort that may arise here. When we have a balance between Leo and Aquarius, we act from our heart and our creativity while daring to create new templates that can benefit society as a whole.

There are three houses in the birth chart that relate to our inner depth, our transformation and our spirituality. It is houses 4, 8 & 12. House four shows what we carry from family and lineage. House eight shows how we undergo transformation during life but also what healing abilities we have. House twelve shows what we carry in our subconscious and what energy we need to lift up and make conscious. If we have planets in one of these houses, the energy and focus there becomes even stronger.

With the ascendant in Leo, we have our spiritual houses in Scorpio, Pisces & Cancer. This means that the spiritual houses are in water signs. When these houses are in water signs, we get a great depth and a great sensitivity. Many individuals with water in these houses have great abilities in mediumship and healing. There is an ability to sense what lies beneath the surface, both for ourselves and for other people.

With this combination we can see several important aspects. Behind the easy-going and self-confident Leo energy, there is often a great depth and complexity, which shows itself through the fourth house. The fourth house represents our childhood and what we carry with us from there. When this house is in Scorpio, we have had experiences that were intense, deep and often even traumatic during our childhood. Here we need to look at what we carry with us and how we can transform what has been challenging and what keeps us in deep trauma patterns.

Combination with the Sun

Now follows a review of the ascendant in Leo in combination with all Sun signs. Look at your ascendant sign in the Birth Chart and then where your Sun is. Combining these two energies gives you a strong indication of what you are here to delve into and manifest in this life. It also gives you guidance for spiritual themes you can develop and understand within yourself and in your life.

The ascendant shows how you have been shaped, how you meet your surroundings as well as important life themes and lessons for you in the course of life.

The sun shows where you are meant to shine in this life and where you have a great opportunity to make an impression with your energy.

Ascendant in Leo & Sun in Aries

With the ascendant in Leo and the Sun in Aries, this means that the Sun is in the ninth house - the house of exploration, travel, adventure, wisdom and belief.

With the Sun in the ninth house, you are here to find your highest truth about yourself and life. You are here to explore and expand, in terms of your beliefs. With this placement, you can feel drawn to different experiences, development and travel – everything that leads you to new insights and new knowledge. The Sun is in Aries, the sign of courage, adventure and leadership. This means that these are qualities that you may need to develop in the course of life and that help you develop your Solar energy. With the Sun here, it is important that you find context and beliefs that resonate with your soul and your energy. Otherwise, you can easily be drawn into other people's preconceptions and lose yourself.

In combination with Leo in the ascendant, you have strong resources when it comes to getting ahead and you can use this energy to lead yourself but also other people - especially when you have healed lower aspects within yourself.

Ascendant in Leo & Sun in Taurus

With the ascendant in Leo and the Sun in Taurus, this means that the Sun is in the tenth house - the house of work, career, life task, manifestation and greater impact.

With the Sun in the tenth house, you are here to make a mark in work and career or through your life's mission. You are here to create something for yourself but also for other people. With this placement, you may feel drawn to invest in your career or find your calling - something that sometimes comes later in life. Part of this placement is also about building your inner authority and freeing yourself from old family patterns that hold you back. The Sun is in Taurus, the sign of stability, patience and creativity. This means that these are qualities that you need to develop and highlight within yourself, to make your Sun shine brightly here. You have creative abilities that you should use in the profession you choose.

In combination with Leo in the ascendant, you have great creative abilities but also strong resources in the form of leadership and other forms of creation.

Ascendant in Leo & Sun in Gemini

With the ascendant in Leo and the Sun in Gemini, this means that the Sun is in the eleventh house - the house of groups, networks, visions of the future, community engagement and innovation.

With the Sun in the eleventh house, you are here to contribute something for the collective and for the great mass. You are not here to fit into the norm, but your task is to find new ways - to contribute to innovation and new thinking. With this placement, you can feel that you are here to contribute something to a higher purpose. You may also feel somewhat out of place and odd among other people, something that you should use to your advantage and development. The Sun is in Gemini, the sign of communication, networking and mental processes. This means that you have strong social skills and by using them you meet the right people who will help you along the way. You should strive to think outside the box and find new solutions to things in life.

With Leo in the ascendant, you have strong resources within you, and you carry a strength that will help you get ahead in the course of life. Here you can use that strength and, together with the Gemini's curiosity, create something big for people around you.

Ascendant in Leo & Sun in Cancer

With the ascendant in Leo and the Sun in Cancer, this means that the Sun is in the twelfth house - the house of subconscious processes, spirituality, dreams and escape.

With the Sun in the twelfth house, you are here to develop your spirituality and to explore deeper layers of yourself. You are also here to make a difference to people, through your sensitivity and through your intuitive ability. With this placement, you are open to external energies, and you can experience yourself that you need a lot of your own time to process things within you. You have great gifts in spirituality, and you can be a powerful healer, especially when healing emotional blockages within yourself. The Sun is in Cancer, the sign of intuition, emotions and family. This means that you are sensitive to what other people need. You feel what people around you are struggling with, and you can pick up on their feelings. Cancer is a cardinal sign, which makes you a strong leader.

With Leo in the ascendant, you have great resources at your disposal. By using Leo's creativity combined with Cancer's intuition, you can create something magical and make a big difference to people.

The Ascendant in Leo & the Sun in Leo
With both the ascendant and the Sun in Leo, they are in the same sign and house, the first house. The first house represents new beginnings, initiation, leadership and our personality.

When both the ascendant and the Sun are in the same sign and house, the energy mixes and they create a strong unity. Our inner core goes hand in hand with our personality and how we were shaped during our upbringing. The Leo energy becomes extra prominent here and we have strong qualities in terms of creativity, leadership and various forms of creation.

With the Sun in the first house, you are here to develop strong leadership and to affirm your personality. Your greatest lessons and insights come when you take the initiative yourself and lead yourself forward towards new goals. Leo is resourceful and with both the ascendant and the Sun here, you have a basic strength that you developed while growing up. You also carry creative abilities, something that you can use to help people. To master the highest energy of Leo and make your Sun shine, you need to find your identity and what gives you energy in life, what touches your heart and soul.

Ascendant in Leo & Sun in Virgo
With the ascendant in Leo and the Sun in Virgo, this means that the Sun is in the second house - the house of material resources, self-worth, money, abundance and scarcity.

With the Sun in the second house, you are here to learn all about your resources, both material resources but also resources that you carry within you. You are also here to understand the difference between lack and abundance and how to create flow in your life. An important task with the Sun here is about how you see yourself, that is, how you value yourself. When you see, know and feel your worth on a deep level, you will attract abundance in different areas of life. To get there you first need to experience the lower energy here, which can be experiences of lack and doubt. The Sun is in Virgo, the sign of perfection, accuracy and service. This means that these are qualities that you should strive to develop in order to make your Sun shine brightly here.

With the Sun in Virgo and Leo in the ascendant, you carry a combination of earth and fire. By using the creative energy of Leo together with the precision and perfection of Virgo, you can build up great resources within yourself - and then manifest it with those around you.

Ascendant in Leo & Sun in Libra

With the ascendant in Leo and the Sun in Libra, this means that the Sun is in the third house - the house of communication, perspective, learning and mental processes.

With the Sun in the third house, you are here to learn all about your divine expression and master the theme of communication. This means that you may grow up in a family where communication is central or prominent in some way. To reach the highest energy of the third house you need to become well aware of what is going on in your thoughts and how you express yourself, towards yourself and others. You learn through challenges and obstacles to find what resonates with you, what you want to express here in the World. The Sun is in Libra, the sign of relationships and balance. This means that many of your big lessons around this theme will come through your relationships and through partnerships. This placement makes you a powerful writer or communicator, especially when you heal yourself and step into your true power.

In combination with Leo in the ascendant, you have great creative and social abilities, something you can use to get ahead among people and in life. It comes naturally to you to spread joy and love.

Ascendant in Leo & Sun in Scorpio

With the ascendant in Leo and the Sun in Scorpio, this means that the Sun is in the fourth house - the house of home, family, security, our roots and our origins.

With the Sun in the fourth house, you are here to find the home within yourself and build your inner secure base. You are also here to free your soul from old family karma and patterns that no longer benefit you. Here it can be positive to review how you grew up and heal what created pain and limitation within you. The Sun is in Scorpio, the sign of transformation and depth. It means that there are intense and emotional aspects within you connected with childhood, something that you need to strive to free yourself from. The placement also makes you a powerful healer and through your own inner work you can help others with transformational processes of various kinds. With the Sun in the fourth house, topics such as security and family are a big theme in your life. You may feel drawn to the family and harbor a great longing to form your own family.

In combination with Leo in the ascendant, you carry great resources and there is a strength within you that helps you achieve your goals. You are strong, persistent and determined. Both Leo and Scorpio need motivation to move forward. To feel energized, you need to find your great passion in life.

Ascendant in Leo & Sun in Sagittarius
With the ascendant in Leo and the Sun in Sagittarius, this means that the Sun is in the fifth house - the house of creativity, sports, creation, expression, children and playfulness.

With the Sun in the fifth house, you are here to affirm your creative side and express it in a concrete form. You are here to express your soul through some form of creative creation, whether it is a book, a piece of art, or through conversation with people. You have strong passionate life energy, and you have the ability to spread joy to those you meet. The Sun is in Sagittarius, the sign of exploration, expansion and travel. This means that there is a searching side within you, and you can be drawn to experiences that lead you towards development

166

and expansion. It can be physical journeys or journeys in your inner self. Sagittarius is generally a very optimistic sign and when it covers the fifth house, we get a mix of passion and expressive energy.

Combined with Leo in the ascendant, this fiery and creative energy is amplified. You have a strength within you, and you have the great gift of spreading joy and uplifting other people. By using Leo's creativity and Sagittarius' search for development, you have the potential to contribute great inspiration – to act as a teacher or mentor of some kind.

Ascendant in Leo & Sun in Capricorn
With the ascendant in Leo and the Sun in Capricorn, this means that the Sun is in the sixth house - the house of health, routines, service, mastery and work.

With the Sun in the sixth house, you are here to learn all about health but also to understand your energetic flow. You are here to find a daily routine that matches your energy frequency and resonates with your soul. With this placement, you may feel drawn to health and service. You may also experience some challenges specifically linked to your health, all so that you can get the insights and lessons that your soul is looking for. By understanding yourself and healing what isn't working, you become a healer with strong abilities to help others. The Sun is in Capricorn, the sign of discipline and determination. This means that you will most likely be determined when it comes to your everyday life, and you are prepared to work hard to achieve your goals.

Combined with Leo on the ascendant, you have a strong drive, and these qualities will help you get where you need to go, if you are prepared to do the work. With Leo and Capricorn, you have a strong masculine energy that helps you manifest your visions. Don't forget to include your feminine aspect in everyday life, so that emotions and intuition can be part of your projects.

Ascendant in Leo & Sun in Aquarius
With the ascendant in Leo and the Sun in Aquarius, this means that the Sun is in the seventh house - the house of relationships, balance, relating and other people. This placement also means that the ascendant and the Sun are opposite each other in the chart.

With the Sun in the seventh house, you are here to learn all about relationships but also to understand your soul through meeting others. Your greatest and deepest lessons in this life come through your relationships, where you learn more about your soul's needs. By understanding your relationship patterns and by freeing yourself from patterns that do not benefit you, you achieve great spiritual expansion and development. From that knowledge, the gift will help other people. The Sun is in Aquarius, the sign of innovation and new thinking. This means that you can feel drawn to people while at the same time feeling somewhat odd or out of the group. You are not here to fit into the norm but to find new paths, for yourself and for others. By affirming your unique side, you become a good leader and guide.

Together with Leo in the ascendant, you have great abilities when it comes to creating and finding new solutions.

You are innovative and creative at the same time. Your tenacity and determination will help you complete the projects you undertake.

Ascendant in Leo & Sun in Pisces

With the ascendant in Leo and the Sun in Pisces, this means that the Sun is in the eighth house - the house of transformation, transformation, shared resources, intimacy and deep aspects of ourselves.

With the Sun in the eighth house, you are here on Earth to discover all the shades of your soul. You are here to explore your inner self, and your learnings and insights usually come through experiences of pain and low frequencies. By learning to master these emotions and lower states, you become master of yourself and what happens in your body. It makes you a powerful healer with abilities to help others in their processes. So, an important task with the Sun in the eighth house is about learning to transform. The Sun is in Pisces, the sign of spirituality, creativity and dreams. This means that you have a great sensitivity with an openness to other people's energies.

Here you can take the help of Leo in the ascendant to protect yourself and your energy when needed. Pisces is extremely open and empathetic in its energy while Leo has the ability to defend itself. Together, Leo and Pisces carry strong creative abilities.

CHAPTER 9
VIRGO IN THE ASCENDANT

Virgo

Qualities: Earth, Mutable, Feminine

Ruled by the planet: Mercury

Connected to house: 6

Soul Archetypes: Fixer, Healer, Organizer

Connection to chakra: Throat chakra

Virgo Characteristics & Energy

Virgo is the sixth sign of the Zodiac and symbolizes themes such as health, routines and service. Other qualities associated with Virgo are perfection, refinement and detail. The sign carries a grounding mutable feminine energy, which means there is a practical and flexible energy here.

Soul archetypes associated with Virgo are the Fixer, the Organizer, and the Healer.

Virgo Ascendant

Virgo is a mutable sign ruled by the planet Mercury, making it a social and communicative sign. Since the sign has earth as its element, there is a grounding and practical energy here. Unlike the sign Gemini, which is also ruled by the planet Mercury, Virgo is generally a bit more reserved energy. So, individuals with the ascendant in Virgo are social, quick thinking and flexible but can also have a tendency to stand a little more in the background and observe.

Virgo has a neutral and natural energy, which creates a calmness in people around. One can express oneself through a certain form of neutrality in both men and women with this sign in the ascendant. So a woman might choose to dress down-to-earth and practical, the same way a man might choose to tone down his super-masculine appearance. This does not mean that individuals who have Virgo are unconcerned about how they are perceived, look or dress - quite the opposite. Virgo is very conscious of their own body and their appearance among other people.

With Virgo in the ascendant, we have a built-in helpfulness, and we are drawn to people and situations where we can help, support and improve things. It is in our nature, and it is also how we were shaped during our upbringing. We have a great accuracy, and we may have a need to create order out of chaos. We want things to be in order and things around us to be in place. The need for perfection can be great, which means that we are good at structuring and arranging things around us. We like to have control over life and what happens around us and other people see us as controlled and collected in our way of being.

This ascendant sign makes us a very good friend but also co-workers in a team, as we care about getting things done properly. We are also keen to help our friends when they seek our help, and we are happy to give advice on how our loved ones can create better conditions for themselves. Virgo has a strong connection to practical service, rather than emotional service – which means we like to help people on a down-to-earth, physical or practical level.

Soul contract/Soul plan
With Virgo in the ascendant, we are here on Earth to master great lessons. One of these teachings is about becoming masters of our physical body and understanding its language. Virgo has a natural connection with the sixth house of the Zodiac, which represents health, body and everyday routines. So, with this ascendant sign we are here to build and create an everyday life, where we become masters of ourselves, our life and our body. It may sound like a big task, and it is. It requires that we create an awareness and that we reflect on how we want our life to look - and that we choose what does not resonate with us. To our advantage, with this ascendant we have a good ability to distinguish things, which means that we often

start to distinguish early on what is good for us. By understanding our body and its unique vibration and what we need to create balance and harmony within ourselves, we become natural healers and mentors to other people.

We are also here on Earth to learn to find peace within ourselves. Peace does not come through external perfection and control, but through an inner feeling – a state that we develop through experiences linked to precisely control.

Childhood & patterns from growing up

When we step into a body here on Earth, we choose a family and an environment that matches our current energy and vibration as well as the lessons we want to learn and deal with during this life. We thus choose a family that helps shape our ascendant.

With the ascendant in Virgo, we have many times had an upbringing where we learned to develop our social skills and a certain form of flexibility. It can be through parents who themselves were social or where we felt that we were appreciated through these qualities. Since Virgo is an earth sign, we have also been shaped to create something or contribute something, for example through service or through achievement. An example is if we have a parent who has high demands on herself, something that is unconsciously transferred to you. As with other ascendant signs, there is a wide spectrum in terms of how we were formed, above all depending on how functional or dysfunctional our childhood was. Some individuals with Virgo Ascendant have experienced harsh control and high demands from their parents, while others have experienced it in a more subtle way.

During our work, we have seen a person in our vicinity who has the ascendant in Virgo. As an adult, she has struggled with strong feelings of need for control and a critical side, towards herself but also towards other people. She has strong opinions about what she thinks is right and wrong. This woman grew up with two parents who were in many ways quite ordinary and simple. But there were strong demands for order in the home while growing up, as well as strong opinions about what was appropriate and not appropriate towards other people. Beyond that, there was a heavy focus on the practical in life, rather than the creative and emotional.

The above is an example of what our upbringing with the ascendant in Virgo might have been like, although there are great differences and nuances.

When we have Virgo Ascendant, we have usually learned early on to discern what is right or wrong, good or bad and so on. It has molded us into a personality where we can be critical, usually of ourselves. We feel that we need to be perfect to be good enough or perform something to have value. This self-criticism means that we place high demands on ourselves in meeting others and in what we do, for example at a job. In some cases, this criticism or perfectionism that we direct towards ourselves can lead to body problems, as Virgo is connected to our physical body in a tangible way. It is not entirely unusual that we had one or two parents who put a lot of focus on their own body and health, regardless of whether it meant that he or she was sick or focused on diet and exercise.

With this ascendant sign, we have learned that thoughts come before feelings and to get ahead in life we need above all to be active

174

mentally and physically. It can cause us to struggle with our emotions and to put logical thinking ahead of our intuition.

If we have grown up in a functional environment, we have acquired the ability to solve things, to find solutions and to take on new things that come our way. There are practical skills that can be of great help to us throughout life. We have also acquired a strong awareness of body and health, which means that we are good at taking care of ourselves on that level. Here it is valuable to review patterns and behaviors as well as the strategies we received from childhood, so that we can step into the higher energy of Virgo.

Common Challenges

With the ascendant in Virgo, we often struggle with high demands, something we described earlier. Usually, these requirements are rooted in two factors. One is that we feel we need to be perfect to be enough or to be loved. The other is rooted in an inner chaos, something that we try to manage through external control and by doing everything right. We search for a sense of peace and balance. In its lower form, this critical part can express itself in strong self-criticism, self-hatred, depression and, in some cases, eating disorders. We can also have an excessive focus on our body and what we put into us, something that can also lead to a controlling in our everyday life.

Another challenge is that we easily get stuck in our thoughts, rather than allowing our emotions to flow. It can lead to physical problems and diseases in the long run, because our emotions and their flow lay the foundation for our general well-being, emotionally, energetically and physically. Here we need to make sure that we let go of control every now and then so that we get access to what is going on inside us.

If we had a tough and challenging upbringing, there is a risk that we also try to control the behavior of those around us. If this is the case, it is extremely important that we look at what is the basis for this and work on inner healing.

Strengths & Gifts

In addition to the fact that Virgo is ambitious and meticulous, there is an ability to see nuances in the environment. So, with the ascendant here, we are experts at seeing what lies between the lines of a conversation but also seeing details that no one else notices. We can look around a room and observe exactly where we can improve something and where there is potential for development.

Of all the signs in the Zodiac, Virgo is the one who is the best at doing that little extra, that thing that makes it a whole. It can be about putting together a book, putting together an education or creating something in, for example, design.

A person in our environment with Virgo ascendant works with web design and helps various companies put together, adjust and improve. She is very thorough and ambitious, which makes her a highly valued employee.

One of Virgo's great gifts lies in its deep interest in service. There is a warmth and a pleasant energy that people around appreciate. Virgos are good at listening and giving advice when someone around them is feeling bad or needs support.

Health & energy flow

There are many important parts to look at in the Birth Chart when it comes to health and two of them are the ascendant sign and the sixth house. The ascendant has a strong connection to our physical body, how we move physically but also how we protect ourselves and absorb energy. The sixth house is the house for health, daily routines and shows what we need in everyday life to get flow in a general way.

Virgo as a sign in itself has a strong connection to health and the routines that surround us in our everyday life. Many individuals who have Virgo in the ascendant have a developed awareness of their health and of what the body needs, unless there are other blocks in the chart that oppose this. For example, if we have a lot of activity in Pisces opposite, there can be a more volatile energy, which causes us to lose a little of our boundaries.

Physically, Virgo has a strong connection with the stomach and our intestines, especially the small intestine. One of the most important tasks for the small intestine in particular is to critically select and sort the food we eat, so that we get the nutrition we need. This means that we should pay extra attention to our stomach and find routines where we take care of our digestion, as that part of us can be a little extra sensitive. Here we can try our way and see which food gives us a light feeling and raises our energy and which food drains us or drags us down in terms of energy.

With Virgo as the ascendant sign, this means that our sixth house is in the sign of Aquarius. The sixth house is connected to our general health and shows what we need in our everyday life to feel good but also to build healthy routines and have flow in our energy. Aquarius as a sign stands for themes such as new thinking, innovation and doing things for a higher purpose. There is an airy and firm energy to this sign, something different from the energy of Virgo.

With the ascendant in Virgo and the sixth house in Aquarius, it is important that we bring in the innovative energy of Aquarius. We cannot keep track of everything that happens in our everyday life, and here we may have to test new things that concern our health during the course of our lives. When Aquarius is in the sixth house, we have seen that individuals may experience some strange or unexplained bodily symptoms and phenomena, as the sign stands for the unexpected. This means there needs to be an exploratory element to this combination.

In order for us to maintain our energy flow and thus create good health with Virgo in the ascendant, it is valuable that we create an awareness of what we put into ourselves without controlling.

Related Chakra

Virgo has a strong connection with the Throat Chakra, which is located in our throat. The chakra represents our communication and our expression, that is, how we make ourselves heard during the course of life. It is also connected with our ability to make decisions and make choices based on our inner voice.

When the Throat Chakra is in balance, we find it easy to express ourselves and take our place when we need it. We can speak up when something doesn't feel right, and we follow our own voice. We know when it's time to talk and when it's time to take a step back.

In the case of imbalance or a blocked Throat Chakra, we may have difficulty making our voice heard. We can feel a lump in our throat and like no one is really listening to what we say.

With the ascendant in Virgo, the Throat Chakra is prominent, and it is valuable that we take care of that part of our energy system a little extra. If we had an upbringing where we had to suppress our expression or where we were silenced in some way, it is especially important to work with the Throat Chakra.

In addition to Virgo, Gemini is also connected with the Throat Chakra, something we touched on in an earlier part. In general, Gemini has a more outgoing energy in the ascendant than Virgo, although both are communicative in nature. This is because Gemini is in the element of air and Virgo is in the element of earth. Air is masculine while earth is feminine. Since Virgo is a communicative sign but still feminine, with this ascendant we tend to have a more closed throat chakra. It can mean that we stay more in the background and take up less space, which can be positive at times. However, it can be valuable to create balance in our Throat Chakra so that we can express ourselves and speak up when we need to.

By finding what feels meaningful to us and communicating it to ourselves and our surroundings, we can maintain the balance in the Throat Chakra, and it also creates good conditions for the rest of our energy system.

The career houses
When it comes to job, career and life path in the Birth Chart, there are many parts to look at, such as our composition of the chart with all the planets and where our power point MC (Midheaven) is located.

But there are some important parts we can look at here. By looking at the qualities and the energy that our ascendant represents, we can see what we need jobwise, to develop. When we know what our ascendant sign is, we can also see what our career houses are, that is, what signs and elements they are in. The career houses are 2, 6 & 10.

With the ascendant in Virgo, the three career houses are in the signs Libra, Aquarius & Gemini, all of which are air signs. Air represents communication, mental processes, knowledge and learning. Having the career houses in air signs means that we have great resources within us when it comes to communication and learning, something we can use to build our career and manifest what we dream of. This is further enhanced if we have the Sun, Moon or other planets in these three houses.

So, what does it mean to have Virgo on the ascendant and the career houses in air signs?

This mix of energies and talents gives us good conditions for working with something where we use our voice or where we are involved in developing something. With Virgo's earth and perfection combined with the analytical ability found in the career houses, we can fit well in professional fields such as health, service, writing, communication, media, technology, data, logistics and learning. Since the career houses are in air, we can be drawn to a profession where we have social interaction and where we can work together with other people in some way. In these meetings with other people, we express our ideas and what we want to create.

The tenth house is one of the career houses and perhaps the most important to look at, in terms of career but also in terms of our life mission – what we are here to manifest in this life.

In this combination Gemini lies in the tenth house, the sign of communication, multitasking and relationships. Both Virgo and Gemini are mutable signs, and this means that we need to have a job where there is some flexibility. We need change and variety, otherwise we will tire quickly. A challenge here can be completing our projects, because of all the mutability there is. We can have a variety of plans and ideas. Here it is important that we also work to execute and complete the projects we embark on.

Spirituality, Transformation & Deep Healing

Traditionally in Astrology, there is a connection between Virgo, the sixth house, and serving other people. In its worst form, we can also call it slavery. Fortunately, we do not have slavery in today's Western society, at least not formally. So why are we bringing this up in the context of Virgo and its spiritual development?

At her lowest energy, Virgo is the one who serves others and who sacrifices herself for others – the one who always stands in the background without getting appreciation for her work. There is a self-defeating energy here that constantly puts the needs of others before their own. We do everything for others to be satisfied with us and what we do. It can eventually lead to bitterness and feelings of failure.

At her highest energy, Virgo uses her accuracy, her perfection, and her service to elevate herself and other people. There is a pride and an ability to back down in certain situations but also to step forward and take the attention that is well deserved. In this energy, Virgo is the natural healer of the Zodiac.

When we have the ascendant in Virgo, it is of the utmost importance that we work with our own sense of value, our divine value that no one can take away from us. Our intrinsic value that lies in our being, rather than in our performance. When we feel and know this value on a deep level within us, then we can find the peace we seek. It can take time, and we can trust that we will meet the very people and situations that challenge us in this - people who do not value us or who demand too much from us.

With the ascendant in Virgo, we are good at focusing on details, which is one of our gifts. If we feel that we get too caught up in the details or if we have difficulty seeing the whole picture, it can be valuable to bring in the energy of the opposite sign, Pisces. While Virgo is meticulous, concrete and focuses on the practical, we see the opposite in Pisces, who in many ways is limitless with a broad overview. In the field of medical Astrology, it has been seen that individuals who have Virgo strongly in their birth chart have a tendency to develop eating disorders in the form of anorexia, while individuals with Pisces develop eating disorders in the form of bulimia. This means that Virgo can be too critical, while Pisces can be too limitless and open, regardless of whether it concerns food, relationships or otherwise. So based on that, it is important to find a balance where we are critical and where we choose what should enter our life. But sometimes we also need to let go of our focus on details and see things from a higher perspective - we need to let go of control and trust that we will end up where we need to be, rather than living life through control. Virgo and Pisces lie in what we refer to as the axis of service and there is a strong theme of service and healing with both of these signs.

During our ascension, we need to work a lot with the concept of trust when we have Virgo as the ascendant sign. It helps us dare to try new things and step outside of our comfort zone, even though we are afraid of making mistakes or failing.

There are three houses in the Birth Chart that relate to our inner depth, our transformation and our spirituality. It is houses 4, 8 & 12. House four shows what we carry from family and lineage. House eight shows how we undergo transformation during life but also what healing abilities we have. House twelve shows what we carry in our subconscious and what energy we need to lift up and make conscious. If we have planets in one of these houses, the energy and focus there becomes even stronger.

With the ascendant in Virgo, we have our spiritual houses in Sagittarius, Aries & Leo. This means that the spiritual houses are in fire signs. When these houses are on fire, we get a strong penetrating and fiery energy. Many individuals with fire in these houses have great abilities in energy work and an ability to transform strong energy.

In this combination, we can have strong and dramatic emotions within us, as our deep houses are covered in fire. With Virgo in the ascendant, there can be a tendency to control precisely emotions and the inner spontaneity that comes with fire. Here we may need to practice becoming more permissive, so that we welcome our inner power and the feelings that lie within us and that need to come to the surface from time to time.

With this combination, it is also important that we allow ourselves to have a little fun, that we don't get stuck in jobs or what we call "duties". Sagittarius in the fourth house shows that we have an aspect within us that seeks joy and adventure, that longs to discover things and develop new insights about ourselves and life. By affirming that part within us, we bring in spontaneity and joy during the course of life.

Combination with the Sun

Now follows a review of the ascendant in Virgo in combination with all Sun signs. Look at your ascendant sign in the Birth Chart and then where your Sun is. Combining these two energies gives you a strong indication of what you are here to delve into and manifest in this life. It also gives you guidance for spiritual themes you can develop and understand within yourself and in your life.

The ascendant shows how you have been shaped, how you meet your surroundings as well as important life themes and lessons for you in the course of life.

The Sun shows where you are meant to shine in this life and where you have a great opportunity to make an impression with your energy.

Ascendant in Virgo & Sun in Aries
With the ascendant in Virgo and the Sun in Aries, this means that the Sun is in the eighth house - the house of transformation, transformation, shared resources, intimacy and deep aspects of ourselves.

With the Sun in the eighth house, you are here to explore the deepest parts of yourself. You are here to learn how to transmute pain and lower energy frequencies into higher ones. By learning the art of transformation, you become master of your energy, and you become a powerful healer. With this placement, you may face some obstacles along the way and many of your great lessons come through crises, all to get you what your soul is seeking. The Sun is in Aries, the sign of leadership and courage. This means that these are qualities you need to develop, in order for your Sun to develop and shine. You are a powerful soul with a strong life energy.

Virgo in the ascendant helps you to ground yourself and to create a structure in everyday life. By using the accuracy found in your ascendant sign, you can build your skills in whatever you choose to do. Service and healing are strong themes for you in this life.

Ascendant in Virgo & Sun in Taurus

With the ascendant in Virgo and the Sun in Taurus, this means that the Sun is in the ninth house - the house of exploration, travel, adventure, wisdom and belief.

With the Sun in the ninth house, you are here to find the higher meaning of life and to expand your soul. You are here to gain knowledge and insight, something that will ultimately make you a powerful teacher or mentor. With this placement, you may feel drawn to experiences or travel of various kinds, anything that leads you towards development. You may also be drawn to education and courses where you learn more about yourself and your soul. Since the ninth house is connected to beliefs, there can be a common thread through your life, which is about finding your inner truth about what you believe. The Sun is in Taurus, the sign of stability and endurance. Based on the fact that Taurus is calm and grounded in its energy, you have the ability to combine your search with a certain security in life. You want to discover, but you also need to have your safe point.

In combination with Virgo in the ascendant, which is also an earth sign, you have great qualities when it comes to building things up in a purely practical way. You know the art of manifesting something on a physical plane. You are thorough and you put time into what you do. Based on that, you can build a foundation to stand on during the course of life. Don't forget to include your feelings and your intuition in what you do, so that you build things based on your heart and what is important to you.

Ascendant in Virgo & Sun in Gemini

With the ascendant in Virgo and the Sun in Gemini, this means that the Sun is in the tenth house - the house of work, career, life mission, manifestation and greater impact.

With the Sun in the tenth house, you are here to contribute something in career, work or through your life task. You are here to create something, and you may have a longing to invest in your career or find your calling in life. An important task with this placement is about building your own authority and freeing yourself from family patterns that limit you in some way. The Sun is in Gemini, the sign of communication, flexibility and multitasking. This means that you have social skills, and you are good at seeing things from different perspectives. You can do several things at the same time, and you can easily jump from project to project. With the Sun here, you have the opportunity to become a strong communicator or work with people in some way.

In combination with Virgo in the ascendant, you have a great accuracy, and you know what people around you need. Communication and service are important themes for you in this life.

Ascendant in Virgo & Sun in Cancer

With the ascendant in Virgo and the Sun in Cancer, this means that the Sun is in the eleventh house - the house of groups, networks, visions of the future, community involvement and innovation.

With the ascendant in the eleventh house, you are here to find your unique and innovative expression. You are here to break old patterns and find new ways that benefit the great mass and thus the collective. To achieve this, you need to be brave and dare to go against the collective. When you affirm your individuality and what makes you different, you fill up with life energy. You gain strength and you become a strong inspiration for others. The Sun is in Cancer, the sign of security, family and intuition. This means that there is a part of you that seeks security and another that seeks freedom. By building a strong sense of security in yourself, you can choose to free yourself from what limits you and do things your way. Here it can be important that you free yourself from family patterns that can hold you back in an excessive need for security.

With Virgo in the ascendant, you have a grounding energy, and you strive to help and contribute with service. Through the placement of the Sun and through the ascendant here, you may find some form of service where you help humanity in a way that is a little outside the box.

Ascendant in Virgo & Sun in Leo

With the ascendant in Virgo and the Sun in Leo, this means that the Sun is in the twelfth house - the house of subconscious processes, spirituality, dreams and escape.

With the Sun in the twelfth house, you are here to explore your inner depths and to understand your subconscious processes. You are here to bring awareness to what is going on within you, to use that energy in your everyday life. This can be a challenge and with the Sun here, you may feel locked into yourself in some way. You may need a lot of time for yourself, and you carry a sensitivity to other people and their energies. With this placement, you have great intuitive abilities, and you can become a strong healer, especially when you learn to work with your own inner self. The Sun is in Leo, the sign of passion and creativity. This means that you have a strong life energy within you, which can sometimes be a bit challenging to channel and express. Creativity in any form can help you develop your Sun and make it shine.

In combination with Virgo in the ascendant, you have fine abilities in the form of accuracy and perfection, something that ultimately leads you to self-knowledge and health balance - if you consciously work on it.

Ascendant in Virgo & Sun in Virgo
With both the ascendant and the Sun in Virgo, they are in the same sign and house, the first house. The first house represents new beginnings, initiation, leadership and our personality.

When both the ascendant and the Sun are in the same sign and house, the energy mixes and they create a strong unity. Our inner core goes hand in hand with our personality and how we were shaped during our upbringing. Virgo's energy becomes extra prominent here and we have strong qualities in details, service and health. There can be a great focus on the body and the health aspect as well as a deep longing to contribute with service or help to others.

With the Sun in the first house, you are here to develop strong leadership and to live out your personality. You are also here to lead yourself forward in a conscious way. With this placement, many of your big and deep lessons come when you act yourself and take initiative forward. With both the Sun and the ascendant in Virgo, you are helpful, and you see what people around you need. One piece of advice is to lower the demands on yourself, so that you find joy and passion in what you do. Service, healing and health are important themes for you in this life.

Ascendant in Virgo & Sun in Libra
With the ascendant in Virgo and the Sun in Libra, this means that the Sun is in the second house - the house of material resources, self-worth, money, abundance and scarcity.

With the Sun in the second house, you are here to learn all about your resources, both in terms of inner resources and material ones. You are here to understand your soul's relationship to resources. An important task for you involves understanding the difference between lack and abundance. Lack comes when you undervalue yourself or when you learn that you are limited. Abundance comes when you see and know your true worth on a deep level. So, with this placement you are also here to work on your view of yourself, how you value yourself in relation to external things – for example money. If you consciously work with these themes, you can go from lack to abundance in different areas of life. The Sun is in Libra, the sign of relationships and balance. This means that many of your lessons here come through meeting others, through experiences in relationships. It is of great importance that you find the value within yourself in relation to others.

In combination with Virgo in the ascendant, you have a precision and a structured energy. It helps you to see things clearly and to move forward in a conscious way. The critical energy of Virgo is very valuable at times, and it helps you sort out what is not good for you.

Ascendant in Virgo & Sun in Scorpio
With the ascendant in Virgo and the Sun in Scorpio, this means that the Sun is in the third house - the house of communication, perspective, learning and mental processes.

With the Sun in the third house, you are here to learn all about communication and to find your higher form of communication. You have your divine expression and part of your journey is about finding this. With this placement, you can have a great interest in seeking new knowledge and you can be drawn to anything that gives you new insights. The Sun is in Scorpio, the sign of depth and transformation. This means that there will be some challenges in this area that you need to learn to transform and heal. It could be, for example, that you struggle with negative thoughts about yourself or that you are afraid to remain in your expression. There may also be blockages or limitations from childhood that you need to work on, in order for your Sun to shine brightly here.
Together with your ascendant sign Virgo, you have an inner depth but also a more clairvoyant and analytical side, something that you can use to move forward and achieve your goals. You can become a powerful writer and healer with this combination.

Ascendant in Virgo & Sun in Sagittarius

With the ascendant in Virgo and the Sun in Sagittarius, this means that the Sun is in the fourth house - the house of home, family, security, our roots and our origins.

With the Sun in the fourth house, you are here to create a security within yourself and thus find home within yourself. You are also here too free yourself from dysfunctional family patterns and build new patterns that resonate with you and your soul. Here, it is valuable to review the patterns you brought with you from home and transform those that limit you in your everyday life. With this placement, you can feel drawn to home and family, regardless of whether it concerns your growing up environment or creating your own family. You need a safe base, a place where you can land and navigate from. The Sun is in Sagittarius, the sign of expansion, belief systems and freedom. This means that these are important themes for your soul's development. There may also be strong belief systems or beliefs that you brought with you from home, which may be valuable to review. Strive for freedom and expansion and you will get where you need to go.

With the ascendant in Virgo, you can use your accuracy and grounding energy to build yourself up and the security you need. Use your critical side to sort out what doesn't resonate with you, while welcoming what is good for you and your development.

Ascendant in Virgo & Sun in Capricorn

With the ascendant in Virgo and the Sun in Capricorn, this means that the Sun is in the fifth house - the house of creativity, sports, creation, expression, children and playfulness.

With the Sun in the fifth house, you are here to affirm your creativity and express it in the World. You are here to reconnect with the creative energy that your soul carries. You have a strong life energy and when you work in a creative way, your energy comes out even more. The Sun is in Capricorn, the sign of discipline and determination. This means that you should strive to develop these qualities over the course of your life. Through solid work, you have great potential to create something big in this area. You can use your creativity and expression to help others, whether it's through books, through diet, or through conversations with people.

Together with the ascendant in Virgo, you have an attraction to service. Your thoroughness, which recurs in both Virgo and Capricorn, allows you to create exactly what you long for. There is a grounding energy here that will help you get through the challenges that may come along the way.

Ascendant in Virgo & Sun in Aquarius
With the ascendant in Virgo and the Sun in Aquarius, this means that the Sun is in the sixth house - the house of health, routines, service, mastery and work.

With the Sun in the sixth house, you are here to learn all about health and to understand the flow of energy in your body. You are here to build a daily routine with routines that resonate with your soul and vibration. With this placement, you may experience some challenges related to your health, in order for you to gain the knowledge your soul is seeking. By learning signals and tendencies in yourself, you will eventually become an expert in helping others - in the form of service and healing. The Sun is in Aquarius, the sign of innovation and new thinking. This means that you should seek alternative approaches to health, rather than following the patterns that already exist in society. You are not here to fit into the norm but to break it. By affirming your unique energy, you fill up with life energy and your Sun develops.

With Virgo on the Ascendant, you have a strong theme of service and health during this lifetime. Use the precision and perfection that Virgo possesses combined with the innovative power of Aquarius.

Ascendant in Virgo & Sun in Pisces

With the ascendant in Virgo and the Sun in Pisces, this means that the Sun is in the seventh house - the house of relationships, balance, relating and other people. This placement also means that the ascendant and the Sun are opposite each other in the chart.

With the Sun in the seventh house, you are here to learn all about relationships. You are also here to understand patterns in your relationships and free yourself from what limits you. With this placement, many of your great lessons come precisely through your relationships and through partnerships. The Sun is in Pisces, the sign of spirituality, creativity and emotions. This means that you have a great sensitivity to other people's energies. Here it is important that you find ways to protect your energy and that you set clear boundaries when necessary. With the Sun here, you have strong intuitive abilities, and you can become a powerful healer or therapist. You know what people around you need to feel good.

Together with Virgo on the ascendant, you have strong healing abilities and service is a big theme for you in this lifetime. Strive for a balance where you affirm your sensitivity in Pisces but also the

193

critical energy found in the ascendant. It helps you sort out what drains you or takes your energy.

CHAPTER 10

LIBRA IN THE ASCENDANT

Libra

Qualities: Air, Cardinal, Masculine

Ruled by the planet: Venus

Connected to house: 7

Soul Archetypes: Peacemaker, Therapist, The Artist

Connection to chakra: The Heart chakra

Libra Characteristics & Energy

Libra is the seventh sign of the Zodiac and symbolizes themes such as balance, relationships and how we relate to other people. Other qualities associated with Libra are aesthetics, beauty and an analytical ability. The sign carries an airy cardinal masculine energy, which means that there is a strong initial energy and a great focus on what is happening in the environment and in relation to other people.

Soul archetypes associated with Libra are the Peacemaker, Therapist and Artist.

Libra as ascendant

Libra has a natural connection with the seventh house of the Zodiac, which is the house of relationships and how we relate to other people. Based on that, Libra is the sign that most represents relationship themes in life.

With Libra ascendant, we usually have outstanding social skills and when it comes to knowing what people around us want from us. We know how to act when meeting another person, something we learned early in life. Libra is an air sign and with the planet Venus as the ruling planet, it becomes a major relationship focus in our life, something that can take shape on many different levels. With this ascendant sign, we are good at seeing things from the other's perspective and we are experts at understanding a dilemma from all sides and angles. So, if we have a discussion with two friends who have different opinions about something, we are usually the ones who understand both sides. We can see behind their words and actions, allowing us to see the underlying energy and motivation. This means that we are often perceived as a good friend, and we find it easy to get along with many different people. We are perceived as easy-going, and our loved ones know that they can come to us with their problems. We are the bridge between different opinions and the therapist who is happy to give of our time and energy.

Just like the other air signs, there is an analytical ability in Libra, which means that individuals with this ascendant spend a lot of time on thoughts, mental processes and analysis - something that can be their great gift but also lead to purely intellectual decisions.

When we have Libra in the ascendant, we have a strong aspect within us that longs for harmony and balance. We want to enjoy the beauty and magic around us. To satisfy that part of us inside, we might engage in something creative, for example interior design or art. There are many artists with strong elements of Libra in the birth chart. We place and usually great focus on creating balance and harmony in our closest relationships.

Soul contract/Soul plan

With Libra in the ascendant, we have great lessons to master in this lifetime. These teachings are about understanding relationships on a deep energetic level. It can be the relationship with ourselves, relationships with other people but also our relationship with life and how we look at it. We are here to achieve a deep spiritual balance within ourselves, a balance that comes through authenticity and through life experience. When we find the balance within ourselves, that balance will be reflected in all the relationships around us - and we become masters of relationships for real. These lessons come through experiences and contrasts in the relationships we encounter and with this ascendant we need to learn to see who we are. We need to see and feel all parts and spectrum within us, even the parts that cause discomfort, friction and pain. It's about making friends with our shadow sides and being able to stay in low frequencies long enough for transformation to take place.

Childhood & patterns from growing up

When we step into a body here on Earth, we choose a family and an environment that matches our current energy and vibration as well as the lessons we want to learn and deal with during this life. We thus choose a family that helps shape our ascendant.

With Libra as the ascendant sign, we usually come from a background where relationships have been central in some way, usually relationships in the form of one and one. Depending on what the family dynamics looked like, it will determine how we built these relationship patterns. In some cases, we have seen that individuals with Libra here grew up in an environment where everything in everyday life revolved around relationships in the family, in a rather destructive way. It can be about strong discussions, conflicts or even co-dependency in their lower energy.

Individuals with this ascendant sign learn early to mediate, adapt and facilitate the other person in the meeting. It is common for there to be other family members with a strong or prominent personality here. Since Libra is ruled by Venus, one of the most feminine planets, there is often a strong dynamic and connection to the mother or the one with the most feminine energy in the family.

A woman near us has the ascendant in Libra. She grew up in a family where there was a lot of conflict between all the different parties and above all between the mother and other family members.

The mother in this case had great difficulty in regulating her own emotions and had traits of narcissism in her way of acting. This led to the daughter early learning to act based on the mother's rules and she learned to agree, act as a mediator and not be a nuisance. As an adult, she generally has a close and good relationship with her mother. They socialize and have similar interests. She has many classic traits of Libra in the ascendant, such as an interest in beauty, aesthetics and she easily adapt and gets at ease with most people around her.

The above example shows several things, and an important aspect here concerns the beautified image that Libra sometimes has of his upbringing and in some cases of his mother. There is an image that everything was okay and there is also no major focus on sorting out or trying to understand what happened during childhood. How is it so? There are several reasons for that. With Libra as ascendant, we have learned to focus on the beautiful and fine in life. We have somehow learned through circumstance that pain and discomfort are something dangerous, something that we should hide deep within ourselves. This means that we can have a tendency to focus on what happens in everyday life and what gives us positive vibrations. It protects us from coming into contact with darker aspects of ourselves. We have seen many examples of individuals with Libra Ascendant who experienced trauma and tough things in childhood, but it can take a long time for them to open up and dare to face these parts within themselves.

When we have this ascendant sign, we have learned to focus on what is outside of ourselves and that includes other people. We have learned to put the needs of others before our own, which means that it comes naturally within us to help and support others.

We know a man who has Libra in the ascendant. He grew up in an environment where there was a lot of discussion and where he was the youngest child. Based on that, he quickly learned to stay a bit in the background and to step into the role of the easy-going one. As an adult, he is analytical, helpful, and he finds it easier to handle meetings with one person than larger groups.

Here it is important that we look at what our childhood looked like and what patterns we entered into, unconsciously in order to feel seen, loved and protected from the outside world.

Common Challenges

A common challenge when we have the ascendant in Libra is that we easily go into adaptation, that is, we put others before ourselves. It can be shown by us becoming like a chameleon, where we agree with the person we are with at the time. At worst, we can enter very dysfunctional relationships with codependency or even abuse in some form. For that reason, it is extremely valuable to become aware of the patterns and behaviors we carry and transform them into more effective strategies. The reason we can get into this type of situation is because it's familiar. We feel safe in giving to others and by being there for another person we avoid the discomfort that may arise in the other person or in ourselves. We may carry a fear of conflict that makes us avoid confronting someone or saying no when necessary. It allows us to let other people cross our boundaries, in a way that hurts us in different ways.

Because we have learned to consider other people, there can be uncertainty about what we ourselves think, what is our own opinion in relation to others. Therefore, it is quite common for us to lose our own person and direction when we are with someone else. We are so used to giving up our own needs and, in the end, we no longer know what our needs really are. We can also have difficulty getting in touch with our feelings and our inner depth, as we have learned to be in thought and to focus on our surroundings.

Strengths & Gifts

Individuals with this ascendant sign spread joy, peace and harmony around them, which is needed in the times we live in. There is a gift that is about seeing the bright and hopeful in everything that happens.

With Libra in the ascendant, we have great qualities within us and when we follow our heart, we can create magic and expansion for ourselves and for others. We have an ability to make people around us feel well taken care of and seen, in a soft and at the same time stripped-down way. We know how to use our words to lift others and create harmony.

When we have this ascendant sign, we have the ability to see the beauty in everything around us. It allows us to see the good and the highest in our partner or friend. We see it through a filter of harmony and balance. In the same way, we can see exactly what is needed on a painting, to get that magical feeling or what is needed to create magic in a room. This is where our aesthetic power comes in, a power that we can use to create something that touches.

Health & energy flow

There are many important parts to look at in the Birth Chart when it comes to health and two of them are the ascendant sign and the sixth house. The ascendant has a strong connection to our physical body, how we move physically but also how we protect ourselves and absorb energy. The sixth house is the house for health, daily routines and shows what we need in everyday life to get flow in a general way.

Libra as a sign has a strong connection to our balance in the body, i.e. balance between different body systems. This also includes the body's hormones and its balance. This makes it extra valuable to review and take care of these parts of the body during the course of life. In order to maintain a hormonal balance and have well-functioning glands, we need to review how we deal with stress. Prolonged and strong stress affects our hormones and creates an imbalance in the long term.

When we have the ascendant in Libra, it is important that we find a way to live, where we maintain a certain integrity, towards other people but also towards life. Due to the fact that we have learned many times to be at the mercy of others and to cater to the needs of others, we can easily become burnt out or lose our own energy. We can enter stress patterns that affect our body and its balance on many different levels. By looking at where our boundaries are, we can build an everyday life where we start from our own capacity and our needs. We can save energy and spend it on what feels important to us, not on what is expected of us.

Since Libra is an air sign, we deal with a lot of our stress through our thoughts. It usually happens quickly and unconsciously because it is a pattern we learned growing up. So, when we get stressed or feel threatened, we are quick to think out what to say, how to do or how we should act so that things are calm in the environment. In many ways, it can be a good strategy for dealing with stress, but we need to make sure that we don't get stuck only in our thoughts. Sometimes we may have to let go of what is going on in our thoughts and dare to face the stress we have around us, regardless of whether it is connected to a person or situation. We need to draw our focus down to the body to see and feel what is going on there. This means that we get both heart and brain into what we do.

With Libra as the ascendant sign, it means that our sixth house is in the sign of Pisces. The sixth house is connected to our general health and shows what we need in our everyday life to feel good but also to build healthy routines and have flow in our energy. Pisces as a sign stands for themes such as imagination, dreams, creativity and emotions. It is also connected with our intuition and empathic ability. There is a moving and watery energy in this sign, something very different from the energy of Libra.

With the ascendant in Libra and the sixth house in Pisces, we get a fusion of water and air, thought and feeling, feminine and masculine energy. This reinforces what we were talking about earlier - the importance of finding balance physically but also between our thoughts and feelings. When we find routines in everyday life that help us find this balance, we will approach good health and get flow in the body and energy system.

Since both Libra and Pisces have a tendency to cross their own boundaries to help others, it is extremely important here that we work with just that. Otherwise, there is a big risk that we let other people pass far beyond our borders, which in the long run can make us sick. We can also pick up other people's pain and energies, if we are too open.

Creativity is also a prominent watchword with this mix. We feel good about getting some form of creativity into our everyday life. It helps us fill up with energy and strengthen us on all levels.

Related Chakra

Libra has a strong connection with the Heart Chakra, which makes it extra important to maintain balance here.

The heart chakra is the chakra that lies in the middle and thus forms the area around our heart in the body. The heart chakra is our strongest and most powerful energy center in the body, as it is a direct link to our soul and thus our purpose here on Earth. When we create from our heart, we get flow in this chakra and there is enormous power in what we do from the heart. If, on the other hand, we have blockages or a closed heart, we may experience that we are generally closed and that we feel disconnected from life and our true essence. We can also find it difficult to be close to a person and experience the depth that we need to get close to someone purely spiritually.

Since the Heart Chakra is prominent in Libra, it is important with this ascendant sign that we constantly go back and land in our heart. If we only act and live based on our thoughts, it can become mechanical and the choices we make can become logical, rather than true.

Many individuals with Libra in the ascendant state that they easily lose themselves. They do not know who they are behind what is happening on the surface. This is usually a clear sign that we focus too much on thought processes and that we have too little contact with the heart. The heart is our direct contact with the soul and our higher self, which means that we find home within ourselves at that contact. Our thoughts, however, have a different function. Our thoughts are a powerful tool that we have at our disposal here on Earth. They help us understand, structure, plan and find strategies. But we cannot live only through them, because they are almost always created from our imprints and the patterns we brought with us from home.

Our heart chakra symbolizes the relationship with ourselves but also the relationship with others and with life. This means that relationships are a strong theme when we have Libra in the ascendant. We are here to experience love, drama and passion in relationships to ultimately find a higher form of love within us. To get to the higher form of love and ultimately pure self-love, we may have to experience the opposite first in the form of tough and draining relationships.

The career houses

When it comes to job, career and life path in the Birth Chart, there are many parts to look at, such as our composition of the chart with all the planets and where our power point MC (Midheaven) is located. But there are some important parts we can look at here. By looking at the qualities and the energy that our ascendant represents, we can see what we need jobwise, to develop. When we know what our ascendant sign is, we can also see what our career houses are, that is, what signs and elements they are in. The career houses are 2, 6 & 10.

With the ascendant in Libra, the three career houses are in the signs of Scorpio, Pisces & Cancer, all of which are water signs. Water represents intuition, flow, emotions and creativity. Having the career houses in water signs means that we have great resources within us when it comes to emotions and knowing what people need, something we can use to build our career and manifest what we dream of. This is further enhanced if we have the Sun, Moon or other planets in these three houses.

So, what does it mean that we have Libra in the ascendant and the career houses in the water signs?

Libra here gives us strong skills and gifts when it comes to social interaction and meeting people where they are. When we have water in the career houses, we should engage in something where we also get our emotions in, where we get in touch with our creativity and our flow. This mix of energies creates very good conditions for work in healing, therapy and developing conversations with people.

We also have a good prerequisite for becoming a good manager or leader. We know what our employees need, and we have the ability to see things from different nuances and perspectives. Here, however, we need to build ourselves up enough that we can remain in our own power - we need to know who we are and remain in that energy when things get shaky around us.

The tenth house is one of the career houses and perhaps the most important to look at, in terms of career but also in terms of our life mission – what we are here to manifest in this life.
With this combination, the tenth house is in Cancer, the sign of emotions, intuition, home and family. Both Libra and Cancer are cardinal signs, and this means that we have good leadership skills

when it comes to work. However, Cancer is the sign of home and security, which means that we need to feel a certain form of security and stability in what we do. When we have the tenth house in Cancer, we fit well in professions where we can devote ourselves to some form of care or care. It can be healthcare, but it can also be work at a preschool or something else where we come into contact with this part of ourselves. If we apply for professions where we experience meetings with people and where we can contribute with service, help or support in some way, we have a great chance of finding the right one.

Spirituality, Transformation & Deep Healing

With Libra as the ascendant sign, we are more or less forced into a journey that is about relationships, especially during our spiritual ascent. We will encounter situations with people where we will have the opportunity to create a greater awareness of ourselves and how we relate.

At its lowest energy, Libra is a copy of its surroundings and a result of the patterns and behaviors that existed during childhood. In this case, we have a hard time knowing who we are, and we can easily become dependent on other people, because we build our whole personality through them.

At its highest energy, Libra has enormous power and a deep ability to understand itself and other people. There is a balance in meeting those we meet, and we move in and out of relationships without losing ourselves. We help and support without going beyond our own boundaries.

To achieve the higher energy of Libra we need to release patterns of adaptation and developing our authentic side. If we constantly follow the needs of others, we tend to get stuck in our development. We do everything we can to keep ourselves in old templates and we close our eyes to the part of us that yearns for expansion. When we let go of these templates and direct our focus to our heart and our innermost needs, our innermost longing - then we undergo a great transformation process. We get in touch with our intuition, which becomes our guide in everyday life.

To get balance with Libra, it can be valuable to take in the energy of the opposite sign, Aries. While Libra is the sign of relationships and balance, Aries is the sign of independence and our own will. Aries is spontaneous and does things based on their needs, even if it means that people around them may disagree. This is Aries' strong point, but of course it can also lead to exaggeration. If we feel that we get too caught up in analysis or that we weigh our surroundings too much, we can practice using the Aries qualities and bring in more spontaneity, fire and courage when we do things.

There are three houses in the Birth Chart that relate to our inner depth, our transformation and our spirituality. It is houses 4, 8 & 12. House four shows what we carry from family and lineage. House eight shows how we undergo transformation during life but also what healing abilities we have. House twelve shows what we carry in our subconscious and what energy we need to lift up and make conscious. If we have planets in one of these houses, the energy and focus there becomes even stronger.

With the ascendant in Libra, we have our spiritual houses in Capricorn, Taurus & Virgo. This means that the spiritual houses are in earth signs. When these houses are in earth, we get an earthy energy here, something that allows us to work with our inner self and at the same time be grounded. Many individuals with earth in these houses are drawn to work with inner development and spirituality, where there is a closeness to nature or to the physical body. There is an inner calm and stability, which we can use when we heal our inner self but also when we help other people.

When the spiritual and deep houses are in the earth, we can sometimes experience it challenging to get in touch with our feelings and our inner depth. This is because we have learned to have a practical but also mental starting point and foundation throughout life. We have seen individuals with this combination who had difficulty getting in touch with their emotional life, due to external protection and defense mechanisms. It can be shown by us focusing on practical or external things when we feel bad rather than taking the time to feel what is going on. With Libra in the ascendant, we are also used to solving things in our thoughts. If we dare to go beyond the superficial and the practical, we will discover new parts within us and when we do, we have our earth here to help us find grounding and stability. When we have water in these houses it can sometimes be overwhelming with emotion and depth, but with earth we usually find it easier to ground ourselves.

In this combination, the twelfth house is in Virgo. It allows us to use Virgo's qualities of service, accuracy and structure to reach out with our spiritual messages. The energy between the twelfth house and Virgo makes us well suited to work with healing or spirituality, in a way where we come into contact with the physical body - for example massage, body therapy or healing with physical elements.

Combination with the Sun

Now follows a review of the ascendant in Libra in combination with all Sun signs. Look at your ascendant sign in the Birth Chart and then where your Sun is. Combining these two energies gives you a strong indication of what you are here to delve into and manifest in this life. It also gives you guidance for spiritual themes you can develop and understand within yourself and in your life.

The ascendant shows how you have been shaped, how you meet your surroundings as well as important life themes and lessons for you in the course of life.

The Sun shows where you are meant to shine in this life and where you have a great opportunity to make an impression with your energy.

Ascendant in Libra & Sun in Aries
With the ascendant in Libra and the Sun in Aries, this means that the Sun is in the seventh house - the house of relationships, balance, relating and other people. This placement also means that the ascendant and the Sun are opposite each other in the chart.

With the Sun in the seventh house, you are here to learn all about relationships as well as to understand relationship patterns. You are also here too free yourself from dysfunctional patterns related to relationships, such as those you have brought with you from childhood and previous lives. With the Sun here, many of your greatest lessons and insights come through relationships and partnerships. Through the meeting with another person, you get to know yourself. The Sun is in Aries, the sign of independence, courage and strength. This means that these are qualities you should strive to develop in order to make your Sun shine brightly here. This placement gives you social skills, something you can use to make connections or in some kind of relief work.

Since Libra in the ascendant also represents relationships, it is clear that relationships are central themes for you in this life. You have great opportunities to dissolve old karma and create relationships based on a higher energy, the energy that matches your vibration and soul.

Ascendant in Libra & Sun in Taurus

With the ascendant in Libra and the Sun in Taurus, this means that the Sun is in the eighth house - the house of transformation, shared resources, intimacy and deep aspects of ourselves.

With the Sun in the eighth house, you are here to explore deeper parts of yourself and to learn how to transform energy. To get there, you need to face some challenges that drag you down into lower emotions and maybe even pain. It may sound tough, but by learning to transform pain into knowledge and darkness into light, you become a powerful healer. You are given great gifts to help others. The Sun is in Taurus, the sign of stability and determination. This means that you need to develop these qualities to get ahead and to make your Sun shine. If you find a balance between security and development, you can use the stability found in Taurus to reach deeper layers within yourself.

Combined with Libra in the ascendant, you have great abilities when it comes to seeing what other people need. You find it easy to meet people where they are, and this makes you an empathetic person and a dedicated healer.

211

Ascendant in Libra & Sun in Gemini

With the ascendant in Libra and the Sun in Gemini, this means that the Sun is in the ninth house - the house of exploration, travel, adventure, wisdom and belief.

With the Sun in the ninth house, you're here to find a higher meaning to your existence, whether that's through education, spirituality, or other experiences. You are here to find your inner truth and who you are here on Earth. With this placement, you may feel drawn to experiences that lead you towards expansion and new insights in life. Through your own experiences, you build up a wisdom in yourself, something that ultimately makes you a good teacher or mentor. The Sun is in Gemini, the sign of communication, curiosity and learning. It means that you have strong social skills within you, something that you can use to write books or teach people. With the Sun here, you will most likely be drawn to education and courses to learn more about yourself and you yearn for new paths for development.

Combined with Libra in the ascendant, you have a great gift for seeing people. You know how to meet people where they are. Since both the Sun and the ascendant are in air signs, you have a strong analytical ability, so you should think about including your emotions in what you do.

Ascendant in Libra & Sun in Cancer

With the ascendant in Libra and the Sun in Cancer, this means that the Sun is in the tenth house - the house of work, career, life task, manifestation and greater impact.

With the Sun in the tenth house, you are here to contribute something in career, work or through your life task here on Earth. You may be drawn to building something or investing in your career. With this placement, you may also have a longing to find your calling or your unique mission in this life. The sun is in Cancer, the sign of security and family but also intuition and emotions. This means that you have a great sensitivity to what other people need. You can be highly sensitive and experience a need to have your own time to process things happening around you. With the Sun in Cancer, you can have a strong attachment to your family, something that can be positive or negative depending on how you grew up. Here it is important that you work on freeing yourself from dysfunctional imbalances that affect your family and thus release family patterns that limit you. You need to build your own authority within yourself so that you lead yourself forward, rather than being led by others.

With Libra in the ascendant combined with Cancer, you are incredibly sensitive to what people need. Use your empathy and social skills to develop and to create relationships and jobs that resonate with you. You can help many people you meet in the course of life.

Ascendant in Libra & Sun in Leo
With the ascendant in Libra and the Sun in Leo, this means that the Sun is in the eleventh house - the house of groups, networks, visions of the future, community engagement and innovation.

With the Sun in the eleventh house, you are here to contribute something to society and the collective, through your unique and creative energy. You are not meant to fit into predetermined templates, but you are meant to be unique. This means that it is positive for you to dare to go outside the box, regardless of whether it concerns work, relationships or everyday life. The Sun is in Leo, the sign of creativity and creation but also pride. This means that these are qualities you should develop to make your Sun shine brightly here. You have social skills, and you find it easy to create joy in people around you.

With Libra in the ascendant, you are good at dealing with meeting people. In combination with the Sun in Leo and the eleventh house, you can use your creative ability and your ability to innovate to fill up with life energy and get where you want.

Ascendant in Libra & Sun in Virgo
With the ascendant in Libra and the Sun in Virgo, this means that the Sun is in the twelfth house - the house of subconscious processes, spirituality, dreams and escape.

With the Sun in the twelfth house, you are here to explore deep parts of yourself and to develop your spirituality. You have a sensitivity, and you can sense people around you with this placement. You may find that you have a need to recover more than people around you and you do that best through your own time. The Sun is in Virgo, the sign of service, health and accuracy. It means that you are here to contribute some kind of service or healing. Virgo is an earth sign, which means that there is a practical side to you where you like to have a certain structure. You are good at seeing details and you may struggle with high demands on yourself.

With Libra in the ascendant and the Sun in Virgo, service is a strong theme, especially with the Sun in the twelfth house. You have a sensitivity but also the grounding and structure you need to move forward in Virgo.

Ascendant in Libra & Sun in Libra
With both the ascendant and the Sun in Libra, they are in the same sign and house, the first house. The first house represents new beginnings, initiation, leadership and our personality.

When both the ascendant and the Sun are in the same house and sign, the energy mixes and they create a strong unity. Our inner core goes hand in hand with our personality and how we were shaped during our upbringing. Libra's energy becomes extra prominent here and we have strong qualities when it comes to relating, understanding people and seeing things from different perspectives. We can also carry great artistic and creative abilities.

With the Sun in the first house, you are here to develop strong leadership and affirm your personality. You are also here to lead yourself forward and to express your energy strongly in the world. With both the Sun and the ascendant in Libra, you have great lessons in relationships waiting in this life. Many of your great insights come through meeting others and finding balance in relationships. An important task for you involves working a lot on your relationship with yourself, so that you have your own security and position while at the same time being able to be there and help others. You are analytical and you see things from different angles, often before other people notice. To replenish energy in life, you should affirm your creative energy and find ways to express it.

Ascendant in Libra & Sun in Scorpio

With the ascendant in Libra and the Sun in Scorpio, this means that the Sun is in the second house - the house of material resources, self-worth, money, abundance and scarcity.

With the Sun in the second house, you are here to learn all about your own resources, both material and emotional. You are here to learn more about your soul's relationship to resources. With this placement, you are very likely to experience themes of scarcity and abundance, all for your soul to have the experiences and insights it seeks. An important task with the Sun here is about seeing your inner value, your true value that reflects your soul. When you see and feel your true worth, you will attract abundance in different areas of life. The Sun is in Scorpio, the sign of deep emotion and transformation. Based on that, this is a life with great opportunities for inner healing and transformation. You may have to face some lower aspects of yourself and heal deeply, in order to develop your Sun here and make it shine.

With Libra in the ascendant, you are analytical, and you are sensitive to what the people around you need. Be sure to set boundaries when necessary. With Libra and Scorpio, you have access to deep emotions and a strong intellect. With balance here, you can use these gifts to help people in their development.

Ascendant in Libra & Sun in Sagittarius

With the ascendant in Libra and the Sun in Sagittarius, this means that the Sun is in the third house - the house of communication, perspective, learning and mental processes.

With the Sun in the third house, you are here to learn all about communication and to find your divine expression.

Through development and through some challenging experiences, you will find your inner communication, the one that comes from your soul. By channeling it to your surroundings, you become a strong communicator but also a skilled healer. The Sun is in Sagittarius, the sign of travel, expansion and learning. This means that your Sun develops and is energized by these themes. With the Sun in this placement, you have great potential to become a good writer or teacher, in the subject that interests you.

In combination with Libra in the ascendant, you have strong social skills, and you are good at making others feel seen. You are optimistic and you can get along with different types of people. Be sure to find the beliefs that resonate with you on an energetic level.

Ascendant in Libra & Sun in Capricorn
With the ascendant in Libra and the Sun in Capricorn, this means that the Sun is in the fourth house - the house of home, family, security, our roots and our origins.

With the Sun in the fourth house, you are here to build a solid and secure base within yourself and to find home within yourself. Family and roots are a big theme for you and there may be family patterns that you need to review in order to heal yourself and reach your full potential. With this placement, there is very likely some form of karma from past lives with family members, something that creates strong bonds. Look at the patterns you brought with you that limit you and create new ones that resonate with you and your vibration. The Sun is in Capricorn, the sign of discipline, purposefulness and structure. This means that these qualities are something you should strive to develop over the course of your life. Through methodical work and through planning, you can free yourself from the old but also build your own stable foundation, perhaps through your own family.

Together with Libra in the ascendant, you have strong leadership skills and through this combination you know the art of meeting people and at the same time have the structure needed to face life's challenges.

Ascendant in Libra & Sun in Aquarius
With the ascendant in Libra and the Sun in Aquarius, this means that the Sun is in the fifth house - the house of creativity, sports, creation, expression, children and playfulness.

With the Sun in the fifth house, you are here to find your divine creative expression and share it with the world. You are here to affirm your creative energy and when you find a way to express it, you can help yourself and people. With this placement, you are here to explore what makes you happy and what sparks your passion. Through that life energy, creation can take place. The Sun is in Aquarius, the sign of innovation and creativity. It means you are here to go your own way and do things outside the box. You are not here to follow ready-made templates but to contribute with your unique energy. When you create with the help of Aquarius energy, you help your Sun develop in the best way.

Together with Libra in the ascendant, you have great opportunities to create harmony and joy for people. You are responsive but also innovative. If you find yourself stuck in the mediating role of Libra, remember to boost up the Sun in Aquarius, where you do things your way.

Ascendant in Libra & Sun in Pisces

With the ascendant in Libra and the Sun in Pisces, this means that the Sun is in the sixth house - the house of health, routines, service, mastery and work.

With the Sun in the sixth house, you are here to learn all about health and to understand the flow of energy in your body. You are here to become master of your own body and find everyday routines that resonate with you. In order to get here, you will most likely need to experience some challenges connected with your health and your everyday life. It could be that you are struggling with some kind of health problem or that you have a hard time replenishing your energy. These challenges can be tough, but they lead you towards the search for new solutions and the lessons your soul seeks. The Sun is in Pisces, the sign of emotions and spirituality but also of escape. This means that you have a great sensitivity to other people's energies. There may also be a sensitivity to certain types of food or substances. With Pisces here, there may be a tendency to run away or difficulty with routines. Look at how you can get into routines where you will stay in your feelings but also where there is some kind of structure. Together with Libra in the ascendant, you have great gifts when it comes to seeing the needs of other people. You are responsive and open in meeting those around you. Here, it can be particularly important that you work with integrity and protect yourself, so that you remain in your own power.

CHAPTER 11
SCORPIO IN THE ASCENDANT

Scorpio

Qualities: Water, Fixed, Feminine

Ruled by the planet: Pluto

Connected to house: 8

Soul Archetypes: Detective, Psychologist, Athlete

Connection to chakra: The Sacral chakra

Scorpio Characteristics & Energy

Scorpio is the eighth sign of the Zodiac and symbolizes themes such as deep resources, shared resources, transformation and spiritual depth. Other traits and qualities associated with Scorpio are exploration, getting below the surface, and black or white thinking. The sign carries a watery firm feminine energy, which means there is a very penetrating and emotional aspect here.

Soul archetypes associated with Scorpio are the Detective, the Psychologist and the Athlete.

Scorpio as ascendant

Scorpio comes after the sign Libra in the Zodiac. While Libra tends to seek the beautiful, balanced and harmonious in life, Scorpio seeks the opposite - the raw, the deep and the painful. There is an intense and deep energy in Scorpio that people around can sense immediately in the meeting. Just like the other water signs in the ascendant, there is a great sensitivity with Scorpio as an ascendant sign. The difference is that Scorpio is generally very good at protecting itself and sorting out what enters the energy field. The sign is fixed in its energy, which means that there is a stubbornness and a steadfastness, something that makes it less influenced by the environment.

With the Ascendant in Scorpio, we often have a complex personality, and we are drawn to what is more complex in terms of knowledge and relationships. We search for that which gives a sense of meaning and this means that we tend to get stuck in two different modes - a mode where we do something fully and a mode where we become passive. Based on that, people around us can usually perceive us as withdrawn and somewhat cautious or, on the contrary, intense and extremely determined. Scorpio is ruled by the planet Pluto, which is the most intense and profound of all the planets in the Zodiac. This means that there is a lot of depth, contrasts, intensity and sensitivity with this ascendant.

A man in our environment has the ascendant in Scorpio and he has a somewhat complex and deep character. He likes to stay in the background and can sometimes be perceived as passive. He has explained in his own words how he finds it difficult to get involved in everyday things that feel meaningless. If, on the other hand, he is drawn to something, he can go into it one hundred percent. In his case, the planet Pluto is also in the first house near the ascendant, giving a double energy of the same theme.

With Scorpio in the ascendant, we are loyal in what we do, once we decide to commit to something. This means that we can go far in a certain area, as there is a strong endurance and strength within us. This also means that we like to stay in close relationships for a long time once we have decided to invest in a person.

Because of our proximity to the depths of life, we have an ability to see the depths of other people. We can see and feel the pain of those around us, making us exceptionally skilled therapists and healers, if we choose to transform imbalanced parts within ourselves first.

Soul contract/Soul plan
Scorpio is the deepest sign of the Zodiac and that means we have great and deep lessons to master with this ascendant sign. One of them is about learning how to transform heavy and dark energy. Scorpio has a natural connection to the eighth house of the Zodiac, which is the house of the hidden, transformation, crises, healing and

even death. By going through emotional crises and by experiencing lower energies within ourselves, we can help other people do the same. We become a transformer for different forms of energy here on Earth.

When we have the ascendant in Scorpio, we are here to learn to understand patterns of power and control - and to find balance in these areas. In English, we have the term power struggle, which describes what this is about. We will very likely come across situations where we feel powerless or where we feel that others are trying to exercise control over us, all so that we can learn to find our way back to this within ourselves. We need to learn to be in our own power in a balanced way, in order to create good for ourselves and other people.

Childhood & patterns from growing up
When we step into a body here on Earth, we choose a family and an environment that matches our current energy and vibration as well as the lessons we want to learn and deal with during this life. We thus choose a family that helps shape our ascendant.

When we have our ascendant in Scorpio, we often had a childhood with some kind of intense energy. It could be, for example, that we experienced some kind of emotional trauma in the meeting with a parent or that our parents themselves had great challenges. Since our ascendant gives information about our birth and our first encounter with the outside world, there may have been some kind of trauma or intense emotions connected with our birth, with us or with our mother.

During our work with Birth Charts, we have seen a pattern where individuals with Scorpio in the ascendant often have an intense or strong relationship with the mother (can also be the father). What the relationship looks like can vary greatly, but generally there are elements of dysfunctionality here, where the mother herself carries trauma, is overprotective or controlling of the child. It can also be shown by the mother herself having strong or intense feelings within her, something that the child picks up and senses. It is also common that the mother has a strong attachment to the child and that this attachment binds the child to the mother as the child grows up.

It could also be that we grew up in a family situation where there was a complex or intense relationship between our parents, which meant that we were forced to face strong emotions and aspects of ourselves early as children.

During our work we came into contact with a child, a little girl with the ascendant in Scorpio. Normally, our ascendant usually becomes more clear as we approach adulthood, but sometimes we can see tendencies and behaviors clearly even in children. The girl was withdrawn and very cautious in her appearance. She was almost attached to her mother and refused to be close to other people. The mother of this child herself had experienced trauma and complex things in her childhood, which meant that she carried strong unhealed feelings inside her. She was determined to be there for her own child, which she was – all the time, every minute. There is no judgment in this, however we can see a pattern of intensity and strong emotions that are created early in the child in this situation. The mother in this case had strong fears connected with her own feelings and there was a lot of inner pain involved in the picture.

Another example concerns a man with the ascendant in Scorpio who also had a close relationship with his mother. The mother had a strong concern for her son and because the son developed a serious chronic illness as a child, there were strong fears in the mother. It led to overprotective tendencies. She did everything to help and support her son even in adulthood, even at the expense of her own well-being.

Based on the fact that many individuals with the ascendant in Scorpio grow up with a certain complexity in their closest relationships, this becomes a theme that continues throughout life. So, we may be drawn to complex or intense relationships, or we may avoid close relationships because of inner fears. We can struggle with fear of closeness and abandonment when we get very close to someone. With Scorpio in the ascendant, we often come into contact early on with great and deep emotions but also pain. These experiences lead us into life's big questions, and they make us in a way prepared for a life of great contrasts and great shades of emotions.

Common Challenges

Scorpio often has a strong protective side which causes it to put up a defense against the outside world, which in turn can lead to feelings of isolation and loneliness. People with this ascendant can even be perceived as hard or cold precisely because of the defenses that are there. Behind this shell is a great sensitivity.

When Scorpio is our ascendant sign, we can have a tendency to drag ourselves down into negative and destructive spirals – whether in thoughts, feelings, relationships or other areas of life. Scorpio is fixed in its energy and that means we can have a hard time breaking patterns once we get into one. Based on that, we can also end up in various forms of self-sabotage, where we unconsciously drag ourselves down into things that limit us. We can also get stuck in feelings of resignation or passivity if we feel that our existence feels too stagnant or meaningless. For that reason, it is extremely important that we find an everyday life that feels rewarding and developing, so that we put ourselves in favorable patterns.

Strengths & Gifts

Individuals with Scorpio Ascendant carry great inner resources, resources that can make them masters in their chosen field. Many people who have reached extreme levels in spirituality, sports and other fields have strong elements of Scorpio and Pluto in their birth chart. So, in the same way that Scorpio can get stuck in its passive energy, it can get to the top of the mountain when the underlying motivation is there. Passion and motivation are important watchwords here. So, with the ascendant here, we need to put a lot of emphasis on exploring where our passion lies. Without it, we find it difficult to push ourselves through a project or a task.

Scorpio is extremely intuitive and there is strong instinctive feeling in the sign. So, with the ascendant here, we have the ability to see and feel things that other people miss. We look behind the facade and we see the true motive of a person standing before us.

Individuals with this ascendant sign have the ability to touch people on a deep level and they can, through their presence and energy, initiate healing processes in the person they meet. There is a strong magnetic force, and the energy here carries a great transformative power.

Health & energy flow

There are many important parts to look at in the Birth Chart when it comes to health and two of them are the ascendant sign and the sixth house. The ascendant has a strong connection to our physical body, how we move physically but also how we protect ourselves and absorb energy. The sixth house is the house for health, daily routines and shows what we need in everyday life to get flow in a general way.

Something that is important for all water signs in the ascendant is to work with the flow in the body, that is, the flow in our emotions but also purely physically. We need to keep our water clean in the same way that we need to cleanse our body of toxins of various kinds. Since Scorpio is a fixed sign, the meaning of flow becomes extremely important here. We can get stuck in our heavy emotions and if we get stuck in our emotions without being able to transform them, it leads to stagnation within us. Stagnation can eventually lead to depression and physical symptoms for the body. In order to flow, we need to be willing to attend to our emotions and learn to transform heavy states of emotion into acceptance and higher energies. We also need to make sure that our physical body has the opportunity to clean out rubbish from time to time, for example through physical activity, movement or through a conscious choice of food and nutrition.

Scorpio as a sign represents our reproductive organs and the purification of toxins that takes place through our intestines. This means that it can be valuable to give our stomach and intestines extra care, so that we can maintain balance in that area. In general, Scorpio has a strong resistance to illness and stress, just like the other fixed signs of the Zodiac. We have seen that there is a connection between

Scorpio and health problems that comes through heredity and through our DNA.

With Scorpio as the ascendant sign, this means that our sixth house is in the sign of Aries. The sixth house is connected to our general health and shows what we need in our everyday life to feel good but also to build healthy routines and have flow in our energy. Aries as a sign stands for themes such as spontaneity, strength, discovery and physical activity. There is a fiery and initiating energy in this sign, something very different from the energy of Scorpio.

With Scorpio in the ascendant and Aries in the sixth house, we get a great need for movement in everyday life. We need movement, both physically and emotionally. It is connected to what we described earlier that Scorpio easily accumulates lower energies within itself. When Aries is in the sixth house, it shows that we need to bring in the very fire and spontaneity that comes with that sign. Both Aries and Scorpio have a strong connection to the instinctive and what arouses our passion. This means that we should strive for an everyday life and routines where we get the opportunity to do something we are passionate about and where there is an opportunity for discovery and exploration.

Related Chakra

Scorpio has a strong connection to the Sacral Chakra, which is the second chakra from the bottom of our chakra system. The Sacral Chakra represents our emotions, relationship patterns and how we relate to other people and physical things. It is also related to intimacy, creativity and emotional attachment.

When we have balance in our sacral chakra, we usually have healthy relationships without negative emotional ties. We have learned to separate ourselves from others and we are not dependent on other people. We find it easy to be close to someone we like and find it easy to be in our creative energy.

With blockages or stagnation in the Sacral Chakra, we can experience imbalances in terms of relationships and the patterns we have there, especially in our close and intimate relationships. We may struggle with patterns of codependency or adaptation. Different forms of addiction also have their roots in this chakra, for example abuse of food, alcohol, sugar or exercise.

Since Scorpio quite often has somewhat complex relationship patterns, there is a risk of challenges in our closest relationships. We may struggle to find balance in this area, making it black or white, on or off. When it comes to intimate relationships with partners, we can struggle with patterns between distancing and the opposite, becoming too emotionally involved with a partner. If we feel that we end up in this dynamic, it is valuable to look at how our relationship patterns looked during our childhood and look at where we need to heal that part within ourselves. We may also need to look at how it looks with our trust in other people, as that part can sometimes be damaged while growing up.

We may also need to review our relationship with food, sugar and other substances, which could become a substitute for our inner pain and emotional blockages.

We can create balance in our Sacral Chakra by working with balance in our relationships, working with trust and healing lower emotional aspects of ourselves. The reason why emotions and various forms of addiction are related to the same chakra is because of their strong connection. When we carry a lot of weight and unprocessed emotions, it's easy to turn to something external to get emotional relief. By becoming aware of what we carry, we can consciously work to heal our emotions and raise our general vibration.

The career houses

When it comes to job, career and life path in the Birth Chart, there are many parts to look at, such as our composition of the chart with all the planets and where our power point MC (Midheaven) is located. But there are some important parts we can look at here. By looking at the qualities and the energy that our ascendant represents, we can see what we need jobwise, to develop. When we know what our ascendant sign is, we can also see what our career houses are, that is, what signs and elements they are in. The career houses are 2, 6 & 10.

With the ascendant in Scorpio, the three career houses are in the signs of Sagittarius, Aries & Leo, all of which are fire signs. Fire represents power, creativity, energy, passion and inspiration. Having the career houses in fire signs means that we have great resources within us when it comes to motivating and inspiring people as well as starting ongoing projects, something we can use to build our career and manifest what we dream of. This is further enhanced if we have the Sun, Moon or other planets in these three houses.

So, what does it mean to have Scorpio in the ascendant and career houses in fire signs?

With fire and water combined, we always get a strong creative and transforming energy. There is power and an intense energy with these elements together. This means that we can be drawn to and fit well in professions where our creative abilities come to the surface. It can be areas within artistry, music, motivator, coaching, inspirer, leadership, energy healing and sports. We have a great opportunity to go far in the field we choose, if we feel passion for it and if it gives us a sense of meaning.

The tenth house is one of the career houses and perhaps the most important to look at, in terms of career but also in terms of our life mission – what we are here to manifest in this life.

In this combination the tenth house lies in Leo, the sign of creativity, self-expression, entertainment and leadership. Both Scorpio and Leo are fixed signs and they both have strong resources within them. This means that there are great opportunities for us to go far and become masters of what we do in terms of work. There is a noticeable difference between Leo and Scorpio! Scorpio can be somewhat more subdued and may have a hard time with external attention. Leo, on the other hand, generally has a greater attraction to getting attention and making his voice heard. Here we can experience an inner conflict where part of us wants to do something outwardly while another part wants to hide under the covers. Here it is positive to let both of these aspects emerge and integrate them as part of us. It means that we have our private side, but we go outside our comfort zone and create things that are good for ourselves and for other people.

Spirituality, Transformation & Deep Healing

As we mentioned earlier, we have great lessons to learn with Scorpio as the ascendant sign. We are on a lifelong journey that gives us great opportunities in the form of development and transformation.

We have the opportunity to go from victim to teacher, from inner blockages to masters of pain. We can only do that by first ending up at the bottom and then rising again, slowly but surely.

At its lowest energy, Scorpio is isolated and stuck in its pain and its experience of hopelessness. It leads to passivity and if we get stuck here for too long, we can develop disease states of various kinds, both emotionally and physically.

At its highest energy, Scorpio is perhaps the most powerful healer in the Zodiac. Through own experiences of darkness and pain, there is a deep understanding of life and the transformation processes that take place and that lead to development of various kinds.

To get to the highest energy of Scorpio we need to learn that we have the power and control over our life. This means that we have the power over our own body and our energy. We can transform the most heavy and low-frequency feeling into a high-frequency feeling. We can transform fear into love, through our power and through our conviction - as well as through solid work with ourselves.

When we have the ascendant in Scorpio, our ascension process is about understanding our energy and what it takes to be able to heal and transform. Another theme that can come up strongly during our spiritual journey is relationships. We need to heal the pain and fear that can be with us from childhood, above all that which concerns trust and closeness.

There are three houses in the Birth Chart that relate to our inner depth, our transformation and our spirituality. It is houses 4, 8 & 12. House four shows what we carry from family and lineage. House eight shows how we undergo transformation during life but also what healing abilities we have. House twelve shows what we carry in our subconscious and what energy we need to lift up and make conscious. If we have planets in one of these houses, the energy and focus there becomes even stronger.

With the ascendant in Scorpio, we have our spiritual houses in Aquarius, Gemini & Libra. This means that the spiritual houses are in air signs. When these houses are in the air, there is a depth in our thoughts, and we analyze a lot about ourselves and our inner self. There are often great abilities in mediumship, and we can receive intuitive guidance, healing and information just through our thoughts or in writing.

When the ascendant is in Scorpio and the spiritual houses in air, we get a mix of feelings and thoughts, depth and intellect. Scorpio is very intuitive and senses nuances and vibrations even from a distance. When our spiritual houses are in air signs, we generally have intuitive abilities connected with our thoughts and we can be experts at reading people. We feel through Scorpio, and we get intuitive information through our thoughts, through the air signs. This allows us to meet people both in their thoughts and feelings.

Sometimes we can get stuck in our thoughts and on the mental plane when our deeper houses are up in the air. If we feel that we fall into negative loops or get stuck in thoughts that limit us, it is valuable to work on it. The more we heal and transform thought blocks here, the purer and clearer our intuition and medial messages become.

Combination with the Sun

Now follows a review of the ascendant in Scorpio in combination with all Sun signs. Look at your ascendant sign in the Birth Chart and then where your Sun is. Combining these two energies gives you a strong indication of what you are here to delve into and manifest in this life. It also gives you guidance for spiritual themes you can develop and understand within yourself and in your life.

The ascendant shows how you have been shaped, how you meet your surroundings as well as important life themes and lessons for you in the course of life.

The Sun shows where you are meant to shine in this life and where you have a great opportunity to make an impression with your energy.

Ascendant in Scorpio & Sun in Aries
With the ascendant in Scorpio and the Sun in Aries, this means that the Sun is in the sixth house - the house of health, routines, service, mastery and work.

With the Sun in the sixth house, you are here to become the master of your health and your body. You are here to learn more about your bodily needs and what you need to maintain a high energy flow in everyday life. To get there, you may need to go through some challenges in this area, in order for your soul to receive the lessons it seeks. For example, you may experience an attraction to the area of health but also struggle with some kind of health problem or lack of energy. Through your own experiences, you become an expert on your body and its needs, which makes you a powerful healer or health advisor. You may also feel drawn to service with this placement. It is important that you find an everyday routine with routines that resonate with your soul and energy, regardless of whether it concerns health, relationships or work. The Sun is in Aries, the sign of vitality, spontaneity and courage. There is also a leadership here. These are qualities that you should strive to develop in order to feel good in everyday life and to make your Sun shine and develop.

In combination with the ascendant in Scorpio, you have a deep and intense energy. You have the ability to see what people need, both in terms of practical help and on a deep spiritual level.

Ascendant in Scorpio & Sun in Taurus

With the ascendant in Scorpio and the Sun in Taurus, this means that the Sun is in the seventh house - the house of relationships, balance, relating and other people. This placement also means that the ascendant and the Sun are opposite each other in the chart.

With the Sun in the seventh house, you are here to learn all about relationships and your relationship patterns. You are also here to learn to transform dysfunctional patterns in your relationships and choose what gives you a positive flow of energy. With this placement, many of your deepest lessons come in meeting other people and through partnerships. By exploring this area, you will learn what resonates with your soul and what does not. With this placement, it is important that you work on the relationship with yourself so that it becomes strong and stable. Through a healthy relationship with yourself, external healthy relationships are created. Balance is an important watchword here. The Sun is in Taurus, the sign of stability, determination and resources. This means that these are qualities that you should develop in order to strengthen your Sun and manifest it in the best way.

In combination with Scorpio in the ascendant, you have great resources, and you are a strong soul. There is a stubbornness and a firm conviction within you, which helps you – when the conviction is right for you. Sometimes you need to dare to break free from old patterns and try new paths outside your comfort zone.

Ascendant in Scorpio & Sun in Gemini
With the ascendant in Scorpio and the Sun in Gemini, this means that the Sun is in the eighth house - the house of transformation, transformation, shared resources, intimacy and deep aspects of ourselves.

With the Sun in the eighth house, you are here to understand all the nuances of your soul. You are here to learn how to transform energy and when you master it you can transform any state within you. To get there, you need to dare to face discomfort, pain and heavy feelings that may be inside you. Many of your great lessons in this life come through emotional crises or through events that lead you into growing. You carry strong healing abilities with this placement. The Sun is in Gemini, the sign of communication and learning. This means that you are analytical while there is depth in your thoughts.

Combined with Scorpio in the ascendant, themes of transformation and healing are strong themes for you in this life. You have a strong life energy, something you can use to help yourself and other people in their development. There are great plans for your soul in this life.

Ascendant in Scorpio & Sun in Cancer
With the ascendant in Scorpio and the Sun in Cancer, this means that the Sun is in the ninth house - the house of exploration, travel, adventure, wisdom and belief. With the Sun in the ninth house, you are here to find the higher essence of your life, a higher meaning that

guides you towards expansion. You are here to find your inner truth about yourself and about life. With this placement, you can feel drawn to different forms of learning, knowledge or experiences that make you develop. Through your own experiences and through the insights you gather, you can become a good teacher or mentor to other people. You easily see things from a perspective, and you can see both sides of what people struggle with.

The sun is in Cancer, the sign of security and family but also emotions. This means that you have a sensitivity and a strong intuition. You empathize with other people, and you have an ability to know what people around you need. With Cancer here, there may be strong beliefs or opinions that you brought with you from home, something that you need to free yourself from - to find your own beliefs about life.

With the ascendant in Scorpio, you have strong spiritual gifts, and you have an instinctive knowledge of things. Use your creativity, your sensitivity and your inner resources in the form of intuition, to develop your Sun in the ninth house.

Ascendant in Scorpio & Sun in Leo
With the ascendant in Scorpio and the Sun in Leo, this means that the Sun is in the tenth house - the house of work, career, life mission, manifestation and greater impact.

With the Sun in the tenth house, you are here to make a mark in work, career or through your life's task. You are also here to build your inner authority and free yourself from dysfunctional family patterns that limit or hold you back. With this placement, you may feel a longing for your calling in life and you may be drawn to invest in a job or career. The Sun is in Leo, the sign of leadership and creativity. Leo is a proud sign with a lot of creative resources. This means that these are qualities that you should strive to develop in order for your Sun to shine and manifest in a powerful way here.

Combined with the ascendant in Scorpio, you have strong resources within you, and you have enormous creative talents, something that you should use in the profession of your choice. By affirming your inner depth in the ascendant together with the leadership of Leo, you can create something great for yourself and for other people.

Ascendant in Scorpio & Sun in Virgo

With the ascendant in Scorpio and the Sun in Virgo, this means that the Sun is in the eleventh house - the house of groups, networks, visions of the future, community engagement and innovation.

With the Sun in the eleventh house, you are here to contribute something that helps the greater mass or society as a whole. It can be something grand on the outside but also something smaller, for example a unique style of clothing or a health book with innovative methods. With the Sun in this house, you are not here to fit into the norm, but you should strive to find your own way, to do things outside the box. The Sun is in Virgo, the sign of health and service but also of perfection. So, you may feel drawn to some kind of service where you can improve things for people. By using the perfection of Virgo in combination with the theme of innovation in the eleventh house, you can create something new, something that contributes to a better society and a better future.

Scorpio in the ascendant gives you the conditions to dig deep and access what lies beneath the surface. It is important that there is passion in what you choose to do - your feelings need to be included in the picture, regardless of whether it concerns everyday life, relationships or work.

Ascendant in Scorpio & Sun in Libra
With the ascendant in Scorpio and the Sun in Libra, this means that the Sun is in the twelfth house - the house of subconscious processes, spirituality, dreams and escape.

With the Sun in the twelfth house, you are here to affirm your inner self and develop your spirituality. You are here to learn how your inner processes affect your life, both in terms of negative and positive states. With this placement you have a great sensitivity, and you have a lot going on in your subconscious. You may find that you need a lot of your own time to process your experiences. Here it is important that you learn to master what is going on inside you, by working with inner healing. The more balance you get within yourself, the more you can help other people. You have strong intuitive abilities, and you can become a powerful healer. The Sun is in Libra, the sign of relationships and balance. This means that many of your great lessons in life come through relationships, in meeting others. You may also experience some challenges in relationships before you find balance within yourself.

In combination with Scorpio in the ascendant, you are a deep person, and you learned early on to fend for yourself. You may find it difficult to trust other people, something that makes you keep deep intimacy at a distance. Trust is an important keyword for you in this lifetime. Dare to be in the unknown and dare to trust people, even if you have previously been hurt or experience fear.

Ascendant in Scorpio & Sun in Scorpio
With both the ascendant and the Sun in Scorpio, they are in the same sign and house, the first house. The first house represents new beginnings, initiation, leadership and our personality.

When both the ascendant and the Sun are in the same, the energy mixes and they create a strong unity. Our inner core goes hand in hand with our personality and how we were shaped during our upbringing. Scorpio's energy becomes extra prominent here and we have strong qualities when it comes to getting below the surface, looking into the deep and we carry strong emotional resources.

With the Sun in the first house, you are here to understand your life energy and to develop strong leadership. You are here to affirm your personality and find expression for it here in the World. With this placement, many of your deepest insights and lessons come as you take initiative and lead yourself forward. With both the ascendant and the Sun in Scorpio, you have deep emotional resources within you. You see what people need, probably before they see it themselves. Here, it is important that you find what awakens your passion in life. Through your passion and through your strong life energy, you can help many people around you. Be aware of situations of stagnation and make sure you are moving forward.

Ascendant in Scorpio & Sun in Sagittarius

With the ascendant in Scorpio and the Sun in Sagittarius, this means that the Sun is in the second house - the house of material resources, self-worth, money, abundance and scarcity.

With the Sun in the second house, you are here to learn all about resources, both in the form of inner and outer resources. You are here to learn how to create abundance in different areas of life. To get here you may have to experience different spectrums of scarcity and abundance. An important task for you is about really seeing your true value, the value that reflects your soul. When you realize that you are worthy of the highest and best, you can create abundance in finance but also in other areas. The Sun is in Sagittarius, the sign of learning, belief systems and expansion. This means that these are elements that you need to bring into your life - to develop your Sun and fill up with life energy. By seeking new knowledge and through various forms of experiences, you will eventually find your inner truth and you will find home within yourself.

Together with Scorpio in the ascendant, you have the depth and exploratory energy you need to develop and find new approaches. Use the depth of Scorpio and the searching of Sagittarius to reach your goals and expand your soul.

Ascendant in Scorpio & Sun in Capricorn

With the ascendant in Scorpio and the Sun in Capricorn, this means that the Sun is in the third house - the house of communication, perspective, learning and mental processes.

With the Sun in the third house, you are here to learn all about communication but also to find the expression of your soul. When you express yourself through your soul, a high vibration is created in your voice, and you contribute healing in the meeting with people. With this placement, you have abilities in communication, and you can be drawn to new knowledge and perspectives. In order to find the highest energy here, it is important that you free yourself from limiting thoughts and views, about yourself but also about life. It can be valuable to review what thought patterns you brought with you from home, so that you can find your own view of things. The Sun is in Capricorn, the sign of determination and hard work. This means that these are qualities that you should develop during life to make your Sun manifest strongly. Through strategic work, you can go far with what you choose to do with this subject.

The Ascendant in Scorpio helps you dig deep and get below the surface when needed. With your deep sensitivity and your strong intuition, you will be drawn to situations and people that contribute to your highest development through life.

Ascendant in Scorpio & Sun in Aquarius

With the ascendant in Scorpio and the Sun in Aquarius, this means that the Sun is in the fourth house - the house of home, family, security, our roots and our origins.

With the Sun in the fourth house, you are here to understand your roots and build a security within yourself – to find home within yourself. You have a great need to land in yourself and in your own presence you can fill up with energy. With this placement, it is important that you heal blockages and free yourself from dysfunctional family patterns. Through that healing process, you can find approaches that suit you and that resonate with your soul.

The sun is in Aquarius, the sign of chaos, innovation but also of revolt. This means that these are elements that you need to bring into your life to strengthen your Sun. You need to think outside the box and find alternative paths most of the time. You are not here to fit into the norm but to break away from old templates. By affirming the uniqueness in you, you will finally find home in yourself.

Scorpio in the ascendant helps you get below the surface and find what you need within yourself to develop. Use your depth and intuition here to heal trauma and imbalances within you. Through that work, you can build a home, and a base based on your true needs.

Ascendant in Scorpio & Sun in Pisces

With the ascendant in Scorpio and the Sun in Pisces, this means that the Sun is in the fifth house - the house of creativity, sports, creation, expression, children and playfulness.

With the Sun in the fifth house, you are here to find your creative expression and then express it in the world. It can be an expression in the form of art, artistry, books or conversations with people. You have strong gifts in creativity and when you use these you can help people in a powerful way. The Sun is in Pisces, the sign of spirituality and creativity but also escape. This means that you have a great sensitivity, and you are extremely open to energies around you. There is a wide range of emotions and nuances within you that you need to express. When Pisces is in their lower energy, it can manifest in the form of flight and confusion. Based on that, it is important that you work actively to build up your power. You can do that through clear boundaries and through strong integrity. With the Sun in Pisces in the fifth house, you are a strong healer and by using the creative and dreamy energy within you, you can create anything.

With the ascendant in Scorpio and the Sun in Pisces, you have great emotional depth. Your enormous strength lies in your emotions and your ability to transform them. Be aware of situations or states of stagnation or flight. Learn to face all emotions and thus become master of your energy. Your spirituality and creativity can be meaningful to many people.

Sagittarius

Qualities: Fire, Mobile, Masculine

Ruled by the planet: Jupiter

Connected to house: 9

Soul Archetypes: Adventurer, Teacher

Connection to chakra: Crown Chakra

Sagittarius Characteristics & Energy

Sagittarius is the ninth sign of the Zodiac and symbolizes themes of discovery, learning and various forms of travel – both inner and outer. Other qualities associated with Sagittarius are expansion, development and curiosity about life. The sign carries a fiery mutable masculine energy, which means that there is an outward, expansive and searching energy here.

Soul archetypes associated with Sagittarius are the Adventurer and the Teacher.

Sagittarius as ascendant

The sign Sagittarius is ruled by the planet Jupiter, the planet of expansion and opportunity. We usually say that Jupiter as the planet magnifies and expands everything it comes into contact with in our Birth Chart. So, when we have Sagittarius in the ascendant with Jupiter as the ruling planet, we usually have big life themes and big hopes for life. We are drawn to different experiences, and we may have a strong desire to discover new things or places. It can also be about discovering a specific belief, for example within the spiritual.

When we have Sagittarius as ascendant, we have a fiery and mutable energy which makes us searching and flexible. We long for the next adventure, regardless of whether it is a longer journey in the world or a new online course.

Individuals with this ascendant sign are generally very optimistic and there is a built-in belief that things will work out in life, if there is not much weight in the chart otherwise. Sagittarius has a connection to everything that gives expansion and new insights and thus development in some form.

With the ascendant in Sagittarius, we are generally perceived as positive and quite exciting by those around us. People around us sense our high energy and they sense our aura of positivity. Because we like to share our knowledge and our experiences with those around us, we are perceived as interesting when meeting others.

We have a woman in our vicinity with the ascendant in Sagittarius and she has all the characteristics of this sign. It will not be as clear for everyone, because it depends on how our birth chart looks as a whole and what we carry with us from our upbringing. This woman is around 35 years old and the years between 20 and 30 her whole life revolved around various trips and experiences. She traveled practically all over the world and as soon as she came back to Sweden, she felt bored with everyday life and its routines. That meant she was soon out on a new trip again. She has it easy to talk to people and is perceived as optimistic and alive in her energy. In addition to travel, she also has an interest in learning more about the spiritual, which she has done in the form of yoga, healing and various courses. She herself has stated that her motivation and driving force lies in experiencing something new and experiencing that feeling of excitement that comes with a fresh start.

Soul contract/Soul plan

With the ascendant in Sagittarius, we can have a sense that we are here for something special, with a mission. Through our search and through life experiences, we eventually get closer to what we are looking for. An important lesson of this ascendant sign is about finding our innermost convictions about ourselves and life, our inner soul truth. When we find what resonates with our innermost vibration and essence, we also become great teachers for others. We get the opportunity to teach our knowledge and wisdom to people who need it in our surroundings. To get here, we need to give ourselves time and space to integrate what we experience in the course of life. We need to let things land within us and learn to sort out what does not resonate with us.

It is not unusual for individuals with Sagittarius in the ascendant to be drawn into various "negative" contexts, before they find what actually suits them. It is part of the journey we need to make and learn from.

Childhood & patterns from growing up

When we step into a body here on Earth, we choose a family and an environment that matches our current energy and vibration as well as the lessons we want to learn and deal with during this life. We thus choose a family that helps shape our ascendant.

With the ascendant in Sagittarius, it is common that we had a childhood where we were shaped into the positive, the one who looks at things optimistically and who makes things easier for other people. For example, it could be that we grew up in an environment where there were some kind of difficulties at home – a sick parent, an unstable parent or a sibling who took up a lot of space. We learn not to complain, and we become experts at behaving in a way that creates ease for others. How this looks will differ a lot from individual to individual, but we have seen that there are common patterns that can be included in the picture.

When we have the ascendant in Sagittarius, we have learned to facilitate and help others, but we have much more difficulty helping ourselves, especially on a deeper emotional level. It's not because we can't or don't have the ability, but because we put more focus on our surroundings than on our inner self.

During our work we came into contact with a woman whose ascendant is in Sagittarius. We studied her experiences and patterns in childhood. She grew up in an existence where her father was an alcoholic and where there were a lot of heavy things in the family. They were three siblings who grew up under the same roof. One sister had emotional problems and chose to take her own life when she got a little older. The other sister developed mental illness, and she also started drinking alcohol when she got older. The third sister, the woman with Sagittarius in the ascendant entered the role of the positive, helpful and optimistic. She decided (perhaps unconsciously) not to follow the same path as the rest of the family and she didn't either. However, she developed a host of physical problems and illnesses later in life. It is not entirely unusual for individuals with this ascendant to develop physical health problems, which we will return to later.

Another woman with the ascendant in Sagittarius grew up in a family where she more or less took care of her parents. Both parents had major problems with themselves, which meant that the woman early as a child became the strong one, the one who is able to solve things for herself and for others.

When we have Sagittarius as ascendant, it can also be the case that we had parents with strong beliefs about life or who were involved in some form of religious or spiritual belief. It has shaped us into themes around life and we are drawn to themes related to this during the course of life.

Common Challenges

Since Sagittarius is always moving towards the next experience or towards the next lesson, there can be a difficulty in stopping and integrating things internally. We can easily get stuck in an existence where we jump from thing to thing, without really giving ourselves time for reflection. When we attend an education or course, we need to take the time to let knowledge and information become a part of us, a part of our inner self and the way we look at things. But if we are constantly on the go, we miss the important process within us.

With the ascendant in Sagittarius, we can get stuck in a state where we become the constant seeker and where we never feel satisfied with our everyday life. We can become bored and restless when we are forced to face everyday life and in the long run we can experience an inner feeling of rootlessness. Here it is valuable that we stop once in a while and look at where we are going and what we think is important to us in life - what we want to spend our time and energy on, which gives us meaning.

Strengths & Gifts

Sagittarius has an exceptional ability to maintain a high energy in meeting others and there is a sense of hope, which people around are drawn to and feel. This doesn't mean we always have to be on top or be positive with this ascendant sign, but we have a natural aspect within us that brings joy to other people.

Because we are constantly in motion, whether that means movement physically or mentally, we gather many different lessons and perspectives - something that we can share with those around us. We know how to make another person feel uplifted and inspired in the meeting. Here we have a great opportunity to create inspiration and hope for others. It can be part of our everyday life or part of our life task here on Earth.

Health & energy flow

There are many important parts to look at in the Birth Chart when it comes to health and two of them are the ascendant sign and the sixth house. The ascendant has a strong connection to our physical body, how we move physically but also how we protect ourselves and absorb energy. The sixth house is the house for health, daily routines and shows what we need in everyday life to get flow in a general way.

Sagittarius is a fire sign and, in the same way as for other fire signs, there is a fairly good resistance, due to our physical strength but also our tendency to physical activity. However, Sagittarius is a mutable sign, and we have seen that mutable signs as the ascendant have a tendency to run away from heavy emotions and what is uncomfortable.

Individuals with the ascendant in Sagittarius are generally good at hiding their inner pain through a positive and optimistic attitude. They like to radiate and prove that they can do well on their own and that they don't need any help. Although it is a nice thought, we have seen how it can create problems in terms of health, especially physically. We previously mentioned the example of the woman who was taught to be positive and strong, but who during the course of her life developed a number of different medical conditions. How is that? With Sagittarius in the ascendant, we often have three patterns that mean we have an increased risk of having health problems, especially if we are highly sensitive. The first is that we are overly positive, which causes us to shut down feelings of heaviness and pain. The second is that we like to fend for ourselves and that means we don't ask for help when we are having a hard time. The third is that we find it easier to help people around us than to help ourselves. If we feel that we have these patterns within us, it can be valuable to review them and practice integrating and facing our feelings of depth and pain that may be hidden within us. By allowing all emotions and energies to be within us, we can integrate them as part of us – we build up our physical body and our general flow of energy.

With Sagittarius as the ascendant sign, it means that your sixth house is in the sign of Taurus. The sixth house is connected to our general health and shows what we need in our everyday life to feel good but also to build healthy routines and have flow in our energy. Taurus as a sign stands for themes such as practical things, construction and stability. There is a grounding, stable and practical energy in this sign, something very different from the energy of Sagittarius.

With the ascendant in Sagittarius and the sixth house in Taurus, we get a perfect mix of movement and stability. Taurus helps us to come down to Earth and to anchor our body in the ground we walk on. Since the ascendant in Sagittarius can make us somewhat ungrounded and restless, it is very valuable to bring the energy of Taurus into our everyday life. We need stability in everyday life to feel good and to create good health. We also need to find some kind of routine, where we land in the body and where we find calm. Taurus is in no hurry, but there is time to take in and process everything that happens in peace and quiet. If we can find an everyday life where we have room for excitement as well as stability, we have the conditions to find a balanced existence.

Related Chakra

Sagittarius has a strong connection with the Crown Chakra, the top chakra located just above our head. The Crown Chakra is the energy center that represents thoughts, beliefs and our spiritual connection. It is also related to our expansion of our energy as well as our spiritual growth.

With balance in this chakra, we seek contexts that resonate with our soul and its vibration. We generally hold high thoughts that lead us towards development and expansion. We know who we are while there is an openness to new insights.

When the Crown Chakra is out of balance, we can hold too tightly to our beliefs. We become rigid and have a tendency to try to convince others of our view, what is true for us. When imbalanced, we can also feel confused and overwhelmed, as if we are taking in everything and everyone around us. We find it difficult to sort and we are easily drawn into other people's opinions and belief systems.

Since Sagittarius is strongly connected with the Crown Chakra, it is valuable for us to take good care of it – that we strive for balance here. It is common for us to experience a certain form of imbalance in this chakra (and other chakras) in the first part of life, especially if we experienced dysfunctional things during childhood. Not infrequently, we have our parents and their ideas as a basis at the beginning of life, before we find our own. With Sagittarius in the ascendant, it is important that we strive towards what feels true to us, what gives us meaning and which raises our energy and vibration. When we make choices and actions that resonate with our inner self, we fill up with energy. Here we can pay a little attention to what we choose to spend our time and energy on, so that we are not drawn into things that drag us down, rather than help us. If we grew up in a family where we learned heavy and negative patterns, it is important that we break away from it and create beliefs that support us and that feel important to us.

The career houses

When it comes to job, career and life path in the Birth Chart, there are many parts to look at, such as our composition of the chart with all the planets and where our power point MC (Midheaven) is located. But there are some important parts we can look at here. By looking at the qualities and the energy that our ascendant represents, we can see what we need jobwise, to develop. When we know what our ascendant sign is, we can also see what our career houses are, that is, what signs and elements they are in. The career houses are 2, 6 & 10.

With the ascendant in Sagittarius, the three career houses are in the signs Capricorn, Taurus & Virgo, which are all earth signs. Earth represents the practical and material things around us, what we can touch. Having the career houses in earth signs means that we have great resources within us when it comes to creation and building, something we can use to build our career and manifest what we dream of. This is further enhanced if we have the Sun, Moon or other planets in these three houses.

So, what does it mean to have Sagittarius in the ascendant and career houses in earth signs?

When we have the ascendant in Sagittarius and our career houses in earth, we get a nice mix of earth and fire. Fire creates a creative and initiating energy while Earth helps to build and manifest. Here we can use the knowledge and experience we carry to bring it out into physical manifestation, for example through our workplace or through our own company. Examples of professions that can fit with this combination are teacher, self-employed, tour guide, health coach, spiritual service and service in general.

The tenth house is one of the career houses and perhaps the most important to look at, in terms of career but also in terms of our life mission – what we are here to manifest in this life.

In this combination the tenth house lies in Virgo, the sign of service, health, detail and perfection. Since both Sagittarius and Virgo are mutable signs, there should be some form of flexibility and variety in the work we choose to do. Service and inspiration are strong watchwords for these two signs together. Here we can use our ability to inspire through Sagittarius and our service ability through Virgo in the tenth house.

Spirituality, Transformation & Deep Healing

When Sagittarius is our ascendant sign, we have great tasks to accomplish and master in this lifetime. It may sound overwhelming, but we will get through it – as the planet Jupiter guides us towards opportunities and helps us along the way. An important theme that recurs here and that creates a common thread for Sagittarius is precisely higher learning and expansion. We will very likely spend a large part of our existence trying to understand ourselves but also life as a whole. Big life questions are close to our hearts and by trying to answer these questions we have the opportunity to get closer to ourselves.

Sometimes Sagittarius tends to get caught up in the big things – in the search for big experiences, big insights and big opportunities. In that case, it is valuable to bring in the energy of the opposite sign of the Zodiac, which is Gemini. While Sagittarius focuses on the big questions of life, Gemini focuses on what happens in everyday life, in the meeting with others. We need to have both perspectives to have balance in everyday life. Sometimes it is positive to go deeper into things and sometimes we need to allow ourselves to be here, in what is happening here and now around us.

At its lowest energy, Sagittarius can get stuck in rigid and fixed beliefs, where there is a need to convince others. It can be about a spiritual faith or beliefs about how we should live in different areas.

At its highest energy, Sagittarius is a great inspirer and teacher, following its own truth but keeping an open mind. There is a curiosity and an ability to bring other people's perspectives and opinions into the meeting.

There are three houses in the Birth Chart that relate to our inner depth, our transformation and our spirituality. It is houses 4, 8 & 12. House four shows what we carry from family and lineage. House eight shows how we undergo transformation during life but also what healing abilities we have. House twelve shows what we carry in our subconscious and what energy we need to lift up and make conscious. If we have planets in one of these houses, the energy and focus there becomes even stronger.

With the ascendant in Sagittarius, we have our spiritual houses in Pisces, Cancer & Scorpio. This means that the spiritual houses are in water signs. When these houses are in water, we get a great depth and a great sensitivity. Many individuals with water in these houses have great abilities in mediumship and healing. There is an ability to sense what lies beneath the surface, both for ourselves, and for other people.

With water in our spiritual houses, we bring a deeper and more emotional aspect into our lives. It shows that we have a sensitive side within us, which needs to be allowed to participate in our everyday life. Our eighth house which represents our capacity for transformation is in Cancer. We need to allow ourselves to feel pain and get in touch with our inner vulnerability in order to transform crises and obstacles that come our way. If we run over our emotions, we skip over our inner transformation and thus our true expansion.

When we have our deepest houses in water, we have great abilities in spirituality and mediumship. We have the ability to sense and know what people around us need. We can feel energies and if we want, we can use this in healing work.

Combination with the Sun

Now follows a review of the ascendant in Sagittarius in combination with all Sun signs. Look at your ascendant sign in the Birth Chart and then where your Sun is. Combining these two energies gives you a strong indication of what you are here to delve into and manifest in this life. It also gives you guidance for spiritual themes you can develop and understand within yourself and in your life.

The ascendant shows how you have been shaped, how you meet your surroundings as well as important life themes and lessons for you in the course of life.

The Sun shows where you are meant to shine in this life and where you have a great opportunity to make an impression with your energy.

Ascendant in Sagittarius & Sun in Aries
With the ascendant in Sagittarius and the Sun in Aries, this means that the Sun is in the fifth house - the house of creativity, sports, creation, expression, children and playfulness.

With the Sun in the fifth house, you are here to find your creative expression and share it with the world. You are here to affirm your playfulness and joy. You have a strong life energy, and you find it easy to spread joy around you. With this placement, you carry strong creative abilities, something that tends to get stronger over the course of life. The Sun is in Aries, the sign of spontaneity and courage but also leadership. This means that these are qualities that you should develop in order to make your Sun shine brightly here. With this placement, you also have social skills that can help you make positive connections.

With the ascendant in Sagittarius and the Sun in Aries, you have a lot of energy, and you need some kind of adventure or activity to express this energy. There needs to be passion and development in what you do. Through your optimistic and creative energy, you can create great change for people around you. Be sure to bring your emotional aspect into everyday life along with grounding - so that you land in body and feeling.

Ascendant in Sagittarius & Sun in Taurus

With the ascendant in Sagittarius and the Sun in Taurus, this means that the Sun is in the sixth house - the house of health, routines, service, mastery and work.

With the Sun in the sixth house, you are here to learn all about health and to understand the flow of your energy. You are here to find an everyday life and routines that resonate with your soul. To get there, you may experience some challenges, especially the first part of life. It can be health problems, a lack of energy or something else - which forces you to review your existence. By understanding your body and your needs, you become an expert in this area. You become a skilled healer with gifts to help others find balance in life. With this placement, you may feel drawn to health and service of some kind. The Sun is in Taurus, the sign of stability and determination. This means that these are qualities that you should develop in order to have a form of stability with routines in everyday life. The challenge for you with this placement may be to strike a balance between security and development. If it becomes too stable, it can lead to stagnation. If it becomes too flexible, it will be difficult to maintain routines.

Sagittarius in the ascendant helps you maintain an optimistic attitude towards life and through your interest in development you will gain the insights and knowledge you need - to understand your needs and thus build a foundation for helping others.

Ascendant in Sagittarius & Sun in Gemini

With the ascendant in Sagittarius and the Sun in Gemini, this means that the Sun is in the seventh house - the house of relationships, balance, relating and other people. This placement also means that the ascendant and the Sun are opposite each other in the chart.

With the Sun in the seventh house, you are here to learn all about relationships, including your relationship with yourself. You are here to understand different forms of relationship patterns and find what resonates with you and your soul. With this placement, many of your deepest lessons come through your relationships and through partnerships. The Sun is in Gemini, the sign of communication, and flexibility but also learning. This means that you have social skills, and you are good at reading what people around you expect or want from you. You are flexible and quick-thinking.

Combined with Sagittarius in the ascendant there are strong themes of learning, development, expansion and social relationships. An important task for you here involves learning to distinguish which knowledge and which beliefs resonate with your inner self. When you do that, you can contribute important lessons and knowledge to people. You also need to learn to stand in your truth in your closest relationships, so that you don't become too flexible and adapt.

Ascendant in Sagittarius & Sun in Cancer

With the ascendant in Sagittarius and the Sun in Cancer, this means that the Sun is in the eighth house - the house of transformation, shared resources, intimacy and deep aspects of ourselves.

With the Sun in the eighth house, you are here to explore your inner self and experience all its nuances and vibrations. You are here to learn the art of transforming emotions and developing your intuition. To get there, you first need to face some tough experiences and resistance. It can happen through some kind of crisis or trauma in growing up, but it can also come later. It may sound like a tough challenge, but by learning to face deep pain, you learn to master your body and your emotions—ultimately your energy. You become a skilled and powerful healer. The Sun is in Cancer, the sign of emotions and intuition. It reinforces this theme, and you are here on Earth to understand your emotional nature. Your emotions can affect you in a variety of ways, depending on how you choose to relate to them.

In combination with Sagittarius in the ascendant, you have both your inner sensitivity, and the curiosity needed to reach deeper development. Using your range of emotions in Cancer to help others and your fire in Sagittarius, to expand and acquire new experiences.

Ascendant in Sagittarius & Sun in Leo

With the ascendant in Sagittarius and the Sun in Leo, this means that the Sun is in the ninth house - the house of exploration, travel, adventure, wisdom and belief.

With the Sun in the ninth house, you are here to find your higher truth about yourself and about life. You are here because your soul is seeking expansion and development. There may be a longing for travel or experiences that make you feel alive and that give you the feeling of "aha". You get bored easily when things get mundane and you're always longing for the next adventure, whether it's a long physical journey or a new course. With this placement, it is important that you find beliefs and belief systems that resonate with your soul and inner being. Be sensitive to what raises your energy and what lowers your energy. The Sun is in Leo, the sign of passion and creativity but also leadership. This means that these are qualities that you need to feel good and to fill up with vital energy in life.

With the ascendant in Sagittarius and the Sun in Leo, you have a lot of fire within you, which means a lot of life energy. You need to find ways to help you channel this energy in a positive way. With so much fire, it is important that you find a way to ground yourself once in a while, so that you land in yourself and your body.

Ascendant in Sagittarius & Sun in Virgo
With the ascendant in Sagittarius and the Sun in Virgo, this means that the Sun is in the tenth house - the house of work, career, life mission, manifestation and greater impact.

With the Sun in the tenth house, you are here to make a mark in work, career or through your life's task. You may feel drawn to invest in your job and you may have an inner longing to find your calling in life. With this placement, you are also here to build your inner authority and free yourself from negative family patterns that can limit you. Here you need to look at what you carry with you from growing up to see what can affect you. It can be especially important to look at patterns of flight, as the fourth house of home and family is in the mutable sign of Pisces. The Sun is in Virgo, the sign of service, and accuracy but also perfection. This means that these are qualities you should develop to make your Sun shine here. You are here to contribute some form of service, to help people improve their lives in a concrete way.

With Sagittarius in the ascendant and the Sun in Virgo, you have a combination of curiosity but also seriousness, which can help you build the life you long for. Service, knowledge and precision are important watchwords for you in this life.

Ascendant in Sagittarius & Sun in Libra
With the ascendant in Sagittarius and the Sun in Libra, this means that the Sun is in the eleventh house - the house of groups, networks, visions of the future, community engagement and innovation.

With the Sun in the eleventh house, you are here to contribute something outside the box, something that can serve as an inspiration and guide for other people. It can be something big on the outside but also something smaller, for example by writing a book or daring to wear different clothes. To develop your Sun here, you need to dare to find your own unique path and go against the flow. It requires courage and a certain determination. With this placement, you are a soul with a certain originality. You may find that you don't really fit in with larger groups and even when you are among people you may feel different. The Sun is in Libra, the sign of relationships and balance. This means that you find it easy to put yourself in other people's perspectives. You are sensitive and can quickly see the needs of a person you are having a conversation with. Here it is important that you work with balance, so that you start from your own spiritual needs, rather than becoming a follower of others.

With the ascendant in Sagittarius and the Sun in Libra, you have the gift of lifting people up. You inspire and you make people feel seen. To get your Sun to develop in the eleventh house, you need to bring in your unique and sometimes rebellious energy, where you work towards innovation and new thinking.

Ascendant in Sagittarius & Sun in Scorpio

With the ascendant in Sagittarius and the Sun in Scorpio, this means that the Sun is in the twelfth house - the house of subconscious processes, spirituality, dreams and escape.

With the Sun in the twelfth house, you are here to explore your inner self and develop your spirituality. You have a great emotional depth and to fill up with life energy you need a lot of time for yourself. You carry strong inner resources, in the form of dynamic emotions and a strong energy. With this placement, it can be difficult to get your energy out at times and this is because the twelfth house represents precisely the subconscious. An important task for you in this life involves starting to "unpack" what is hidden within you. It can be blockages, pain from childhood or things that you were forced to silence in childhood. The Sun is in Scorpio, the sign of depth and contrasts. This means that much of your great learning and important insights come through periods of transformation. You may experience emotional crises or tough situations that lead you towards development and emotional healing.

With Sagittarius on the ascendant and the Sun in Scorpio, people around you may perceive you as more secure than you feel deep down. You are extremely good at making other people feel seen and understood, while it takes a lot for you to show your deepest vulnerability to someone. To strengthen your Sun, you can use your curiosity and your optimistic energy that you have through the ascendant to heal your inner self - and thus become the powerful healer that you are.

Ascendant in Sagittarius & Sun in Sagittarius

With both the ascendant and the Sun in Sagittarius, they are in the same sign and house, the first house. The first house represents new beginnings, initiation, leadership and our personality.

When both the ascendant and the Sun are in the same house and sign, the energy mixes and they create a strong unity. Our inner core goes hand in hand with our personality and how we were shaped during our upbringing. The energy of Sagittarius becomes extra prominent here and we have strong qualities when it comes to seeing things from a higher perspective and exploring different aspects of life.

With the Sun in the first house, you are here to affirm your own life energy and to develop strong leadership. With this placement comes many of your deep insights and lessons as you lead yourself forward and take initiative in things. With both the Sun and the ascendant in Sagittarius, you are truly here to experience life on many different levels. You need to give yourself permission to explore what sparks your passion and longing, to find what is important and true to you. You have a strong life energy and other people get energy from being around you. When you find something that resonates with your soul, share it with those around you. Once you land in your inner wisdom, your knowledge can be meaningful to many that you meet.

Ascendant in Sagittarius & Sun in Capricorn

With the ascendant in Sagittarius and the Sun in Capricorn, this means that the Sun is in the second house - the house of material resources, self-worth, money, abundance and scarcity.

With the Sun in the second house, you are here to learn all about resources. You are here to learn more about your soul's relationship to resources here on Earth. Resources can be everything from money, material things but also resources in the interior - such as emotions, creativity and your intuition. An important task with this placement involves understanding the difference between scarcity and abundance. To understand this on a deep level, we may need to experience some kind of lack in our life, to understand what it is like to be in that state. With the Sun in this house, you need to work on how you value yourself. When you see and know your true worth, you will create abundance in different areas of life. It can apply to money but also to work, health or relationships. The Sun is in Capricorn, the sign of discipline and determination. This means that these are qualities that you should develop in order to work strategically in this area. Through time and through work, you build yourself up. You create new resources within yourself, and you create what you want in your surroundings, because you know you are worth it.

Sagittarius in the ascendant helps you maintain an optimistic outlook on life. By looking for new experiences, you get the opportunity to work with your inner self and heal what comes your way. Sagittarius gives you fire, and Capricorn gives you the determination you need to get you where you need to go.

Ascendant in Sagittarius & Sun in Aquarius
With the ascendant in Sagittarius and the Sun in Aquarius, this means that the Sun is in the third house - the house of communication, perspective, learning and mental processes.

With the Sun in the third house, you are here to learn all about communication and to find your divine expression here on Earth. You are here to contribute with your communication or with your views, in a way that can lift and help people. To get there, you may need to work on freeing yourself from lower parts of this theme. You need to let go of mindsets and approaches that limit you or that drag you down into dysfunctional patterns. The Sun is in Aquarius, the sign of innovation and new thinking. This means that you need to find a unique nuance to what you convey to the world. You need to go outside the norm and dare to be different to make your Sun develop here. This may mean that you dare to raise topics that no one else dares or write a book with innovative information.

With the ascendant in Sagittarius and the Sun in Aquarius, you find it easy to see other people as they are. You have no need to change people, but you respect other people's differences. With Sagittarius' search for development and the Sun in Aquarius in the third house, you have great opportunities to create something big through your communication.

Ascendant in Sagittarius & Sun in Pisces
With the ascendant in Sagittarius and the Sun in Pisces, this means that the Sun is in the fourth house - the house of home, family, security, our roots and our origins.

With the Sun in the fourth house, you are here to build a sense of security within yourself and find a home within yourself. You are here to explore themes around roots and family. With this placement, it is important that you free yourself from negative and dysfunctional family patterns that limit you. It could be strong opinions or fears from your parents that don't resonate with you and your soul. The Sun is in Pisces, the sign of spirituality, emotion and of escape. This means that there may be things in your upbringing that were not quite as they appear to the outside. Perhaps one of your parents has had challenges with themselves or moved in everyday life. With the Sun in Pisces, you are extremely open to other people's energies, and you feel most of what is going on around you. For this reason, it is extremely important that you learn to protect your energy when needed – that you learn to set boundaries and say no. You may also need some time of your own to process what is happening.

With the ascendant in Sagittarius and the Sun in Pisces, you are creative, open and sensitive to other people. You know what people around you need to replenish their energy. Use your fiery and searching energy in the ascendant to strengthen your Sun in Pisces. Through a balance of security and seeking, you will find the balance you need to develop your Sun in the best way.

CHAPTER 13

CAPRICORN IN THE ASCENDANT

Capricorn

Qualities: Earth, Cardinal, Feminine

Ruled by the planet: Saturn

Connected to house: 10

Soul Archetypes: Master, Builder, Boss

Connection to chakra: Root Chakra

Capricorn Characteristics & Energy

Capricorn is the tenth sign of the Zodiac and symbolizes themes such as discipline, construction and structure. Other traits and qualities prominent in Capricorn are its ability to climb mountains when needed and to get things done, even when challenges arise. The sign carries a grounding cardinal feminine energy, which means there is a lot of leadership, calm and determination here.

Soul archetypes associated with Capricorn are the Master, the Builder and the Boss.

Capricorn Ascendant

Capricorn is ruled by Saturn, the planet that represents hard work, discipline and mastery. From that we get a pretty good idea of what this ascendant sign is all about. Capricorn is strong and tough, just like in real life. There is a striving towards material security and towards some form of mastery during the course of life. Capricorns like to build something and leave some kind of mark, usually in work and career.

With Capricorn in the ascendant, we have a strong ability to plan, set goals and make sure we reach them. We have a logical mindset that helps us deal with adversity and we don't shy away from working hard, especially if it's something worth fighting for. We are efficient and we make sure to finish things that we start, both in terms of private projects and in work. It makes us very loyal and trustworthy in different areas, even when it comes to relationships.

Capricorn carries an inner power, and this power is felt by people around us. It commands respect and makes people listen, especially when we have healed our inner imbalances and stepped into the higher energy of the sign. In the meeting we are usually perceived as stable and safe, because of our earth energy but also because of our cardinal energy which gives us leadership qualities. Because Capricorn is a feminine sign, we are rarely perceived as extremely outgoing or colorful, but rather as grounded and strategic. This can change if we have a lot of other explosive energy in the chart.

With Capricorn ascendant, we are prepared to put time and energy into what we strive for and we are very likely to get what we want, although some things may come later in life.

Soul contract/Soul plan

When we have the ascendant in Capricorn, we are here to learn to master things and not just any things, but what we truly believe. We are here on Earth with an important task, to work hard to achieve our goals. By doing that, we have the opportunity to build something big and at the same time we are building a huge capacity within ourselves.

The planet Saturn can be limiting initially, but once we work through the challenges that come our way, we become masters of what we do. We become a mentor and a leader who can inspire other people in our chosen field.

Another important lesson with this ascendant sign is about finding a balance between hard work and enjoyment. We should strive to work hard for what we believe in while allowing ourselves to enjoy life and the beauty around us - whether it's relationships, food or experiences.

Childhood & patterns from growing up

When we step into a body here on Earth, we choose a family and an environment that matches our current energy and vibration as well as the lessons we want to learn and deal with during this life. We thus choose a family that helps shape our ascendant.

With Capricorn ascendant, we usually had a childhood where we learned to perform and to meet certain demands from our parents. It could be that we grew up in an existence where our parents had high demands on us and where we felt that our performance was important or even decisive in some way. What this looks like will differ, but in our work in Astrology we have seen specific patterns that underlie this ascendant sign. It is common for us to grow up quickly and take on a lot of responsibility early on, perhaps for a parent or for siblings in the home. We have also learned that we need to work hard to cope with life and to get where we want, which means that we have high demands on ourselves.

During our work we came into contact with a woman who had the ascendant in Capricorn. She grew up as the big sister to many siblings, which meant that she quickly had to become an adult and take on responsibility for her siblings. She described it herself as having to put aside play and spontaneity to step into the role of responsible older sister. In this case, her mother was also ill, which made the situation even more crucial.

It is not entirely unusual for individuals with this ascendant to have had a similar situation at home. The positive thing is that the child learns early on to cope with things and become strong. The more challenging part is that the child more or less skips parts of play and creativity, which makes it difficult to get in touch with these parts later in life. We learn that life is serious and that we need to be responsible in everything we do.

Another person with the ascendant in Capricorn learned early on the importance of hard work, which resulted in that the man started his own business in adulthood, a business that expanded across several continents. He became great at what he did and, in many ways became a leader in his field. He stated, however, that in retrospect he wished he had had more fun in life and that he took life too seriously even as a young man.

It could also be that we grew up in a family where the focus was on the practical, for example that we lived on a farm with a lot of responsibility and practical work.

Common Challenges

When Capricorn is our ascendant sign, we can experience challenges coupled with high demands and perfection. Because we somehow learned that we need to handle things on our own, we can struggle with excessive demands on ourselves. These requirements can be about our person, how we act, how we relate to life or how we solve things in everyday life. So, we may think that we should be able to do more than we do or that what we do is not always enough. If we do not work with our inner self through awareness and reflection, these demands can also be transferred to other people. We may have an opinion that people around us should do more, work harder, etc.

Capricorn can also carry traits of perfectionism, which can lead us into burnout and drain, as we always want to do things a little better and a little more. We may also find it difficult to relax and enjoy life, due to our responsible side. If this is the case, it is valuable to see how we can bring more joy and spontaneity into our everyday lives.

Another challenge we've seen with this sign is a difficulty showing their vulnerability. Many times, we can carry a great sensitivity within us with the ascendant here, but we have learned to hide it through practical action. This means that people around us can perceive us as stronger or more resilient than what we feel deep inside.

Strengths & Gifts

Capricorns have an outstanding ability to lead themselves and people, through their leadership and through their strong convictions. When we have a Capricorn Ascendant, we have the ability to see and know what it takes to reach our final destination. It is something that inspires people we meet. There is promise in what we do and people around us can lean on us and what we do.

We also have the gift of creating something big from something small. So, we can take an abstract idea and manifest it in physical form. It can be about turning an idea into a business or creating a good relationship based on a strong positive intention.

Generally, we have seen that individuals with earth ascendant signs are good with money and with the material things around them. It lays a very good foundation for creating good financial conditions during the course of life. Capricorns are good at planning and acting accordingly. This means that we rarely enter patterns where we become too spontaneous or fiery in our actions.

Health & energy flow

There are many important parts to look at in the Birth Chart when it comes to health and two of them are the ascendant sign and the sixth house. The ascendant has a strong connection to our physical body, how we move physically but also how we protect ourselves and absorb energy. The sixth house is the house for health, daily routines and shows what we need in everyday life to get flow in a general way.

Capricorns have strength and perseverance in their way of facing obstacles in everyday life. There is a strong resistance in the physical body, just as with the other earth signs of the Zodiac. The ability to stay grounded and in touch with physical reality makes us in a way protected from stress and other people's energies.

Because of this strength, we can sometimes build up emotional blocks when we have Capricorn here. We protect ourselves fiercely and we don't like to show our vulnerability, if we even know it ourselves. It is common for individuals with this ascendant to focus so much on the practical that the inner emotional life comes to the fore. If we shut down our emotions over time, we increase the risk of serious medical conditions, such as autoimmune diseases, various pain symptoms and stress-related medical conditions. We need to feel our whole body – the physical but also what is going on deep down. As we previously described, it is common that we grew up in an environment where we took on a lot of responsibility or where we learned early on that emotions are superfluous - it is our performance that counts. Here it can be valuable to review patterns from childhood and life to see how we manage the flow of our emotions.

With Capricorn in the ascendant, we can easily work beyond our own limits and capacities, which increases the risk that we will be drained of energy over time. Our sense of purpose and our sense of duty can lead us into dysfunctional patterns where we do everything to prove to ourselves (and to others) how much we can do.

Capricorn as a sign represents the skeleton in our body and above all our knees. If we look at the skeleton purely symbolically, it is the very foundation of our body. It is our skeleton that builds the very foundation of our physical system and here it is of the utmost importance that we maintain a certain mobility, so that we can move forward in life. In the same way, we need to be aware of getting stuck in rigid patterns or stagnation with Capricorn. We need to work to create flow, and we do that through openness, curiosity, creativity and by being in our emotions.

With Capricorn as the ascendant sign, this means that our sixth house is in the sign of Gemini. The sixth house is connected to our general health and shows what we need in our everyday life to feel good but also to build healthy routines and have flow in our energy. Gemini as a sign stands for themes such as flexibility, communication and learning of various kinds. There is a moving and airy energy in this sign, something very different from the energy of Capricorn.

With the ascendant in Capricorn and Gemini in the sixth house, we return to the theme of flexibility and mutability. We need to bring these themes into our everyday lives to keep our body and general flow in good shape. Unlike Capricorn, who can be somewhat principled, Gemini carries exactly the openness and curiosity that we need access to here. There is also a playfulness in Gemini, and in Astrology, the sign Gemini is usually referred to as the eternal child.

There are always new questions and new thoughts to which we seek the answers.

Related Chakra

Just like Taurus, Capricorn has a strong connection to the Root Chakra in our energy system. The Root Chakra is our lowest chakra (at least of our seven main chakras) and is located at the bottom of the spine. The chakra is connected with our inner security, stability, our roots and our connection with the physical body. It is also related to our ability to feel grounded and to bring out energy in a physical manifestation - that is, manifesting things in our life.

When the Root Chakra is out of balance, we may experience that we are ungrounded and that we have difficulty finding inner peace. We can also find it difficult to build things in the material world and feel generally restless. We can also have an excess of energy in the Root Chakra, creating an excessive need for stability and structure.

When the chakra is balanced, we have a natural calm within us, and we move forward in a systematic and grounded way. We have our basic security within us, something that is there regardless of the stress in our surroundings.

Since the Root Chakra is prominent in Capricorn, it is valuable to take care of it a little extra. When we have Capricorn in the ascendant, there are mainly two areas we need to review. One is that we don't become too rigid, just like we mentioned before. We can use our ability to build our existence in a positive and constructive way, without getting stuck in a square box. The second concerns material security. While Cancer, on the other hand, tends to get stuck in the search for emotional security, Capricorn tends to get stuck in the search for material security. It can be shown by us putting too much focus on building up our existence purely materially - to hold tight to our money, to make sure that our plans go exactly as we want, etc. If this is the case, we need to create new patterns where we work with trust in the process and where we can handle unexpected events.

The career houses

When it comes to job, career and life path in the birth chart, there are many parts to look at, such as our composition of the chart with all the planets and where our power point MC (Midheaven) is located. But there are some important parts we can look at here. By looking at the qualities and the energy that our ascendant represents, we can see what we need jobwise, to develop. When we know what our ascendant sign is, we can also see what our career houses are, that is, what signs and elements they are in. The career houses are 2, 6 & 10.

With the ascendant in Capricorn, the three career houses are in the signs Aquarius, Gemini & Libra, all of which are air signs. Air represents communication, mental processes, knowledge and learning. Having the career houses in air signs means that we have great resources within us when it comes to communication and learning, something we can use to build our career and manifest what we dream of. This is further enhanced if we have the Sun, Moon or other planets in these three houses.

So, what does it mean to have Capricorn ascendant and career houses in air signs?

When we mix earth and air, we get a mix of stability, structure, mental processes, relationships and communication. Here we can use our grounding practical energy from Capricorn and together with the air signs build social relationships and networks. When we have this combination, we fit well in professions where we meet other people and where we have the opportunity to build up some form of leadership. This may mean that we work as a manager or leader in a workplace or that we are our own leader through our own company. Examples of professional areas that fit well here are logistics, networking, communication, management, banking, advertising, coaching, innovation, technology and service.

The tenth house is one of the career houses and perhaps the most important to look at, in terms of career but also in terms of our life mission – what we are here to manifest in this life.

In this combination the tenth house lies in Libra, the sign of relationships, balance and creativity. Both Capricorn and Libra are leadership signs, which means there is a lot of power here. Capricorn is focused on the work itself, while Libra tends to focus more on the relationship part of work and career. By using both of these qualities, we can strive to build up our career or our life's task at the same time as we build up the social part of what we do. Libra is also a sign with a strong sense of aesthetics and creative processes, something that we can feel good about bringing into what we do.

Spirituality, Transformation & Deep Healing

Just like with other signs in the Zodiac, it can take time before we learn to find balance in our lives, whether it's about work, relationships or inner development. Many times, we tend to live out the lower energy of our Ascendant early in life, before evolving and healing lower aspects of ourselves.

In the lowest energy of Capricorn, we are far too rigid in our way of thinking and conveying our communication. We stick too tightly to our principles, which means that we are perceived as hard or inflexible. We can also sabotage ourselves by depleting our energy through hard work.

In the highest energy of Capricorn, we are a powerful leader, a role model that shows that anything is possible to achieve in life. By getting through the most difficult challenges and mastering them, we become masters of what we do. We make it to the top of the mountain with our willpower and with our determination.

To get to the highest energy of Capricorn, we need to open up to our inner vulnerability and allow our emotions to be part of our guidance. This is where our intuition comes into play and without it our projects become static and mechanical. Here it can be positive to take in the energy from Cancer, which is opposite in the Zodiac. Cancer precisely represents our emotions, our intuition and our ability to sense what is going on in our surroundings. There is a nurturing and motherly energy here. These qualities can help us find a middle ground where we maintain our determination and purposefulness but bring our intuition and emotions into the picture.

There are three houses in the Birth Chart that relate to our inner depth, our transformation and our spirituality. It is houses 4, 8 & 12. House four shows what we carry with us from family and lineage. House eight shows how we undergo transformation during life but also what healing abilities we have. House twelve shows what we carry in our subconscious and what energy we need to lift up and make conscious. If we have planets in one of these houses, the energy and focus there becomes even stronger.

With the ascendant in Capricorn, we have our spiritual houses in Aries, Leo & Sagittarius. This means that the spiritual houses are in fire signs. When these houses are on fire, we get a strong penetrating and fiery energy. Many individuals with fire in these houses have great abilities in energy work and an ability to transform strong energy.

When we have the ascendant in Capricorn and our spiritual houses in fire signs, we carry a strong transformative energy within us. There can be explosive feelings and a strong passion within us that needs to be expressed. Fire in particular is a strong energy, and we have seen that individuals who suppress strong emotions and hold back their creative expression often lose their energy and become burnt out. To learn to master our emotions and our subconscious, we need to be willing to face all the nuances within us. We need to allow ourselves to feel anger, sadness, joy, fear and other important expressions. By experiencing them and befriending them, we can transform our inner selves – we become strong healers with the abilities to help others in that process.

Combination with the Sun

Now follows a review of the ascendant in Capricorn in combination with all Sun signs. Look at your ascendant sign in the Birth Chart and then where your Sun is. Combining these two energies gives you a strong indication of what you are here to delve into and manifest in this life. It also gives you guidance for spiritual themes you can develop and understand within yourself and in your life.

The ascendant shows how you have been shaped, how you meet your surroundings as well as important life themes and lessons for you in the course of life.

The Sun shows where you are meant to shine in this life and where you have a great opportunity to make an impression with your energy.

Ascendant in Capricorn & Sun in Aries
With the ascendant in Capricorn and the Sun in Aries, this means that the Sun is in the fourth house - the house of home, family, security, our roots and our origins.

With the Sun in the fourth house, you are here to find security within yourself and find home within yourself. You are here too free yourself from dysfunctional family patterns and build your own person. With this placement, it is extremely important that you look at how you grew up. It is also valuable that you work on your inner healing, especially if you know that there have been imbalances in some form. The Sun is in Aries, the sign of independence and leadership but also of courage. This means that these are qualities and characteristics that you should strive to develop during life, in order to find a home in yourself and to fill up with life energy.

With Capricorn in the ascendant and the Sun in Aries, you have a strength within you that can take you far in this life. There is a leadership energy that you can use to achieve the goals you aim for. Use Capricorn's drive and strategic qualities in combination with Aries' courage and spontaneous energy, and you'll get a nice balance here.

Ascendant in Capricorn & Sun in Taurus

With the ascendant in Capricorn and the Sun in Taurus, this means that the Sun is in the fifth house - the house of creativity, sports, creation, expression, children and playfulness.

With the Sun in the fifth house, you are here to develop your creativity and share it with the outside world. It can be in the form of a book, art, spirituality or through something else. Creativity has no boundaries or templates, but you can use your creative power in any field. With this placement, you are here to affirm your ability to build and create in this world. The Sun is in Taurus, the sign of beauty and creativity as well as stability. Taurus is an earth sign with a strong stubbornness. This means that these are qualities that you should develop and bring into your life to nourish your Sun. With the Sun in Taurus, you also need to allow yourself to enjoy life and the beauty around you. It helps replenish life energy and power.

With Capricorn in the ascendant and the Sun in Taurus, we get double the amount of earth elements. You have a grounded energy and an ability to get practical things done. If you can find a way to get your creativity out in a practical form, for example through a job or business, you can go far in whatever you choose to do in this area.

Ascendant in Capricorn & Sun in Gemini

With the ascendant in Capricorn and the Sun in Gemini, this means that the Sun is in the sixth house - the house of health, routines, service, mastery and work.

With the Sun in the sixth house, you are here to learn all about health and understand how energy flows through your physical body. You are also here to contribute with service and to find an everyday life that resonates with your soul. To get there, you may have to experience a number of challenges in your everyday life during the first part of your life. For example, it may be about health problems or challenges at work. By healing yourself and through insights into what you yourself need to feel well, you can understand other people's needs. You are becoming a powerful healer with gifts to help. The Sun is in Gemini, the sign of communication and learning but also of flexibility. This means that these are qualities that help you develop your Sun here. You are quick-thinking and you find it easy to talk to different types of people.

With the ascendant in Capricorn and the Sun in Gemini, you need to combine strategic work with curiosity and flexibility. The earth you possess through Capricorn helps you stay grounded with the body and its needs.

Ascendant in Capricorn & Sun in Cancer
With the ascendant in Capricorn and the Sun in Cancer, this means that the Sun is in the seventh house - the house of relationships, balance, relating and other people. This placement also means that the ascendant and the Sun are opposite each other in the chart.

With the Sun in the seventh house, you are here to learn all about relationships and about the relationship with yourself. You are here to learn how to create healthy relationships that are based on love and a high frequency, rather than dysfunctional patterns and behaviors. To master this area, you will most likely have to face some challenges in the course of life, connected with your relationships. You will also notice that many of your great and deep lessons come precisely through your relationships and through partnerships. The Sun is in

Cancer, the sign of security and emotions. This means that you have a great sensitivity in your relationships, and you are open to what a partner needs from you. Here it is important that you build your relationship patterns on intuition rather than on old patterns that do not resonate with you on a soul level. You may also need to watch out for co-dependency or excessive responsibility in your closest relationships. The Sun here makes you an empathetic and skilled therapist, as you feel and know what others need.

With Capricorn in the ascendant and the Sun in Cancer, you have a fine balance between earth and water. Capricorn can help you set the boundaries that you may need when the Sun is in Cancer, especially in the house of relationships. Strive for a balance between Capricorn's strategic approach and your strong intuition.

Ascendant in Capricorn & Sun in Leo

With the ascendant in Capricorn and the Sun in Leo, this means that the Sun is in the eighth house - the house of transformation, shared resources, intimacy and deep aspects of ourselves.

With the Sun in the eighth house, you are here to learn all about your inner self and understand the nuances of emotions that exist within you. This placement makes you a skilled and powerful healer, especially when you have learned the art of inner transformation and healing lower aspects of yourself. With the Sun here, you may experience some challenges in life, challenges in the form of emotional crises or states of pain. Through these experiences, you have a great opportunity to learn to understand the processes that are going on within you and that may be directing the direction of your life. The Sun is in Leo, the sign of leadership and creativity but also pride. This means that these are qualities that you should develop in order to develop your Sun here. By leading yourself forward and by finding creative solutions, you can transform heavy conditions in your interior and thus become master of your energy.

The Ascendant in Capricorn helps you find strategies and move forward methodically and in a grounded way. To make your Sun shine, you sometimes need to let go of the seriousness that can be in Capricorn and allow Leo to be in its playfulness. A balance between hard work and joy leads you towards development and success in what you do.

Ascendant in Capricorn & Sun in Virgo
With the ascendant in Capricorn and the Sun in Virgo, this means that the Sun is in the ninth house - the house of exploration, travel, adventure, wisdom and belief.

With the Sun in the ninth house, you are here to find a higher meaning to life and to your existence here. You are here to build a vision of life that resonates with your soul and your vibration. You may feel drawn to education and new knowledge with this placement. With the Sun in the ninth house, you have an ability to see things from a higher perspective and you can be a great teacher, especially when you have found your inner true vision of life. The Sun is in Virgo, the sign of service and perfection but also accuracy. This means that these are qualities that you can develop and strengthen, to develop your Sun here.

With the Ascendant in Capricorn and the Sun in Virgo, you have a strong earth energy that helps you build structure, maintain your connection with the Earth, and resolve things that come your way.

Use the power and determination found in Capricorn to achieve your dreams and to reach your highest version of yourself and life.

Ascendant in Capricorn & Sun in Libra

With the ascendant in Capricorn and the Sun in Libra, this means that the Sun is in the tenth house - the house of work, career, life task, manifestation and greater impact.

With the Sun in the tenth house, you are here to make a mark in work, career or through your life's task. You may feel drawn to invest in your career or carry a strong longing to find your calling in life. With this placement, you are also here too free yourself from dysfunctional patterns and imbalances from childhood, which limit the way you see the world and yourself. When you let go of old things that drag down your vibration, you find your true guidance and from there you can build your mission in this life. The Sun is in Libra, the sign of relationships and balance but also of beauty. This means that you have strong abilities when it comes to seeing and meeting the needs of other people. You can see both sides of a problem and that makes you a good psychologist or therapist. With the Sun in Libra, it is especially important that you work on finding a balance between you and other people, that is, that you build healthy and balanced relationship patterns that support you on your journey. You carry artistic and creative abilities within you, something that you can choose to find expression for.

With the ascendant in Capricorn, you have the drive and leadership to help you build your dreams and visions in this lifetime. Use Capricorn's methodical way in combination with Libra's humility and understanding of people to get where you want.

Ascendant in Capricorn & Sun in Scorpio

With the ascendant in Capricorn and the Sun in Scorpio, this means that the Sun is in the eleventh house - the house of groups, networks, visions of the future, community engagement and innovation.

With the Sun in the eleventh house, you are here to contribute something to the great mass or collective. You are here to express your unique energy and thereby create something innovative and new thinking. You are not here to fit into the norm, but you make your Sun shine by daring to do things your way. It can be something grand, such as a new structure in society, but also something smaller - for example, that you highlight your point of view on things. By affirming your unique personality, you become a role model and a guide for other people. The Sun is in Scorpio, the sign of transformation and depth. This means that you are a deep and complex soul with many shades. You are here to learn to understand your inner self and through inner transformation you will find who you really are and what your task here on Earth is all about.

With the ascendant in Capricorn and the Sun in Scorpio, you have a good mix of earth and water in your elements. With the drive and structure that Capricorn possesses combined with the depth of Scorpio, you can go far in whatever you do. You have strong resources and a tenacity that leads you forward.

Ascendant in Capricorn & Sun in Sagittarius

With the ascendant in Capricorn and the Sun in Sagittarius, this means that the Sun is in the twelfth house - the house of subconscious processes, spirituality, dreams and escape.

With the Sun in the twelfth house, you are here to explore your inner self and to develop your spirituality. You are here to unlock parts within, things that have been hidden for several lifetimes. You are very sensitive, and you need some time of your own to process what is happening around you. This placement makes you intuitive and you carry great spiritual gifts. But you may have to work a little to get this. The Sun is in Sagittarius, the sign of exploration and expansion. This means that these are qualities that you need to develop and affirm in order to make your Sun develop and shine brightly. With the Sun in Sagittarius, you have a need for great freedom, and you may have a great longing to experience and learn new things - anything that makes you develop. This placement provides strong conditions for becoming a spiritual teacher or mentor of some kind.

With the ascendant in Capricorn, you have the earth and drive you need to move forward and overcome obstacles. You are a strong soul, and you learned early on to take care of yourself. Find a balance where you live out your practical part through the ascendant but where your Sun and your sensitivity get the opportunity to expand and develop over the course of life.

Ascendant in Capricorn & Sun in Capricorn
With both the ascendant and the Sun in Capricorn, they are in the same sign and house, the first house. The first house represents new beginnings, initiation, leadership and our personality.

When both the ascendant and the Sun are in the same house and sign, the energy mixes and they create a strong unity. Our inner core goes hand in hand with our personality and how we were shaped during our upbringing. Capricorn's energy becomes extra prominent here and we have strong qualities when it comes to pushing things through, moving towards our goals and manifesting practical things.

With the Sun in the first house, you are here to affirm your personality and to develop strong leadership. You are here to express your unique energy, in a way that guides you towards your dreams and goals. With this placement, many of your deepest and greatest lessons come as you take initiative and lead yourself forward. With both the Sun and the ascendant in Capricorn, you have a strong ability to make things happen. You are meticulous and you are prepared to work hard to achieve your goals. Strive for a balance where you approve of Capricorn's methodical ways but also bring in your feelings and your intuition. When you get both feeling and thought, you have great possibilities to create exactly what you want.

Ascendant in Capricorn & Sun in Aquarius
With the ascendant in Capricorn and the Sun in Aquarius it means that the Sun is in the second house - the house of material resources, self-worth, money, abundance and scarcity.

With the Sun in the second house, you are here to learn all about your own resources but also to build up new resources in life. You are here to understand your soul's relationship to resources in various forms. An important task with this placement involves learning the difference between states of scarcity and abundance. So, you may experience states of lack throughout life, just to get the lessons around this that your soul seeks. When you realize your true value on a deep level, you can create abundance in all areas of life – finances, but also in relationships and health. The Sun is in Aquarius, the sign of innovation and new thinking. This means that these are qualities that you need to highlight and develop in order to make your Sun shine here. You are not here to fit into the norm but to find new innovative paths, in everything you do.

With Capricorn in the ascendant and the Sun in Aquarius, you are a strong soul with a stubbornness within you. Use this strength to move forward and to build the life you long for. Use Capricorn's methodical energy combined with Aquarius' ability to find new ways.

Ascendant in Capricorn & Sun in Pisces

With the ascendant in Capricorn and the Sun in Pisces, this means that the Sun is in the third house - the house of communication, perspective, learning and mental processes.

With the Sun in the third house, you are here to learn all about communication and to find your divine expression. You are here to understand your thoughts and transform lower states into higher – high thoughts that help yourself and others. The sun is in Pisces, the sign of intuition and sensitivity but also creativity. This means that you are an extremely sensitive soul, and you pick up other people's energies. You are intuitive and there are strong creative abilities within you. With this placement, you need to bring your feelings and your intuition into what you do, in what you express. When you convey something from the heart, you can help many people, whether it is through a book or through a conversation with someone. With the Sun in Pisces, it is important that you learn to protect your energy, set boundaries and say no when necessary.

With Capricorn in the ascendant and the Sun in Pisces, you have built up a shell growing up to protect yourself. This means that you can be perceived as tougher than you sometimes feel deep down. Use the power and earth that Capricorn possesses in combination with the sensitivity of Pisces, and you can achieve a good balance in life.

CHAPTER 14

AQUARIUS IN THE ASCENDANT

Aquarius

Qualities: Air, Fixed, Masculine

Ruled by the planet: Uranus

Connected to house: 11

Soul Archetypes: Rebel, Humanist, Genius

Connection to chakra: Crown Chakra

Aquarius Characteristics & Energy

Aquarius is the eleventh sign of the Zodiac and symbolizes themes such as innovation, new thinking and doing things outside the box. Other characteristics associated with Aquarius are chaos, change but also the collective in society. The sign carries an airy fixed masculine energy, which means there is a determination – an ability to stick to things, even if other people don't always agree.

Soul archetypes associated with Aquarius are the Rebel, the Humanist, and the Genius.

Aquarius Ascendant

Aquarius is ruled by Uranus, the planet that represents chaos, innovation and creativity. Based on that, these qualities are prominent and strong precisely for this sign.

With the ascendant in Aquarius, we have a natural ability to be ourselves and to be a little outside the box. It is not always something we strive for or consciously work against, but it is part of our shaped personality. It may even be that as young people we try to fit into the norm, only to find that it doesn't work.

With this ascendant sign, we are perceived as unique and sometimes somewhat strange by those around us. Individuals may find it difficult to pin down who we are, as we fall outside of what is considered normal. There is an odd touch to what we do, and we rarely blend in completely with the context in which we find ourselves.

Individuals with Aquarius Ascendant often have difficulty following society's templates and there is a longing to do things their way, whether it is work, spirituality or any other area. Because of this, these individuals are often perceived as rebellious. There is a freedom-seeking side to this ascendant and these individuals do not like to be pigeonholed or bossed around. But even though Aquarius has a norm-breaking personality, there is a great acceptance and openness to other people. This means that people around them perceive them as non-judgmental and friendly in the meeting. Aquarius is the sign of future focus and individuals with the ascendant here may have a pull to create something for the future – something that contributes to a better society. For example, it could be about opening up new doors in technology, spirituality, human rights or other areas.

With the ascendant in Aquarius, we have a somewhat detached personality. We are helpful but we like to avoid getting too close to people around us. In this way, it is easier for us to enter into a more observing role than to indulge in passion and closeness. We have strong social skills, unless there is something else in our chart that blocks or limits this. We find it easy to talk to people and we find it easy to create networks around us.

Soul contract/Soul plan

With Aquarius in the ascendant, we are here on Earth to contribute something unique. We are not here to fit in with the big crowd, but our big task is about finding new ways and acting as a guide for other people. The great lesson in this lies in performing this task, with humility and with finesse. We need to be in our unique energy and bring out our innovative side, without running over people around us. So, the great gift we carry with us in this life is the gift of seeing things from a new perspective.

Breaking old patterns and finding new paths requires both courage and humility. We need to find a balance where we are rebellious for a higher purpose, rather than being rebellious just because we can. When we find that balance, we can help people and groups in a penetrating way.

Childhood & patterns from growing up

When we step into a body here on Earth, we choose a family and an environment that matches our current energy and vibration as well as the lessons we want to learn and deal with during this life. We thus choose a family that helps shape our ascendant.

Individuals with Aquarius Ascendant have usually grown up in an environment that was somehow different or a little outside the box. It could be, for example, that we had parents who had an odd upbringing style or that our parents had different occupations. Another example is that we grew up where we experienced a lot of chaos, for example through many moves or through turbulent relationships.

We have a man in our vicinity with this ascendant sign and he was born into a form of chaos as his mother was close to dying at birth. During growing up, there were also a lot of chaotic and different events, including moving between different countries.

A woman we worked with also had the ascendant in Aquarius. She grew up with a mother who was an astrologer, and her friends considered her family very different and a bit strange.

The above example shows what our upbringing might have been like, but there are many different scenarios. Maybe we grew up in a family where technology was important or where there was a "technical" approach to things. Aquarius can be distant in their emotions, which means that we learned to keep a certain distance from our emotions during childhood.

Regardless of what our background looked like; we have been molded into a personality that makes us a little different. We can experience ourselves as the odd bird at times, the one who never fits in with friends or larger groups.

Common Challenges

Aquarius is a fixed air sign, which means that there can be a certain rigidity, especially when it comes to values and opinions. This can make individuals with this ascendant somewhat inflexible and hold their beliefs too tightly at times.

Individuals with this ascendant sign can sometimes be perceived as aloof and a bit cold and this is because they usually keep a certain distance from people around them. It is common for Aquarius to find it easier to have superficial acquaintances around them or a large circle of friends rather than close intimate relationships. Unlike Leo opposite who is looking for passion and warmth, Aquarius stays more in his objective position. It can create a form of alienation and a difficulty in building close and intimate relationships, for example a love relationship. In this way, we need to be careful that we do not become too technical or static in what we do, but that we allow our feelings and our passion to have a place in our life.

Another factor contributing to this challenge is our great need for freedom with this ascendant. We find it difficult to be close to people, because we are afraid of losing our freedom.

Strengths & Gifts

With the ascendant in Aquarius, we have great qualities in leadership, and this is usually something that gets stronger and stronger as the years go by. We see what people need from a higher perspective and our great drive to improve things in society means that we influence many people with our ideas and our way of being.

One of our great gifts lies in our ability to see things as they are without judgment. It can apply to big things in society but also when it comes to relationships and other people. We allow other people to be as they are, without an intention to try to change them. This is precisely why we find it easy to make people feel seen and appreciated for their authentic person. Aquarius acts as a role model by affirming their unique character. So, no matter what we do with this ascendant sign, we will awaken and create questioning in contexts around us.

With this ascendant, we have an optimistic view of things, and we tend to strive for new solutions rather than clinging to the old past. We know that we can create change through determination and by directing our focus to the right things.

Health & energy flow

There are many important parts to look at in the Birth Chart when it comes to health and two of them are the ascendant sign and the sixth house. The ascendant has a strong connection to our physical body, how we move physically but also how we protect ourselves and absorb energy. The sixth house is the house for health, daily routines and shows what we need in everyday life to get flow in a general way.

When the ascendant is in Aquarius, we are close to mental analysis, something that makes us easily lose focus on our inner self and our feelings. As with the other air ascendant signs, it is important to leave the intellect from time to time and get in touch with the subtle nuances that go on inside us - our heart and our emotions. If we get stuck in analyzes or in a technical focus, our body and health can have negative consequences. Aquarius is a masculine sign, and this means that there is a relatively strong protection against external energies and influence from others. The masculine energy can also get in the way of the feminine, which also reinforces the importance of constantly weaving together thoughts and feelings into a unity.

Physically, Aquarius has a connection to the circulatory system in the body. This means that it can be extra valuable to review our circulation. Emotional blockages can create stagnation in the body as a whole and thus circulation will deteriorate. All fixed signs in the Zodiac need to pay extra attention to maintaining a movement in the body, as they have a somewhat increased risk of stagnation.

With Aquarius as the ascendant sign, this means that your sixth house is in the sign of Cancer. The sixth house is connected to our general health and shows what we need in our everyday life to feel good but also to build healthy routines and have flow in our energy. Cancer as a sign stands for themes such as security, emotions and intuition. There is a watery and introductory energy to this sign, something very different from the Aquarian energy.

Aquarius in the ascendant and Cancer in the sixth house reinforce the importance of bringing our emotional life into everyday life. Cancer is empathetic, caring, intuitive and has a feminine energy. By bringing these qualities into our everyday life, it increases our general energy flow, and we can create a balance between the feminine and masculine. We need to have routines where we plan and structure while paying attention to feelings and sensations in the body - regardless of whether it is joy, sadness, anger or pain.

Related Chakra

Aquarius has a strong connection with the Crown Chakra, the top chakra located just above our head. The Crown Chakra is the energy center that represents thoughts, beliefs and our spiritual connection. It is also related to our expansion of our energy as well as our spiritual growth.

With balance in this chakra, we seek contexts that resonate with our soul and its vibration. We generally hold high thoughts that lead us towards development and expansion. We know who we are at the same time as there is an openness to new insights in the course of life.

When the Crown Chakra is out of balance, we can hold too tightly to our beliefs. We become rigid and have a tendency to try to convince others of our view, what is true for us.

Since Aquarius has a strong connection to the Crown Chakra, it can be extra valuable to work with balance and flow in this energy center. Aquarius has an ability to see things from a higher perspective and it is not unusual for us to receive information and ideas from higher dimensions when we have the ascendant here. We think of universal information that benefits society and the collective.

Here we can work on our awareness and make sure we keep an open mind, even if we choose to do things our way. By following our inner convictions while keeping possibilities open to other viewpoints, we achieve balance in the Crown Chakra.

The career houses

When it comes to job, career and life path in the birth chart, there are many parts to look at, such as our composition of the chart with all the planets and where our power point MC (Midheaven) is located. But there are some important parts we can look at here. By looking at the qualities and the energy that our ascendant represents, we can see what we need jobwise, to develop. When we know what our ascendant sign is, we can also see what our career houses are, that is, what signs and elements they are in. The career houses are 2, 6 & 10.

With the ascendant in Aquarius, the three career houses are in the signs Pisces, Cancer & Scorpio, all of which are water signs. Water represents intuition, flow, emotions and creativity. Having the career houses in water signs means that we have great resources within us when it comes to emotions and knowing what people need, something we can use to build our career and manifest what we dream of. This is further enhanced if we have the Sun, Moon or other planets in these three houses.

So, what does it mean that we have Aquarius on the ascendant and career houses in water signs?

With the ascendant in Aquarius and the career houses in water, we get a mix of mental processes, innovation and a form of creativity. Here we can use our unique approach through Aquarius and work in a creative way to create development that benefits people or companies. Examples of professional areas that may be suitable for this combination are self-employment, managerial positions, business development, technical professions, research, design, data, media and various forms of networking. We can also fit well in professions where we help and coach people in their inner development. It can be a job in the form of a healer or therapist.

The tenth house is one of the career houses and perhaps the most important to look at, in terms of career but also in terms of our life mission – what we are here to manifest in this life.

In this combination lies the tenth house in Scorpio, the sign of depth, passion, contrasts and strong emotions. Both Aquarius and Scorpio are fixed signs, which means there can be a strong sense of purpose and a decisive energy. That energy creates great opportunities to build something long-term, something that changes things over time. There are strong resources here that we can make use of, regardless of the field we choose to work in. An important prerequisite for us to thrive and be able to make great achievements is that we choose a job with great freedom - where we can lead ourselves and where there is an opportunity for innovative and creative solutions.

Spirituality, Transformation & Deep Healing

With Aquarius in the ascendant, we have great opportunities to create some kind of change during this lifetime. We have that regardless of our ascendant sign, but with Aquarius this change is written into our soul plane. It can be something big such as societal changes, but it can also be subtle things. It can be about choosing a style of clothing that shows that it's okay to be different. Perhaps we choose to work with spirituality in an innovative way, where we use our unique composite knowledge instead of already specified templates.

At its lowest energy, Aquarius is rebellious and square, without bringing about much positive change for people. It can still be positive in its own way, but often leads to alienation and frustration with ourselves and those around us.

At its highest energy, Aquarius is innovative for a higher purpose and there is a humility in the rebellious. We choose to do things our way and we strive to wake up and inspire - but we respect that people around us do things differently.

As we mentioned earlier, we may experience some challenges related to close relationships with Aquarius in the ascendant. This will not be the case for everyone with this ascendant, but we can see patterns reoccurring. If we feel that we tend to get stuck in our thoughts or if we become too technical in our way of life, it is valuable to take in the energy of Leo, which is opposite. Leo is fiery, passionate and has a tendency to get involved in a variety of things, including relationships. Here we can strive for a balance where we use the more observational energy of Aquarius but bring in the energy of Leo in the form of passion, joy and also intimacy. It can help us maintain our freedom while allowing people who matter to get close.

There are three houses in the Birth Chart that relate to our inner depth, our transformation and our spirituality. It is houses 4, 8 & 12. House four shows what we carry from family and lineage. House eight shows how we undergo transformation during life but also what healing abilities we have. House twelve shows what we carry in our subconscious and what energy we need to lift up and make conscious. If we have planets in one of these houses, the energy and focus there becomes even stronger.

With the ascendant in Aquarius, we have our spiritual houses in Taurus, Virgo & Capricorn. This means that the spiritual houses are in earth signs. When these houses are in earth, we get an earthy energy here, something that allows us to work with our inner self and at the same time be grounded. Many individuals with earth in these houses are drawn to work with inner development and spirituality, where there is a closeness to nature or to the physical body. There is an inner calm and stability, which we can use when we heal our inner self but also when we help other people.

When we have that mix of energies, getting in touch with our grounding is extremely valuable. It is through our grounding that our inner transformation really takes off. If we choose to work with spirituality, we can use our unique approach through Aquarius at the same time as we contribute security through our earth. This combination makes us well suited to work with people on a physical level, for example through massage, acupuncture or something else where we focus on the physical.

Combination with the Sun

Now follows a review of the ascendant in Aquarius in combination with all Sun signs. Look at your ascendant sign in the Birth Chart and then where your Sun is. Combining these two energies gives you a strong indication of what you are here to delve into and manifest in this life. It also gives you guidance for spiritual themes you can develop and understand within yourself and in your life.

The ascendant shows how you have been shaped, how you meet your surroundings as well as important life themes and lessons for you in the course of life.

The Sun shows where you are meant to shine in this life and where you have a great opportunity to make an impression with your energy.

Ascendant in Aquarius & Sun in Aries

With the ascendant in Aquarius and the Sun in Aries, this means that the Sun is in the third house - the house of communication, perspective, learning and mental processes.

With the Sun in the third house, you are here to learn all about communication and find your divine expression. You are also here to understand, and break thought patterns that limit or hold you back in any way. By releasing yourself from the lower energy of this theme, you can enter into the higher energy, that is, communication that comes from within - your soul and higher guidance. With this placement, it is valuable to look over fears and thought patterns you brought with you from home or that limited you during your upbringing in other ways. The Sun is in Aries, the sign of courage and leadership. This means that these are qualities you should strive to develop in the course of life, to make your Sun shine brightly here. You are a strong soul and when you trust your own strength you stand firm in your expression.

With the ascendant in Aquarius and the Sun in Aries, you have a lot to contribute here on Earth. By combining your unique Aquarian energy with Aries courage and strength, you can make a big difference to people, through your voice and through your ideas.

Ascendant in Aquarius & Sun in Taurus

With the ascendant in Aquarius and the Sun in Taurus, this means that the Sun is in the fourth house - the house of home, family, security, our roots and our origins.

With the Sun in the fourth house, you are here to build a sense of security within yourself and find a home within yourself. To find a home within yourself, you need to free yourself from family patterns and imbalances you brought with you, which do not resonate with your soul. It can be about co-dependency, rigid opinions, fears or other things that you brought with you from home. With this placement, you have a great need for your own time where you can process what is happening around you in peace and quiet. The Sun is in Taurus, the sign of stability and determination as well as creativity. This means that you should use the characteristics of Taurus to build up a solid base within yourself, from which you can build everything else in life.

With the ascendant in Aquarius and the Sun in Taurus, you have great resources within you. You are determined and there is a strong conviction within you that leads you forward. To find a balance and achieve your goals, you need to find a good balance between these two signs, where you use your earth and stability in Taurus but also take help from the innovative energy of Aquarius.

Ascendant in Aquarius & Sun in Gemini
With the ascendant in Aquarius and the Sun in Gemini, this means that the Sun is in the fifth house - the house of creativity, sports, creation, expression, children and playfulness.
With the Sun in the fifth house, you are here to affirm your creativity and express it to the world around you - whether it is through a book, a work of art or through conversations with people. You have the ability to spread joy and positive energy to people. With this placement, it is important that you free yourself from limiting ways of thinking about how things should be. Your creativity comes when you have an openness and when you affirm your own energy flow.

The Sun is in Gemini, the sign of communication and movement but also of learning. This means that you find it easy to meet people where they are, and you see things from different perspectives. Knowledge and new lessons are most likely a motivation within you that leads you towards development.

With the ascendant in Aquarius and the Sun in Gemini, you have strong analytical skills, and you are quick-thinking. You are good at finding solutions to things, something you can use to create in life. With this combination, it is important that you find a balance between the firm beliefs of Aquarius and the flexible energy of Gemini. You have great opportunities to influence many people with what you choose to do.

Ascendant in Aquarius & Sun in Cancer

With the ascendant in Aquarius and the Sun in Cancer, this means that the Sun is in the sixth house - the house of health, routines, service, mastery and work.

With the Sun in the sixth house, you are here to learn all about your health and the flow of energy in your body. You are here to become master of your body and to find routines in everyday life that resonate with your soul. To get there, you may have to experience some challenges in life, for example in health or through work. Through these challenges, you learn what works for you and what doesn't. When you heal yourself and find balance in your everyday life, you can help many people do the same. You become a powerful healer with gifts to contribute service. The sun is in Cancer, the sign of intuition and emotions but also of security. This means that you have a great sensitivity in everyday life. You feel people's energies, which makes it extra important to work with integrity and boundaries - that you say no to what doesn't suit you. With this placement, it is valuable that you develop your intuition enough that it can guide you about what your body needs.

With the ascendant in Aquarius and the Sun in Cancer, you have an emotional aspect combined with the intellectual outlook of Aquarius. Use Aquarius to find new approaches to your health and to your life in general, so that you do things your way. At the same time, allow yourself to be in touch with your sensitive side, so that your Sun can develop and shine brightly in your life.

Ascendant in Aquarius & Sun in Leo

With the ascendant in Aquarius and the Sun in Leo, this means that the Sun is in the seventh house - the house of relationships, balance, relating and other people. This placement also means that the ascendant and the Sun are opposite each other in the chart.

With the Sun in the seventh house, you are here to learn all about relationships and to build balanced relationship patterns. This means that you need to become aware of what your relationships looked like during childhood and growing up, in order to clear away things that hold you back. With this placement, many of your great lessons and insights come through your relationships and through partnerships. The Sun is in Leo, the sign of passion and creativity but also of leadership. This means that you are here to experience deep development but also passion through your relationships. You are also meant to develop your leadership so that you retain the power within yourself, even when you have a deep relationship with someone. You are colorful with an ability to raise the energy of people.

With the ascendant in Aquarius and the Sun in Leo, you have strong resources within you that can help people here on Earth. You are a creator of rank and when you use the creativity of Leo combined with the innovative energy of Aquarius, you can create more than you think possible.

Ascendant in Aquarius & Sun in Virgo

With the ascendant in Aquarius and the Sun in Virgo, this means that the Sun is in the eighth house - the house of transformation, shared resources, intimacy and deep aspects of ourselves.

With the Sun in the eighth house, you are here to get to know all spectrums of yourself and your inner self. You are a powerful healer with this placement, but you need to learn the art of transforming and healing yourself – for your Sun to shine here! With the Sun in the eighth house, you will very likely experience some crises or challenges that lead you towards development during life, all for your soul to get the insights it seeks. The eighth house can be one of the most challenging houses to have your Sun in, while also providing opportunities for tremendous expansion and "rapid development". By learning to transform lower energies, emotions and states within yourself, you can help others do the same. You understand energies and you build up your capacity. The Sun is in Virgo, the sign of service and health but also of perfection. This means that you may feel drawn to service and areas within health. It also means that accuracy and perfection are qualities you need to develop within yourself, to get through the challenges that may arise.

With the ascendant in Aquarius and the Sun in Virgo, you have a mix of big thoughts and thoughts down to the detail level. To develop and reach your soul's highest potential, you need to use the grounding and meticulous qualities of Virgo, but also bring in the innovative and grandiose approach of Aquarius. Through the combination, you can create new paths for healing and service, which can be meaningful to many people you meet.

Ascendant in Aquarius & Sun in Libra

With the ascendant in Aries and the Sun in Libra, this means that the Sun is in the ninth house - the house of exploration, travel, adventure, wisdom and belief.

With the Sun in the ninth house, you are here to gather experiences that help your soul expand. You are here to find a higher meaning to your life, that is, what resonates with your soul. With this placement, you can feel drawn to education, development and travel in various forms - everything that leads you towards development. With the Sun here, you have great possibilities to become a good teacher, for example in spirituality or something that you really believe in. The Sun is in Libra, the sign of relationships and balance but also of creativity. This means that these are important themes for your life. It also means that many of your important lessons and decisive experiences come precisely in your relationships. When the Sun is in Libra, it is of the utmost importance that you find a belief system and a philosophy of life that fits with your inner truth, rather than following someone else's opinion. You are sensitive and you have the ability to know what people around you need to feel good. With the

Sun here, you also have a creative or artistic aspect within you that you should find outlet for in some form.

With the ascendant in Aquarius and the Sun in Libra, we get double the amount of air. It makes you an intellectual person with an affinity for analysis. Here it is important that you bring in your emotional aspect from time to time, where you make decisions based on your inner self, that is, that your heart is in the picture. With this combination, you can make a big difference to people through your unique way of looking at things and through your humility.

Ascendant in Aquarius & Sun in Scorpio

With the ascendant in Aquarius and the Sun in Scorpio, this means that the Sun is in the tenth house - the house of work, career, life mission, manifestation and greater impact.

With the Sun in the tenth house, you are here to make a mark in work and career, or through your life's mission. You are here to build something for yourself and other people. With this placement, you may feel drawn to pursue a career or harbor a longing to find your calling in life. To reach your highest potential here, it is important that you look at limiting patterns from childhood, which can hold you back in various ways. It can be about fears or views that make you feel doubt or keep within certain frameworks. The Sun is in Scorpio, the sign of depth and transformation. This means that your Sun needs to undergo some form of transformation during this life, in order to shine brightly in this area - but also in life as a whole. By affirming your sensitivity and the deep contrasts within you, you will find the path that matches your vibration and soul. With this placement, you have a great ability to see things from a deeper perspective. You see and feel what people around you need.

With the ascendant in Aquarius and the Sun in Scorpio, you have strong resources within you. You have great determination, and it can help you move forward in your development. Strive for balance between the analytical innovative energy of Aquarius and the deep emotions of Scorpio, and you will find a powerful balance here. You can help many people in this lifetime.

Ascendant in Aquarius & Sun in Sagittarius
With the ascendant in Aquarius and the Sun in Sagittarius, this means that the Sun is in the eleventh house - the house of groups, networks, visions of the future, community engagement and innovation.

With the Sun in the eleventh house, you are here to contribute something to this world, something that is innovative and outside the box. You're here to do something for a higher purpose, whether it's writing a book, dressing differently, or affirming your unique expression. With this placement, you are not here to follow the norm, but you are developing your Sun and replenishing life energy by doing things your way. Based on that, it is positive for you to dare to go outside the box in what you choose to do, to reach your highest potential on Earth. The Sun is in Sagittarius, the sign of expansion and learning but also of beliefs. This means that there is a longing within you that constantly moves you towards development and new insights. You may feel drawn to experiences or travel that make you feel alive and free. With the Sun here, it is important that you work on developing your own ideas about life, those that resonate with your energy and soul.

With the ascendant in Aquarius and the Sun in Sagittarius, you have an adventurous side but also a strong analytical prominence. You are non-judgmental and you find it easy to make people around you feel seen and appreciated. Both Aquarius and Sagittarius seek freedom, but in slightly different ways. Important keywords for you in this life are expansion, innovation and discovery.

Ascendant in Aquarius & Sun in Capricorn
With the ascendant in Aquarius and the Sun in Capricorn, this means that the Sun is in the twelfth house - the house of subconscious processes, spirituality, dreams and escape.

With the Sun in the twelfth house, you are here to explore your inner self and to develop aspects of your spirituality. You are here to understand how your soul wants to be expressed through your physical body. With this placement, you can experience a high sensitivity, and you may need some time of your own to take in and process what is happening in your everyday life. You have a lot going on in your subconscious, something that you need to learn to channel. When you go deep and bring out what is hidden within you, you can use your enormous power, in a conscious way in everyday life. To get in touch with these deep aspects of yourself, you need to dare to go beyond the physical and behind the mental. You need to learn to face your emotions and the contrasts of emotions that exist within you. The Sun is in Capricorn, the sign of determination and hard work. This means that you need to develop these qualities during life in order to reach your goals and to develop your Sun here. You have strong intuition and mediumistic abilities, but you may need to do some inner work to bring them out and reach your highest potential.

With the ascendant in Aquarius and the Sun in Capricorn, you are a strong soul with many talents. In order to find balance and to make your Sun shine, you need to strive to create a deep connection with your inner self while seeking new unexplored paths through life.

Ascendant in Aquarius & Sun in Aquarius
With both the ascendant and the Sun in Aquarius, they are in the same sign and house, the first house. The first house represents new beginnings, initiation, leadership and our personality.

When both the ascendant and the Sun are in the same house and sign, the energy mixes and they create a strong unity. Our inner core goes hand in hand with our personality and how we were shaped during our upbringing. Aquarian energy becomes extra prominent here and we have strong qualities when it comes to innovation, new thinking and seeing what society needs to create change.

With the Sun in the first house, you are here to affirm your energy and express your personality. You are also here to build strong leadership within yourself. With this placement, many of your great and deep lessons come as you take initiative and lead yourself forward. With both the ascendant and the Sun in Aquarius, you are born to be different, in all areas of life. You will most likely feel like you are living outside the box in some way and if you don't already, now is the time to do so. You are not here to fit into any template, but your Sun receives life energy and power through your unique expression in this world. You are here to create new standards and contribute something to future generations. Find what feels meaningful to you in life and dare to contribute with what you have to give. With both the Sun and the ascendant in Aquarius, it is especially important that you shift your focus from thoughts to feelings every once in a while, so that you are in touch with your inner self. Through the contact with your intuition combined with the innovative thoughts of Aquarius, you can create something new and great for humanity.

Ascendant in Aquarius & Sun in Pisces

With the ascendant in Aquarius and the Sun in Pisces, this means that the Sun is in the second house - the house of material resources, self-worth, money, abundance and scarcity.

With the Sun in the second house, you are here to learn all about resources and to build strong resources within yourself. Resources can be material such as money, physical things or a nice house. But we also have inner resources in the form of emotions, intuition and capacity. An important task with the Sun here is about understanding the relationship to yourself - how you value yourself. Through development and through insights, you build up your power and you expand your inner resources. Important lessons with this placement are about scarcity and abundance. When you see your divine worth on a deep spiritual level, you will be able to create abundance in all areas of life. The Sun is in Pisces, the sign of spirituality and creativity and but also emotions. This means that you have a great sensitivity, and you can pick up energies from people around you. You have strong intuition and strong spiritual abilities, something that becomes even stronger as you learn to set boundaries and build your integrity. When you value yourself and say no to what doesn't resonate with you, you create a shield for your energy. As you use your sensitivity and intuition to grow and expand, your Sun shines brightly here.

With the Sun here, you also have creative and artistic abilities that you can use to recharge your batteries.

With the ascendant in Aquarius and the Sun in Pisces, you are both sensitive and analytical at the same time. Here you can use your creativity and sensitivity in Pisces while trying new paths with the help of Aquarius in the ascendant. You are innovative and you know what people around you need to feel seen.

CHAPTER 15
PISCES IN THE ASCENDANT

Pisces

Qualities: Water, Mutable, Feminine

Ruled by the planet: Neptune

Connected to house: 12

Soul Archetypes: The Volunteer, Dreamer, Artist, Healer

Connection to chakra: Third Eye & our Aura

Pisces Characteristics & Energy

Pisces is the twelfth and final sign of the Zodiac and symbolizes themes such as imagination, intuition, spirituality and creativity. Other characteristics associated with Pisces are dreams, illusions and a great sensitivity. The sign carries a watery moving feminine energy, which means there is a very subtle, sensitive and captivating energy here.

Soul archetypes associated with Pisces are the Volunteer, the Dreamer, the Artist and the Healer.

Pisces as ascendant

Pisces is a mutable feminine water sign which makes it a very receptive and empathetic sign. We have seen in our work that Pisces can be one of the most challenging signs to have as an ascendant, in the same way that it can be one of the most magical - in its higher energy. Pisces as a sign is ruled by the planet Neptune, the planet of infinity, limitlessness, intuition, creation, dreams and imagination. This means that there is an open and almost limitless energy here.

When we have the ascendant in Pisces, we can experience being extremely sensitive and receptive to energies and events around us. We may also have difficulty knowing where our boundaries end and where other people's boundaries begin. We carry a great sensitivity, and this sensitivity makes us very receptive to everything that goes on in our surroundings. We sense all shades of energies, both negative and positive. If we hang out with a person, we can easily enter into the other's mood and feel the other's pain - to the point that we sometimes pick it up as our gene.

We have great mutability in our energy, and we can easily adapt to our surroundings when needed. We are experts at shifting from one role to another, depending on who we hang out with and based on what we think is required of us.

In a way, Pisces can be the most difficult ascendant sign to recognize, due to the fact that individuals with this ascendant shape their personality strongly after others, especially if there are patterns of adaption from childhood.

Pisces is associated with creativity, dreams, music and various forms of creation. With Pisces as the ascendant, we usually have a strong creative ability and we appreciate daydreaming away in everyday life, whether it's listening to music or engaging in spirituality. We have an attraction to the non-earthly and we seek something that fills us with a sense of meaning and magic. We can have difficulty with routines and engaging in the everyday, because we perceive it as boring or meaningless. Like the Sagittarius sign, we search for something more, something bigger.

Because of our reluctance to indulge too much in the mundane, there is a tendency to escapism with this ascendant. This escape can make us escape from our body, escape from our everyday life or even from our reality. We can also run away from ourselves because of our sensitivity and because we find life overwhelming.

We have a woman in our vicinity with Pisces in the ascendant. She is extremely intuitive and medial, to the point that she daily sees and perceives energies and messages from higher dimensions. At the same time, she perceives her existence as chaotic and finds it difficult to remain in her body. Over the years, she has been extremely mobile on all levels – moving a lot, adapting to her surroundings and jumping between different projects. She is physically present in everyday life but constantly longs to be somewhere else, for example on the other side of the Earth. In addition to that, she is very empathetic and sympathetic, which makes her a valued friend.

Soul contract/Soul plan

With Pisces in the ascendant, we are here on Earth to find a purpose and stick with it. Individuals with Pisces in the ascendant often have big dreams and big visions but can get stuck in a constant search or in some form of escape. So, with this ascendant, one of our big lessons is finding something we really resonate with energetically and creating something out of it – something that helps ourselves and other people. We are also here to find a way to express our soul and our creativity – for example through music, art or through dance. This creativity can also come out in our spiritual work or through some form of service.

Another important task that comes with this ascendant sign is about finding and discerning one's energy. Pisces find it easy to merge with other people and their energies, often in a higher philosophy that we are all one. It is true in our opinion that we are all one - on a higher dimensional plane. Here on Earth, however, we need to see ourselves as unique souls with certain conditions and needs. We need to learn to take what we want into our energy system and choose away what we don't want or feel good about.

Childhood & patterns from growing up

When we step into a body here on Earth, we choose a family and an environment that matches our current energy and vibration as well as the lessons we want to learn and deal with during this life. We thus choose a family that helps shape our ascendant.

With the ascendant in Pisces, we have usually grown up in an environment where we were very tuned in to our surroundings. We have learned early on to scan and sense what is going on in our surroundings.

Over the years, we have noticed that individuals with Pisces in the ascendant often had an upbringing with a lot of dysfunctionality or the opposite - an upbringing with supportive and creative parents. However, we have seen that it is more common with the first example, that we had some kind of dysfunctionality. Just as with the other ascendant signs, there will be a wide range of how our experiences have looked, but there are recurring patterns.

When we have Pisces in the ascendant, it is common to have grown up in a family where there was some form of escape in one or both parents. This could mean, for example, that one of our parents had a problem with alcohol or some other addiction problem. It can also mean that we had a parent with their own traumas and imbalances that were overwhelming in some way. Perhaps we have had a mother who was helpless or who herself had difficulty managing herself and her emotions or who was ill. These patterns have made us very aware of our surroundings and we have learned how to be in order to adapt and make it easier for a parent - and by extension for other people.

A woman in our vicinity has the ascendant in Pisces and she grew up in a family where the atmosphere was quite harsh and cold. There were major imbalances between parents and the woman quickly learned to stay in the background and to take up minimal space. Already as a young adult, she developed a form of autoimmune problem, and she has always been extremely sensitive to stress and external demands.

Another woman with the same ascendant grew up in a family where the mother was emotionally unstable and, in many ways, helpless in her personality. She was unable to solve her own everyday life, which made the woman (the daughter) go in and relieve the burden. The mother also had difficulty dealing with stress and as soon as it got difficult, she panicked and went to bed, as a form of escape from life. The father in this constellation was narcissistic and was both aggressive and volatile in his manner. Over the years, this woman has also developed a number of different health problems and a co-dependency in relationships.

The above examples may sound quite depressing, but they show how important it is to become aware of our childhood and the patterns we have there. Through awareness and through inner work we can transform and heal ourselves – we can tap into the higher energy of Pisces which is magical and holds infinite potential.

In some cases, we have also seen that individuals with this ascendant had an environment where they were encouraged to reach their highest dreams, i.e. parents who supported and who saw the potential in their child.

Common Challenges

When we have Pisces as our ascendant sign, we can easily feel overwhelmed by external energies. We can also experience it as overwhelming to live in everyday life with all the demands that are around us. It is usually because we lose ourselves in the encounter with others. We take in other people's opinions as our own, especially early in life before we learn to understand ourselves better.

We can also experience challenges around routines that make it difficult for us to find routines or difficult to stick to them. If this is the case, it is valuable to find some kind of structure in everyday life, where we allow ourselves to be open and creative, but where we also take care of ourselves.

Because of the mutability that comes with this sign, we can get stuck in an existence where we "float" around without knowing where we are going. This condition can be positive at times, as we sometimes need to let go and just flow with what is happening. But if we stay in it for too long, we can experience feelings of rootlessness and confusion about ourselves and our life.

Strengths & Gifts
The great gift of Pisces lies in their amazing ability to empathize with other people. With this ascendant sign we can feel what is going on in our friend, in our partner and what is going on in the world. This means that over time we build up a deep understanding of other people's pain and needs. Overall, we have a somewhat more cautious and withdrawn personality with Pisces in the ascendant, just like the other water ascendant signs. We take in and we feel in rather than acting out in a tangible way. Although it can be a challenge, it is also a great gift, as it makes us good listeners. People come to us if they want to feel seen and appreciated.

Pisces have an ability to transform the mundane and the boring into something magical. There is a subtle, almost ethereal energy in individuals with the ascendant here and these people have strong creative gifts within them. They are good at conveying an emotion in what they do, which makes them good actors if they choose that profession. In addition to that, there is a strong intuition and a strong spiritual energy in Pisces, something that makes individuals with the ascendant here natural healers.

Health & energy flow

There are many important parts to look at in the Birth Chart when it comes to health and two of them are the ascendant sign and the sixth house. The ascendant has a strong connection to our physical body, how we move physically but also how we protect ourselves and absorb energy. The sixth house is the house for health, daily routines and shows what we need in everyday life to get flow in a general way.

With the ascendant in Pisces, there are two key words that are crucial for balanced health – Boundaries and integrity. Because of the sensitivity that exists with Pisces combined with patterns of attunement, it is extremely important that we learn to set healthy boundaries. We need to learn to say no, when necessary, even if it means discomfort for us or for the person we are talking to. Because we have learned to be flexible and responsive during the course of life, it is easy for both people and energies to go right through our defenses and cross our borders. In the worst case, we don't even have a defense, we let everything in. Here, it is valuable to look at what our childhood looked like and how we learned to handle stress and act when meeting another person.

We have seen several examples of individuals with the ascendant in Pisces struggling with physical problems, autoimmune diseases and various forms of pain symptoms. We can connect this problem to several different parts such as stress in growing up, difficulties with boundaries and a tendency to pick up other people's energy/pain. Physically, Pisces is connected to our immune system, the system that protects us from outside invaders. Our immune system and our emotions are connected, and one affects the other. If we don't stand up for ourselves or if we have a hard time saying no, we can see the same pattern in our immune system - behaving in the same way. We allow energetic debris to enter our energy system, and our immune system has difficulty defending against physical invaders. The more we stand up for ourselves on all levels, the more our physical body will support us in life.

Another important factor related to our health is our grounding. With Pisces on the Ascendant, we may have difficulty grounding ourselves, because we perceive our body as uncomfortable to be in. The longer we are ungrounded, the more likely we are to develop some kind of health problem. Here it is extremely valuable that we find a way to land in the body, so that we can meet and feel what is going on there.

To keep our general flow going, we can work on grounding ourselves and finding a creative expression. With this ascendant sign, it is positive to express our feelings through creativity, for example singing, music or dancing.

With Pisces as the ascendant sign, this means that our sixth house is in the sign of Leo. The sixth house is connected to our general health and shows what we need in our everyday life to feel good but also to build healthy routines and have flow in our energy. Leo as a sign stands for themes such as creativity, leadership, playfulness and pride. There is a fiery and fixed energy in this sign, something very different from the energy of Pisces.

With the ascendant in Pisces and the sixth house in Leo, we once again see the importance of bringing creative energy into our everyday lives. Leo is a fixed sign with a certain authority and leadership. Here we can use these qualities to create more balance in everyday life. We can use the determination and power that Leo possesses to build up our stamina and to stick to our routines and what we do.

Related Chakra

Pisces has a strong connection to the Third Eye, the chakra located just above our eyes. There is also a connection with the aura, which can be seen as our energetic immune system.

The third eye represents our inner vision, our truth and our spiritual gifts. When the chakra is in balance, we have a clear vision within us, and we know where we are going. We can distinguish between what is true and what is an illusion.

If there is an imbalance in the chakra, we may have difficulty knowing what we want and what is our path. We can easily get drawn into other people's visions, which can cause us to lose ourselves. We experience confusion about our identity.

With Pisces in the Ascendant, it is valuable to review this chakra a little extra. By freeing ourselves from energies that belong to others and by building up our energy and integrity, we create balance here. We move more towards our own vision and the more we get in touch with our energy - the more we get in touch with our soul.

Our aura surrounds us purely ethereally and we can see it as an extension of our energy system. When we are completely open, we let everything into our aura, even negative energies. This can again lead to us losing our own energy and carrying around weight that is not ours. Through healthy boundaries and building our integrity, we help our aura become more pure and strong.

The career houses

When it comes to job, career and life path in the birth chart, there are many parts to look at, such as our composition of the chart with all the planets and where our power point MC (Midheaven) is located. But there are some important parts we can look at here. By looking at the qualities and the energy that our ascendant represents, we can see what we need jobwise, to develop. When we know what our ascendant sign is, we can also see what our career houses are, that is, what signs and elements they are in. The career houses are 2, 6 & 10.

With the ascendant in Pisces, the three career houses are in the signs Aries, Leo & Sagittarius, all of which are fire signs. Fire represents power, creativity, energy, passion and inspiration. Having the career houses in fire signs means that we have great resources within us when it comes to motivating and inspiring people as well as starting ongoing projects, something we can use to build our career and manifest what we dream of. This is further enhanced if we have the Sun, Moon or other planets in these three houses.

So, what does it mean to have Pisces on the ascendant and career houses in fire signs?

With the ascendant in Pisces and the career houses in fire signs, we get a mix of water and fire – a strong dynamic and creative energy.

Pisces helps us sense and build a vision while the fire in the remaining houses helps us realize and implement this. With fire and water together, it is important that we find a profession where there is passion and where we get to be co-creators in what we do. Examples of professional areas that can fit here are creator, energy healer, coach, artist, service, spiritual teacher or some form of social work.

The tenth house is one of the career houses and perhaps the most important to look at, in terms of career but also in terms of our life mission – what we are here to manifest in this life.

In this combination the tenth house is in Sagittarius, the sign of travel, exploration, higher knowledge and adventure. Both Pisces and Sagittarius are mutable, which means we need to work with something where there is great freedom and the ability to change. Pisces and Sagittarius are both seekers in their own way and when we mix their energy, we get a strong yearning for the great in life, for what creates magic within us. For that reason, we should strive for professions where we get elements of just that – adventure, innovation, exploration and spirituality.

Spirituality, Transformation & Deep Healing

When Pisces is our ascendant sign, it also becomes our filter through which we see and experience the world around us. Unlike the objective sign Aquarius, Pisces has a more subjective and emotional view of the world and things that happen. Nothing is better or worse. Sometimes it's valuable to step back and take a more observant role, just as Aquarius tends to do. But sometimes it is through our subjective assessment that we develop a deep empathetic side.

We feel our way through life and through our feelings we create our reality.

At their lowest energy, Pisces is volatile and absent from everything going on. In this form of escape, we can see different forms of addiction problems where we more or less leave our body and our emotions. Here we can also see patterns of codependency in relationships where we engage in dysfunctional behaviors to elevate our partner.

In their higher energy, Pisces is deeply intuitive and through their presence and contact with Earth can convey this intuitive wisdom to other people. There is a creative energy that we can use to create something for a higher purpose.

The artist Whitney Houston is a good example of a woman who in a way lived in these different contrasts. She was exceptionally musical and fulfilled many people's highest dream through her music career. While living this dream, she struggled (from what we know) with addiction issues and various forms of escapism, something that may even have been her downfall. Whitney had the ascendant in Pisces, and she is a telling example of the higher and lower energy of Pisces.

If we have the ascendant in Pisces, it can be valuable to bring in the energy of the opposite sign in the Zodiac, Virgo. While Pisces has an openness and a tendency to take everything in, Virgo is the opposite, selective and critical. Virgo is an earth sign and there is an organizational side. Both Pisces and Virgo stand for Service in Astrology, and they represent different forms of service. Pisces often has an intuitive, formless and creative form of service, while Virgo generally has a more practical structure in their service. If we can find the balance here, we can help people with healing and inner development - through our sensitivity but also through our ability to build and create routines and a fixed form.

There are three houses in the Birth Chart that relate to our inner depth, our ability to transform and our spirituality. It is houses 4, 8 & 12. House four shows what we carry from family and lineage. House eight shows how we undergo transformation during life but also what healing abilities we have. House twelve shows what we carry in our subconscious and what energy we need to lift up and make conscious. If we have planets in one of these houses, the energy and focus there becomes even stronger.

With the ascendant in Pisces, we have our spiritual houses in Gemini, Libra & Aquarius. This means that the spiritual houses are in air signs. When these houses are in the air, there is often a depth in our thoughts, and we analyze a lot about ourselves and our inner self. There are often great abilities in mediumship, and we can receive intuitive guidance, healing and information just through our thoughts or in writing.

When the ascendant is in Pisces and the spiritual houses in air signs, we get a mixture of water and air. While Pisces helps us feel in, the air signs can help us plan and find strategies for our inner healing but also in our possible work with clients.

Combination with the Sun

Now follows a review of the ascendant in Pisces in combination with all Sun signs. Look at your ascendant sign in the Birth Chart and then where your Sun is. Combining these two energies gives you a strong indication of what you are here to delve into and manifest in this life.

It also gives you guidance for spiritual themes you can develop and understand within yourself and in your life.

The ascendant shows how you have been shaped, how you meet your surroundings as well as important life themes and lessons for you in the course of life.

The Sun shows where you are meant to shine in this life and where you have a great opportunity to make an impression with your energy.

Ascendant in Pisces & Sun in Aries

With the ascendant in Pisces and the Sun in Aries, this means that the Sun is in the second house - the house of material resources, self-worth, money, abundance and scarcity.

With the Sun in the second house, you are here to learn all about resources, which means resources in material form but also resources within you. Important themes for you in this life are scarcity and abundance, understanding the difference in the energy here. This means that you will very likely experience some challenges with lack during the first part of life, in order for you to receive the lessons that your soul seeks. With this placement, you have a big task that is about the relationship with yourself - how you value yourself. Depending on how you value yourself, this will be reflected in different areas of life, for example finances and health. When you see and know your divine worth on a deep level, you gradually begin to create abundance. The Sun is in Aries, the sign of courage and leadership as well as spontaneity. Aries is a fiery and adventurous sign. This means that these are qualities and elements that you need to bring into your life and develop within yourself, for your Sun to shine brightly.

With Pisces in the ascendant and the Sun in Aries, you have a mix of fire and water. To get balance in life, it is important that you approve both your Sun and your ascendant. You can use the courage and leadership of Aries combined with the sensitivity and openness of Pisces - to create what you want and achieve your goals. Use the ascendant to feel in and the Sun to move forward.

Ascendant in Pisces & Sun in Taurus

With the ascendant in Pisces and the Sun in Taurus, this means that the Sun is in the third house - the house of communication, perspective, learning and mental processes.

With the Sun in the third house, you are here to learn all about communication and to find your unique divine expression. To find your divine expression, you first need to free yourself from the lower aspects of this theme. You need to look at how you grew up and free yourself from limiting views or thoughts that do not resonate with you. It could be about fears or negative patterns in communication that you brought with you from home. The more you work on healing this within you, the more your own strong voice will emerge. With this placement you have strong communication skills, and you can become a good writer or teacher of some kind. The Sun is in Taurus, the sign of stability and determination. This means that these are qualities that you need to develop and use in order to strengthen your Sun and make it shine brightly here.

With the ascendant in Pisces and the Sun in Taurus, there is something artistic about you. You have great creative abilities and a strong feminine energy in your being. To create balance and reach your highest potential in life, you need to affirm the energy in both your ascendant and your Sun. Here you can use the strength and purposeful energy of Taurus to move forward in combination with the creativity and empathetic abilities of Pisces. It leads you towards expansion and towards creative creation.

Ascendant in Pisces & Sun in Gemini
With the ascendant in Pisces and the Sun in Gemini, this means that the Sun is in the fourth house - the house of home, family, security, our roots and our origins.

With the Sun in the fourth house, you are here to build a security and foundation in your inner self. You are here to find home within yourself. To get there, you need to free yourself from negativity and dysfunctional patterns you brought with you from home, that is, what is not you. With this placement, there is often some kind of family karma that you need to deal with in order to become strong within yourself. It can be something big and overwhelming that happened growing up but also more subtle things, such as fear-based patterns in your parents. When the Sun is in the fourth house, you have a part of you that is private and you may feel a great need for your own time, to process what happens in everyday life. The Sun is in Gemini, the sign of communication and learning. This means that you may feel a strong desire to learn new things, to accumulate knowledge. You also have strong communicative abilities, something that you can develop over the course of life - above all when you find your unique expression, free from parents and background.

With the ascendant in Pisces and the Sun in Gemini, you have a very mutable energy. You are flexible and you have learned to shift your energy, depending on who you have around you. With this combination, it is important that you find some form of grounding in everyday life, so that you have your base from which you start. To reach your highest potential, you need to affirm the energy from both your ascendant and your Sun. Here you can use the sensitivity and creativity found in Pisces in combination with your analytical and more logical side found in Gemini. Together, they create good conditions for understanding yourself and other people.

Ascendant in Pisces & Sun in Cancer
With the ascendant in Pisces and the Sun in Cancer, this means that the Sun is in the fifth house - the house of creativity, sports, creation, expression, children and playfulness.

With the Sun in the fifth house, you are here to find your creative expression and share it with the world. It can be creativity in the form of art, acting, music, writing or through conversations with people. You have strong creative abilities with this placement and when you create from the heart you can help people raise their energy. The Sun is in Cancer, the sign of emotions and intuition. This means that you have a great sensitivity and strong intuitive abilities. In order for your Sun to develop here, it is important that you work on your inner emotional healing, where you transform old pain and heaviness into flow and acceptance. One way to do this is to use some form of creativity or creation, to heal your feelings.

With the ascendant in Pisces and the Sun in Cancer, you are extremely receptive to energies around you, and it is very important that you learn to set healthy boundaries, in order to maintain your energy and power. With this combination, you are exceptionally good at knowing what people around you need, and you are a strong healer as well as therapist, if you choose to do something within it. Integrity, creation and flow are important keywords for you in this life.

Ascendant in Pisces & Sun in Leo
With the ascendant in Pisces and the Sun in Leo, this means that the Sun is in the sixth house - the house of health, routines, service, mastery and work.

With the Sun in the sixth house, you are here to learn all about your health and to understand the flow of energy in your physical body. You are also here to build routines in everyday life that resonate with you and your soul. To get there, you first need to learn what doesn't resonate with you. This may mean that you experience some kind of health problem or get stuck in routines that make you feel bad - especially the first part of life. With this placement, you may feel drawn to contribute some form of service in life, something that can make people around you feel better. By becoming master of your body and energy, you become a powerful healer with great abilities to help. The Sun is in Leo, the sign of leadership and creativity but also of pride. This means that these are qualities you need to bring out and develop during your life in order for your Sun to shine here. You carry a great inner strength and creative resources, something that you can use to achieve your goals. Look at yourself and your life with pride - it will help you strengthen and expand your energy and your heart.

With the ascendant in Pisces and the Sun in Leo, you have strong creative resources that you can use to help yourself and other people. It may be that you need to work a little to bring out the qualities in

Leo when the ascendant is in Pisces. To reach your highest potential, you need to use your Pisces sensitivity and empathy combined with the power and determination of Leo. You are a creator and healer.

Ascendant in Pisces & Sun in Virgo

With the ascendant in Pisces and the Sun in Virgo, this means that the Sun is in the seventh house - the house of relationships, balance, relating and other people. This placement also means that the ascendant and the Sun are opposite each other in the chart.

With the Sun in the seventh house, you are here to learn all about relationship patterns. You are also here to understand yourself through meeting other people. With this placement, many of your great and deep learnings come precisely through relationships and through partnerships. When the Sun is in the seventh house, you need to review the relationship patterns you brought with you from home, so that you can free yourself from dysfunctional aspects. An important task for you in this life involves building relationships that resonate with you and your soul – relationships that give you energy. The Sun is in Virgo, the sign of service and health but also of perfection. This means that you need to look at how you can develop these qualities in a positive way, in life and in your relationships.

With the ascendant in Pisces and the Sun in Virgo, you are here to contribute some form of service. It is natural within you, and you see the needs of people around you. With this combination, it is important that you find forms of service that work for you and that you avoid being a "slave" for someone else, for example a partner. It may sound harsh, but it is not entirely unusual that we do too much for people around us with this combination. Work on finding balance within yourself and set clear boundaries when necessary. Then you can contribute the kind of help that you are here to do, the help that raises both your energy and that of others. You are a natural healer and therapist in this life.

Ascendant in Pisces & Sun in Libra

With the ascendant in Pisces and the Sun in Libra, this means that the Sun is in the eighth house - the house of transformation, shared resources, intimacy and deep aspects of ourselves.

With the Sun in the eighth house, you are here to learn to understand all parts of yourself – to master all the shades of your energy. To get there you first need to experience pain and lower states of yourself. With this placement, many of your great lessons and insights come in the form of crises and challenges, all for your soul to have the experiences it seeks. It may sound like a tough placement, and it is. But it means that you are a strong soul with great resources at your disposal. With the Sun in the eighth house, you have great healing abilities, and these abilities become stronger the more work you do within yourself. The Sun is in Libra, the sign of relationships and balance. This means that relationships are an important theme for you in this life. You will very likely experience some challenges in relationships, to learn to find balance here.

With the ascendant in Pisces and the Sun in Libra, you are an expert at seeing and understanding other people. You have an openness to people, and you are responsive when meeting people. It makes you a strong healer or therapist. One piece of advice is to review any patterns of co-dependency and adaptation, so that you can use your energy in the highest possible way.

Ascendant in Pisces & Sun in Scorpio

With the ascendant in Pisces and the Sun in Scorpio, this means that the Sun is in the ninth house - the house of exploration, travel, adventure, wisdom and belief.

With the Sun in the ninth house, you are here to find the higher meaning of yourself and your life. You are here to expand your soul and gather profound insights about life. You may feel drawn to learning in various forms and you need to feel alive. With this placement, it is extremely important that you have outlooks and beliefs that resonate with you and your soul. It could mean, for example, that you find a form of spirituality that matches you and your energy. When you find what suits you, you strengthen your Sun here. The Sun is in Scorpio, the sign of deep transformation and healing. This means that you are a strong healer, and you can become a good spiritual teacher, especially when you find your inner truth. With the Sun here, it means that you will go through some transformation and deep processes, before finding your way in life fully.

With the ascendant in Pisces and the Sun in Scorpio, you have twice as much water. It makes you very empathetic and receptive to other people's energies and states. With this combination, it is extremely important that you learn to transmute lower energies and emotions within yourself, so that you create flow rather than stagnation. By working on your own emotional healing, you can become an amazing teacher and healer here on Earth.

Ascendant in Pisces & Sun in Sagittarius

With the ascendant in Pisces and the Sun in Sagittarius, this means that the Sun is in the tenth house - the house of work, career, life mission, manifestation and greater impact.

With the Sun in the tenth house, you are here to make a mark in work, career or through your life's task. You are here to create something that can make a difference to people. With this placement, you may feel drawn to pursue a career or feel a longing to find your calling in life. To reach your highest potential and develop your Sun here, you need to free yourself from limiting attitudes and patterns from childhood. When you do that, you get access to your own capacity and based on it you can build what you long for in life. The Sun is in Sagittarius, the sign of expansion and learning but also of travel. This means that these are qualities and elements that you should bring into your life, to strengthen your Sun and fill up with life energy. You may feel a longing for experiences and adventures that make you feel alive. This placement makes you optimistic and you have a great need for freedom. You can become a good teacher or leader of people around you.

With the ascendant in Pisces and the Sun in Sagittarius, you have a mutable and flexible energy. You find it easy to adapt your energy based on your surroundings. You are empathetic and sensitive to other people, and you are an expert at raising the energy of the person you are having a conversation with. With this combination, it is important that you work on finding what feels true to you and that you learn to sort out and clear things that drain your energy.

Ascendant in Pisces & Sun in Capricorn

With the ascendant in Pisces and the Sun in Capricorn, this means that the Sun is in the eleventh house - the house of groups, networks, visions of the future, community engagement and innovation.

With the Sun in the eleventh house, you are here to contribute something unique, something that opens up new paths in society. It means you are here to act as a guide for others. You are not here to fit into the norm but to create new ways of looking at things. You can contribute to humanity in many different ways. It can be something grand on the outside, but also something smaller - for example, you affirm your unique clothing style or use your voice to awaken new ways of thinking. The Sun is in Capricorn, the sign of hard work and determination but also of structure. This means that these are qualities that you need to develop and use to make your Sun shine here. Through hard work and through awareness, you can create something big, something that has meaning for many people - both here and now but also in the future.

With the ascendant in Pisces and the Sun in Capricorn, you have a mix of sensitivity and structure. It may be that you need to work on developing your Capricorn qualities here. To reach your highest potential, you need to affirm the energy in both your ascendant and your Sun. Here you can use the sensitivity and empathetic ability you have with Pisces in combination with Capricorn's ability to create structure and to work forward.

Ascendant in Pisces & Sun in Aquarius

With the ascendant in Pisces and the Sun in Aquarius, this means that the Sun is in the twelfth house - the house of subconscious processes, spirituality, dreams and escape.

With the Sun in the twelfth house, you are here to understand deeper levels of yourself as well as to develop your spirituality. You are extremely sensitive to external energies, and you may find that you need a lot of your own time to process what is happening in your life. With this placement, you need to learn to affirm what is going on within you, in the form of states, energies and emotions. By exploring your inner self, you also bring out your strong healing abilities that you carry with you. The Sun is in Aquarius, the sign of innovation and new thinking. This means that these are qualities that you should develop and use in order to fill up with life energy and to achieve your full potential. You are not here to fit into the norm, but there is a unique part of you that you need to find and bring out during this lifetime. You have great opportunities to work with healing or some form of spirituality work with the Sun here.

With the ascendant in Pisces and the Sun in Aquarius, you have great sensitivity but also a strong intellect. You are different in your way of thinking, and you may have a feeling that you don't really fit in with other people. With your Pisces empathetic ability in combination with Aquarius' innovative traits, you can make a big difference to people you meet throughout life. Be sure to set the boundaries you need to maintain your power and energy. Dare to affirm your unique energy, and you will reach amazing heights in this lifetime.

Ascendant in Pisces & Sun in Pisces

With both the ascendant and the Sun in Pisces, they are in the same sign and house, the first house. The first house represents new beginnings, initiation, leadership and our personality.

When both the ascendant and the Sun are in the same house and sign, the energy mixes and they create a strong unity. Our inner core goes hand in hand with our personality and how we were shaped during our upbringing. The energy of Pisces becomes extra prominent here and we have strong qualities when it comes to sensing and capturing the energies of others as well as a creative side.

With the Sun in the first house, you are here to affirm and express your own unique energy. You are here to build a strong personality and to develop leadership. With this placement, many of your great lessons come when you take initiative and lead yourself forward. With both the ascendant in and the Sun in Pisces, you are extremely open to energies around you. It is very important that you learn to set clear boundaries when necessary and that you say no when something does not feel right for you. Because you are sensitive and pick up on other people's feelings, you can easily accumulate conditions in your body that are not yours. Here it is valuable to find methods to clear your energy but also to transform lower emotions within you. Since Pisces is a mutable sign, there can be a tendency to run away from the outside world and from the practical. If you find it's a problem, find ways to ground yourself and set concrete goals. You have great creative and spiritual abilities - something that can be of great help to people. When you find balance in Pisces, you have great potential to become a spiritual teacher, a healer or create something grand in the creative world.

PART 3
ADDITIONAL LAYERS
-ASPECTS & CHART RULER

CHAPTER 16

ASPECTS FROM THE ASCENDANT

Once we have gained a deeper understanding of our Ascendant Sign, it is valuable to look at the aspects that go from our Ascendant to the rest of the Birth Chart. If we have one or more planets on or near the ascendant, it will affect our ascendant deeply, and the energy will mix with the planet in question. Generally speaking, planets in the first house will have a big impact and contribute a prominent energy in the Birth Chart and thus in our life.

If we have several harmonious aspects from the ascendant, it shows where we get a little extra help during our life, in form of people, situations or events that come in to our life. If, on the other hand, we have several challenging aspects, they can show where there are blockages and where we may need to work a little extra to get ahead and reach our highest goals.

Usually, we have a bit of each, that is, some harmonious and some more challenging aspect from the ascendant.

Aspects belong to one of the more advanced parts of the Birth Chart and we can go a long way without understanding and interpreting them. If we want to deepen our knowledge about the Birth Chart, the meaning of our ascendant sign but also gain more insights about ourselves and our soul, it can be valuable to understand the basics when it comes to aspects.

What are aspects in the birth chart?

The aspects show the relationship between planets and important points in the Birth Chart. The aspects can be seen as a dialogue between different parts of the chart. The aspects are very valuable to look at in the chart as they make it unique and dynamic. Our idiosyncrasies, deep soul needs and developed gifts emerge through the aspects. It is only when we acknowledge these dynamic movements that our Birth Chart truly comes to life.

Every planet and point in the Birth Chart are on one of the 360° of the Zodiac. This means that planets that are close to each other in degrees, whether next to, opposite or at a different angle, create aspects to each other. If the planet Mercury is at 8 degrees in Aries and the planet Neptune is at 9 degrees in Sagittarius, they are close to each other in degrees and they create a relationship with each other.

There are different types of Aspects in Astrology, and we mainly use the five largest and most common. These five aspect types are called conjunction, sextile, trine, square & opposition.

Each aspect has a more harmonious or challenging energy, which means they are expressed in different ways in the chart. The harmonious aspects have a flowing energy while the challenging aspects have a more intense or dramatic energy.

Now follows a description of the five different aspects and their important keywords.

Conjunction: 1 - 10°

Aspect type: Harmonic

Keywords: Fusion, Mixed Energy, Strength, Double Power

Spiritual meaning: Shows an area of our life with a lot of power and strength.

A conjunction means that two planets are next to each other on the birth chart. The planets should be no more than 10° apart to create this aspect. This aspect causes the energy and qualities of the two planets to blend together.

Sextile: 60°

Aspect type: Harmonic

Keywords: Potential, Opportunity, Collaboration

Spiritual meaning: Shows where we have great potential and opportunities.

A sextile consists of two planets 60° apart. Here we use 8° as the maximum, when it comes to the difference in the number of degrees of both planets. This aspect is seen as harmonious, but we may have to work a little to achieve what we want. We need to put effort into what we do, to achieve our goals.

Trine: 120°

Aspect type: Harmonic

Keywords: Flow, Lightness, Ease

Spiritual meaning: Indicates flow and innate gifts.

A trine consists of two planets 120° apart. Here we use 10° as a maximum limit, regarding the number of degrees. A trine is often seen as the most harmonious and easy-going aspect. The planets in this aspect are in the same element, creating a flowing and easygoing energy. Because of this flow, we see where we have natural gifts and resources, something that comes without much effort.

This aspect helps us attract things, people or situations in life, which can help us in our growth in different ways.

□

Square: 90°

Aspect type: Challenging

Keywords: Inner conflict, Tug of war, Unintegrated energy

Spiritual meaning: Shows where we need to work on healing and transformation of energy.

A square is created by two planets that are 90° apart in the birth chart. Here we use a limit of 10° regarding the number of degrees. A square belongs to one of the more challenging aspects, perhaps the most challenging of all. This is because there is a great disparity in the signs and their energies. We can experience two completely different sides within us, both of which want to take their place and be confirmed. A square is often our great teacher, and it brings us into deep spiritual development. The aspect creates friction and stress within us, which more or less forces us into development. We need to act and do something about it. Challenging aspects are often tough to handle but carry a great transformative power.

Opposition – 180°

Type of Aspect: Challenging

Keywords: Imbalance, Opposites, Polarity, Need for balance

Spiritual meaning: Shows areas of life where we need to find balance.

An opposition is formed by two planets that lie opposite each other in the Birth Chart, that is, 180° apart. Just as before, here we use 10° as the maximum limit when it comes to variation of the number of degrees. An opposition is seen as a challenging aspect, as the planets are in signs with different elements. With this aspect, we can experience a tug of war between two parts of our chart and thus in our inner self.

Aspects as a door to deep Healing

By looking at aspects in the Birth Chart, we gain an awareness of which parts of us we may need to transform or work with, to raise our vibration and frequency. The aspects show us possibilities and potential on our Spiritual journey and in our ascension process. They can be a powerful tool in healing parts within ourselves and stepping into our full power.

By looking at challenged aspects, we get clues as to where we may be carrying an inner vulnerability or where there may be blockages within us. Our Birth Chart is an energetic composition of what we carry from past lives and what we experienced in this life through our childhood. Since our birth time is always (according to us) predetermined to the minute, we will have a chart that exactly matches our vibration and energy - that is, what we need to deal with and balance in this life.

Aspects connected to our Ascendant

Aspects from our ascendant give us more information about our life journey and where there is great activity in relation to the rest of the Birth Chart. The aspects from the ascendant usually show different themes that become extra prominent and that we can be influenced by during life.

The more lighthearted or harmonious aspects such as sextile and trine show where we have extra support, i.e. planets or points in the chart that support us. For example, if we have a trine between the ascendant and Jupiter in the ninth house, we will automatically attract themes connected with the energy of Jupiter. It can manifest itself in a variety of ways, perhaps in the form of a teacher or an education that appears in our life just when we need it.

The more challenging aspects such as square and opposition show where there may be some kind of blockage and where we may need to put in extra effort to get where we need to go.

An example is if we have a square between the ascendant and the fourth house. Since the fourth house represents our family, patterns from growing up and our parents, there may be some block or limitation from childhood that is holding us back.

Specific Planets & their energy

Earlier in the book we have described the 10 planets and the energy they represent in the Birth Chart. Here is a short repetition of the planets with associated keywords. We also look at keywords for the asteroid Chiron and the nodes of the Moon.

The Sun: Light, Power, Life Energy, Vitality, Joy, Center, Purpose, Manifestation, Masculine, Father

The Moon: Receptive, Intake, Feminine, Mother, Intuition, Emotions, Subconscious, Memories, Reactions, Soul Needs

Mercury: Communication, Speech, Writing, Thoughts, Mental Processes, Intuition, Perception, Expression, Receiving Information

Venus: Attraction, Beauty, Balance, Relationships, Money, Values, Self-worth, Material, The physical, Creativity, Resources

Mars: Life Energy, Power, Courage, Strength, Will, Passion, Sexuality, Masculinity, Warrior, Protector, Inspiration

Jupiter: Expansion, Wisdom, Higher Learning, Higher Communication, Travel, Spirituality, Faith, Flow, Luck, Opportunities, Other Cultures

Saturn: Limitation, Mastery, Discipline, Hard work, Master of something, Long-term, Patience

Uranus: Freedom, Liberation, Chaos, Awakening, Higher Thoughts, Rebellious, Innovative, Intelligent, Genius, Innovation, Higher Purpose, Technology

Neptune: Dreams, Creativity, Higher Dimensions, Higher Self, Empathy, Boundless, Unconditional Love, Forgiveness, Escape, Imagination, Illusion

Pluto: Soul Transformation, Kundalini, Rebirth, Healing, Shared Resources, Intimacy, Contrasts, Black or White, Deep Emotions, Crisis

Asteroid Chiron: Blockages from past lives, Deep fears, Great healing potential in this life, Healing abilities

South Node: Patterns and experiences from past lives, what we overdeveloped in past lifetimes, developed gifts

North Node: Destiny point, Opportunity for deep spiritual growth, Shows what energy we need to master in this life

Planets next to the ascendant (Conjunction)

Planets located on or near the ascendant will be positioned in the first house. Planets in the first house always have an important and special meaning, because the first house represents us, our person and strong major life themes. If we have one or more planets in the first house, we should carefully consider them and their characteristics in our personality and how we go forward in life. Planets are always important, no matter where they are in the chart, but precisely in the first house they get a strong power of manifestation. This means that we will meet and attract the energy of the planets in the first house in an intense way.

The closer to the ascendant in degrees that a planet is, the more power there is overall in it. When planets are right next to the ascendant, the energy and the qualities the planet stands for become very prominent and strong in us. If our ascendant sign is Cancer and we have the planet Mercury near the ascendant, we get a strong mix of these energies. Perhaps then we see a somewhat more intellectual or social Cancer, where there is a sensitivity but also a strong communicative side.

Each planet has a lower and a higher energy. This means that we may be somewhere in this spectrum, and we may need to work on developing the higher energy of the planet. So, if we have the Moon in the first house or near the ascendant, it can mean that we are highly sensitive, intuitive and empathic but it can also mean that we are emotional, too much in our emotions or that we pick up a lot of negativity in our surroundings. Based on that, we need to be aware that planets in our first house have a great power in our life and do what we can to learn to master the energy in a constructive way.

Now follows a brief overview of the various planets and what they mean, if they are near the ascendant (or in the first house).

The Moon

If the Moon is near the ascendant or in the first house, it makes us more sensitive and open to the outside world. The Moon is receptive, empathetic and feminine in nature. With the Moon here, we often have a great sensitivity, and we can sense what is going on in our surroundings - both in the form of emotions and energy. When the Moon is in the first house, we have many times been greatly influenced by our mother and there may be a bond here that affects us, positively or negatively.

The Sun

If the Sun is on the ascendant or in the first house, we see a strong personality with a lot of leadership energy. When the Sun and the ascendant are in the same sign, there is a double energy of that particular sign. So, what we are here to express and manifest through the Sun is strongly related to our Ascendant and how we were shaped growing up.

With the Sun in this placement, we are often good at leading ourselves forward or making choices that move us in a certain direction.

Mercury

If the planet Mercury is near the ascendant or in the first house, there is a strong energy of mental processes, flexibility and communication. This can come out through the fact that we are social or that we value meeting other people. This placement can also mean that we are driven and motivated a lot by new knowledge and by learning new things in life.

Venus

If the planet Venus is near the ascendant or in the first house, we can see that themes around relationships, balance and aesthetics can be enhanced. Venus also represents our physical and material resources we have around us so with Venus here we can be good with money or appreciate having nice things around us. When it comes to relationships, we are often the ones who take the initiative and who seek relationships in various forms.

Mars
With the planet Mars near the ascendant or in the first house, we have a strong engine within us that propels us forward through life. We can easily start new projects and there is a fire and passion in our approach to life. Mars here also creates an adventurous energy where we seek things that can make us feel alive.

Jupiter
With the planet Jupiter near the ascendant or in the first house, we can get some unique opportunities in life. Jupiter has an uplifting and positive energy, an energy that can mean luck or rather flow through the choices we make. The planet is also related to education, travel and inner beliefs in our life. With Jupiter here we can have an aspect within us that search for the meaning of life and spends a lot of time and energy exploring and discovering.

Saturn
With Saturn near the ascendant or in the first house, we have a serious side within us, a side that makes us good leaders and responsible for various projects. As Saturn represents limitation, hard work and structure, we may experience some form of limitation within us, especially in the first part of life. With age usually comes a great deal of maturity and we learn to deal with and master challenges within ourselves. When Saturn is in the first house, we have often learned early on to take great responsibility, perhaps for a

parent or over some situation at home. With Saturn here, we can go far in whatever we choose to do, if we are prepared to work and put effort into it.

Uranus

When the planet Uranus is near the ascendant or in the first house, we carry a strong dynamic energy within us, something that people around us can sense. Uranus is the planet of revolution, chaos and innovation. So, with this placement, we often have a strong desire to go our unique way and do things a little outside the box, whether it's health, work or our everyday life in general. We can also be perceived as a bit eccentric and chaotic, precisely because we have a tinge of chaos and electricity in our energy. We have a great need for freedom, and we have a great acceptance of people around us.

Neptune

When the planet Neptune is near the ascendant, we carry a great sensitivity and we are very receptive to what is happening around us, often even more so than with the Moon here. We can be extremely open and pick up what is happening around us, into our energy system and our aura. Because Neptune represents emotions, creativity, dreams, escape, and other dimensions, we can be exceptionally intuitive. With Neptune here, it is of the utmost importance that we get to know our energy and learn to set healthy boundaries in everyday life.

Pluto

With Pluto near the ascendant or in the first house, we have a strong magnetic force, and we are drawn to that which leads us towards depth and transformation – or vice versa. With Pluto here, we can get stuck in black or white, all or nothing thinking, which means we may need to be aware of that aspect of ourselves. When we have Pluto on the ascendant, it is important that we constantly strive towards transformation and if we don't, Pluto will more or less "force" us into it in some way. Very good energy for research or deeper work of any kind.

Asteroid Chiron

With Chiron near the ascendant or in the first house, it means that we carry some kind of block or fear about how we are perceived by people. It can be shown by our low self-esteem or our fear of making mistakes. Here it is important to look at the sign and its characteristics, to see what type of blockage it may be about. Since the ascendant and the first house represent our approach to life and how we get there, we may need to work on healing ourselves here. As we heal this aspect of ourselves, Chiron becomes our great gift and we become a very powerful healer, gifted to help others.

South Node

With the South Node near the ascendant or in the first house, it means that we have had many lives with leadership within us. We have previously developed some form of leadership and in this lifetime, it is about refining this, so that we lead with humility and with love. This placement can also mean that we have a great deal of independence in our personality, something that we developed through upbringing and previous lives. With the South Node here, that means the North Node is in the seventh house opposite, the house of relationships and partnerships. So, in this lifetime we need to open up to explore the theme of relationships and learn to build balance between ourselves and other people. Relationships are a big theme here with this placement and you will very likely experience several fateful encounters with people. Look at the signs in the first and seventh houses to see which energies and qualities are prominent and important to develop.

North Node
With the North Node near the ascendant or in the first house, you are here to develop your leadership in a powerful way. You are meant to understand your own energy and manifest it in what you find meaningful in the course of life. With the North Node here, that means the South Node is in the seventh house, opposite.
It shows that you had many previous lives where relationships were central. It is easy for you to see other people's needs and, in this life, it is important to put your needs first. By prioritizing yourself in a positive way, you can use that to help and support other people in what you choose to do. With the nodes here, it is valuable to look at which signs are involved to see which themes and qualities are important to work with.

A Sextile from the ascendant

If we have a sextile from the ascendant, it usually means that one of the planets involved is in the third or eleventh house, since the distance in this aspect is 60 degrees (two signs away). With a sextile from the ascendant, we have a form of potential within us, which we may need to work a little with to bring out.

If we have a sextile from the ascendant to the third house (the house of communication) it indicates an inner talent in the form of communication. But it takes some effort for us to be able to use this communicative part of us. An example is if we have many ideas and knowledge within us, but that we have a certain fear of conveying this to other people. Through an awareness and through effort, we can get better at this part and get our message out.

If we have a sextile from the ascendant to the eleventh house (the house of groups & friends) we can get opportunities connected with that house and current themes. Sextile as an aspect in the birth chart is usually used to a lesser extent than the others, but it can provide valuable information about us and our life journey. Now follows a brief review of the various planets and what they mean, if they are in a sextile to the ascendant.

The Moon

If we have the ascendant in sextile to the Moon, we have access to an emotional side, but it can be somewhat hidden or invisible, until we choose to highlight it. By welcoming our emotions and the feminine part of ourselves, we gain more insight, knowledge and guidance from our emotions and our inner self. Through this aspect, we can use our emotions and our sensitivity by consciously picking out and developing that part of ourselves.

The Sun

If we have the ascendant in sextile to the Sun, we have a leadership within us, which we may have to consciously pick up and use in our life and everyday life. There is a part within us that longs to shine and that wants to see that our goals and dreams are manifested for us. Here we can look at how we can give this part of ourselves more space, so that it becomes a natural part of us but also in our meeting with other people.

Mercury

With the ascendant in sextile to the planet Mercury, we carry communicative gifts within us, which we may need to work on developing even more. Perhaps we have a longing to get our message across or become clearer in our voice and expression but experience it as a bit challenging. Here it is positive to take the opportunities we get in different contexts and develop this aspect of ourselves more.

Venus

With the ascendant in sextile to the planet Venus, we have a talent or gift when it comes to understanding and meeting other people. We also have something within us who has talent when it comes to creating and manifesting physical things, such as money. To bring out this gift in the best way, it is valuable to spend some time honing it, so that it comes even more naturally to us.

Mars

If the ascendant has a sextile to the planet Mars, it shows that we have a strong passion and willpower within us, which we can bring out and use when we need it. We may be somewhat unaware of this aspect of ourselves, but by becoming aware we can highlight and enhance that quality. Mars carries a forward and an energetic energy and with the help of that energy we can handle challenges and situations where we need to be a little extra strong and in our power.

Jupiter

If the ascendant has a sextile to the planet Jupiter, it means that we can get special opportunities from outside, by daring to bet on opportunities that come to us. These opportunities can be expressed in different ways and many times they can appear in the form of meetings with other people. A sextile to Jupiter can indicate that we have learning and mentoring qualities within us, which we need to pay attention to and highlight.

Saturn

If we have a sextile from the ascendant to the planet Saturn, we have an inner quality of discipline and an ability to make things happen, something that we may need to draw upon when we need it with this aspect. These qualities may not come completely naturally, but when we work with them and use them more and more in everyday life, they gain a strong power and ability to manifest.

Uranus

With a sextile between the ascendant and the planet Uranus, we have a rebellious part within us that we can bring out when we need it. Since the aspect requires a certain effort, it can be that we want to be outside the box and do our thing but can feel like we don't really dare or like something is holding us back in some way. By creating an awareness that this is a part of us, we can use the energy and qualities of Uranus in a more tangible and powerful way.

Neptune

With a sextile between the ascendant and the planet Neptune, we have a sensitive aspect within us, a part that makes us receptive to what is happening around us. We also carry qualities within the creative field, something that we need to address order to bring out in our expression. Neptune stands for the unseen, dreams, visions, the ethereal and the creative flow. Be aware that you have these qualities within you and do something consciously to develop them fully in your everyday life.

Pluto

If we have a sextile from the ascendant to the planet Pluto, we carry a deep and emotional part within us. Pluto's energy of transformation, and strong emotions means that we have the ability to see beneath the surface and we know what others need without them saying anything. There is a clear instinct and a strong intuition, something we may need to work with to fully develop and bring out in our everyday life.

A Trine from the ascendant

If we have a trine from the ascendant, it usually means that one of the planets involved is in the fifth or ninth house, since the distance in this aspect is 120° (four signs away).

This aspect is harmonious in nature, and it shows that there is an ease or flow of energy between the ascendant and the other planet. It is a supporting aspect that allows us to use the energy, and qualities of the planets involved without much effort. We usually find it easy to pick up and use these qualities and attributes in everyday life and in meeting other people.

If we have a trine from the ascendant to the fifth house (the house of creativity, self-expression & playfulness), we have a natural part within us that is drawn to these types of activities and that, on the contrary, draws these types of situations and experiences into our existence. Maybe we do art or enjoy being on a stage. It could also be that we are close to our inner child and that we are good at spreading joy to others, etc.

If we have a trine from the ascendant to the ninth house (the house of travel, belief & learning) we usually have a natural connection with these themes in our life. We may enjoy spending our time in education or we may be drawn to various journeys, either inward or outward. The kind of situations and qualities that come out through this aspect depend a lot on the planet involved. Now follows a review of the various planets and how they affect when they are in a trine with the ascendant.

The Moon

If we have the ascendant in a trine with the Moon, we can naturally get in touch with and channel our sensitivity. Our emotions are generally integrated with the rest of our personality, unless there are other things affecting this in the chart. The Moon represents our emotions, how we express our emotions and how we experience them. In this aspect, we have a strong intuition, and we can use it when meeting other people. So, we can see it as our Moon and our emotions supporting us and they are a superpower we can use to navigate and get ahead.

The Sun

If we have the ascendant in a trine with the Sun, we see a harmonious bond between our outer personality and our inner Core. The Sun shows where we are meant to shine and make a mark in this life and what energy we are here to learn more about. With this aspect we are supported in this by the ascendant and since both the Sun and the ascendant are in the same element (if the Sun is in the fifth or ninth house) this quality becomes strong and a great gift. With the Sun in this aspect, we can also use our leadership to get ahead and to accomplish important things in our everyday lives.

Mercury

If we have a trine between the ascendant and the planet Mercury, we usually have natural abilities related to communication, ideas and knowledge. This aspect allows us to use these characteristics and qualities in a simple and clear way, if we do not have other parts that limit it in the chart. We can be quick-thinking and good at seeing different options in different contexts. Mercury in aspect with the ascendant and our first house also makes us flexible, which can help us as we can adapt to the situation we are in.

Venus

With a trine between the ascendant and the planet Venus, we can appreciate having nice things around us and we will be drawn to relationships or draw relationships into our life that can teach us different things. If we have Venus in the ninth house, for example, we can meet a partner with whom we travel a lot or who helps us with education and higher learning. We also have an ability to create through creativity and to build material things around us.

Mars

If we have a trine between the ascendant and the planet Mars, we often have a strong force that we can use and benefit from in our everyday life. Mars helps us with qualities such as strength, courage and action. With Mars in this harmonious aspect to our Ascendant, we are likely to have a lot of life energy and good physical health, unless we have other elements in the chart that oppose this. Mars in this aspect can also mean that we can be quite direct when dealing with others and we know what we want.

Jupiter

With a trine from the ascendant to the planet Jupiter, we are good at creating flow and attracting positive opportunities. The aspect helps us get opportunities in education, travel and various forms of higher learning. Here it is important to know that we usually need to dare to take the opportunities when they come, as Jupiter does not do that job for us. If we get opportunities, we need to take the step ourselves and invest in our internal development and the areas that apply.

Saturn

If we have a trine between the ascendant and the planet Saturn, we have an orderly, structured and grounding energy in our outer personality. Depending on how our chart looks otherwise and which ascendant sign we have, the energy from Saturn will have varying degrees of influence. Saturn is good at creating structure and setting goals, so this aspect helps us bring out these qualities in our daily lives and in what we do.

Uranus

With a trine between the ascendant and the planet Uranus, we have a rebellious part within us, something that often shines through when individuals meet us. This energy often comes out strongest when Uranus is in the first house of our chart but can also come out through this aspect. Here we can use the energy of Uranus and act with the help of unique ideas and by going outside the box and going through life in our unique way.

Neptune

If we have a trine from the ascendant to the planet Neptune, we have a very sensitive part within us that can shine through when meeting others. We can also find it somewhat challenging to be in situations with loud noises, lots of light or other external phenomena. We can also feel that we pick up energies around us and that it is easy for us to adapt to people in our environment. When we use the positive energy here, we can be in our creative and spiritual energy, in a way that benefits ourselves and other people. We can also become a good psychologist, therapist or healer as it is easy for us to empathize and understand.

Pluto

If we have a trine between the ascendant and the planet Pluto, we have a deep sensitivity within us that allows us to be drawn to deeper things, situations and people. With this aspect, the depth and exploration within us can shine through our personality and we can use these qualities to understand people and get behind what we see on the surface. However, Pluto always means some form of transformation, which means that we can repeatedly end up in situations that cause us to enter a transformation process. If Pluto is in the fifth house, we can experience this especially in our creative expression and, for example, around children.

A square from the Ascendant

If we have a square from the ascendant, it usually means that one of the planets involved is in the fourth or tenth house, since the distance in this aspect is at 90° (three signs away).

An aspect in the form of a square is challenging in its energy and it requires us to consciously work on healing, transforming and dissolving blockages or obstacles within us. The aspect is, in addition to the conjunction, the most powerful and explosive aspect in a birth chart, due to its intensity. This aspect can therefore affect us on many different levels and the more we work with it, the more we can transform its energy into a more harmonious one. Many times, we can experience a square in the form of inner conflict where we have difficulty getting a flow.

If we have a square from the ascendant to the fourth house (the house of family, roots & upbringing) it indicates some kind of stress or blockage connected with these themes. So, this aspect can show that we carry with us some kind of limitation from home or that we felt that our parents were not able to fully support us. It can be anything from a minor blockage to something we really need to resolve and transform within ourselves. Perhaps through growing up we have acquired certain patterns or views that affect our way of being and that create some conflict within us.

If we have a square from the ascendant to the tenth house (the house of work, career and life task), we may carry inner limitations or blockages related to these very themes. As previously mentioned, a square is not negative, but it creates some form of friction within us. This is how we may need to look at how we have been shaped, how we get there and what our big goals and dreams are. It may require us to work hard to achieve these and through awareness we open doors for healing.

The various planets in this aspect provide more information about what we may need to work on and transform within ourselves. Now follows a review of all the planets and how they affect us when they are in a square to the ascendant.

The Moon

If we have a square from the ascendant to the Moon, we have a strong sensitivity within us, but we may need to find a balance in our feelings and how we express them. If the Moon is in the fourth house, there may be an emotional blockage linked to childhood and how we learned to deal with our inner emotional life. If the Moon is in the tenth house, there can be a tension between our emotional needs and how we have been shaped in our personality, above all linked to work and career. Since the Moon in Astrology has a connection with the feminine energy and our mother, there may also be something in the relationship with our mother and how she has influenced us. There is a lot of power in this aspect and when we learn to transform any feelings of chaos and strong emotions into creation and drive, we can go very far.

The Sun

With the ascendant in a square to the Sun, our inner core can be very different from how we were shaped growing up. So, we can have an ascendant that wants something and a Sun that wants something completely different. A friction is created here that we need to work with so that we can be in and use both energies in the best way. If the Sun is in the fourth house, we often have a strong connection to family or what we grew up with and we are also meant to explore that area during the course of life. When the Sun here is in a square with the ascendant, it may be that there have been some contradictions at home or that we are somewhat divided in who we are and what we want. So here it is valuable to look at both the Sun and the ascendant, see what qualities they represent and work towards creating balance between them.

If the Sun is in the tenth house, we are meant to shine in that area of life and possibly make a career or invest a lot in work/life task. With a square to the ascendant here, we may experience that we have difficulty reaching our goals and dreams when it comes to jobs based on how we grew up or how we were shaped. There is some kind of fear or limitation that we need to work with to get more flow.

Mercury

With a square from the ascendant to the planet Mercury, we have a strong communicative side. Due to the aspect's challenging energy, we may have difficulty bringing out these qualities in everyday life or it may emerge uncontrollably. Here we may need to look at what we learned about communication while growing up and if there is anything holding us back in terms of our expression. The throat chakra is valuable to work with for healing. With this aspect we can also have an expression that is very different or a little extreme, something that can be positive and that we can use to break templates and norms.

Venus

If we have a square between the ascendant and the planet Venus, we may experience some kind of blockage or limitation when it comes to relationships but also when it comes to money and material things. We may have grown up in a family where there has been chaos around these subjects or where it has been difficult for parents to create and manifest things materially. Venus is also strongly connected with our self-worth and how we see ourselves. If we have a square between the ascendant and Venus, we can experience a lack within us, a lack of our self-worth that makes it difficult for us to attract what we want in life. Here it is positive to work with our inner value, how we see ourselves and by doing that we can go from lack to balance and abundance in the areas of life.

Mars

With a square between the ascendant and the planet Mars, we have a lot of power and energy within us, something that can be out of balance until we consciously work with it. We may experience that we have a lot of energy, unbalanced energy or that we are restless and stressed. Mars is also related to anger and how we express it in life. With this aspect, there can be some kind of restriction or blockage related to anger and how we express it. Perhaps we have had parents who have expressed a lot of anger or, on the contrary, parents who have not shown anger at all. So, here it is valuable to integrate feelings of anger and use it with our other energy to move us forward in life.

Jupiter

With a square between the ascendant and the planet Jupiter, there can be some kind of limitation or blockage concerning our development and capacity for expansion. Jupiter is the planet of opportunity but also of higher learning, beliefs and raising our consciousness. With this aspect, we may carry with us some kind of experience from childhood that has caused us to limit ourselves in this area. Maybe we had a parent who held us back or who had a hard time motivating us to move forward in life. The aspect can also show itself through the opposite, that we have an excessive need to constantly learn new things and throw ourselves into new things. Here we can work on finding a balance so that we get a more positive energy and thus positive opportunities with the help of Jupiter.

Saturn

With a square from the ascendant to the planet Saturn We may experience a limitation in ourselves and our personality. There can also be a fear of how we are when meeting others and fear of what people will think of us. If Saturn is in the fourth house, it is possible that we had experiences or feelings in childhood that contributed to this fear. Perhaps we have had parents who were critical or who had high demands on us, or parents who themselves had a lot of fears within themselves.

If Saturn is in the tenth house, we may experience difficulty in achieving our goals and ambitions. Maybe we struggle to find the job we want, or we have difficulty realizing and manifesting what we long for.

By consciously working with this part of ourselves, we can transform the aspect into power and gain more flow in ourselves, in the meeting with others and when it comes to work.

Uranus

If we have a square between the ascendant and the planet Uranus, we have a strong rebellious and innovative aspect within us, a part that we may have difficulty bringing out in a balanced way. This aspect can manifest itself in us being extremely rebellious or holding this part of ourselves back too much. If Uranus is in the fourth house, it is possible that we had a childhood with experiences of chaos or where some unexpected things happened. It could also be that we had one or two parents who were different or that the whole family lived outside the box in some way. If Uranus is in the tenth house, there is a need within us to work with some new thinking or something with an innovative orientation. Due to the challenging aspect to the ascendant, we may experience that we have difficulty manifesting this in terms of work and that what we got with us from childhood does not really back up and support this.

Neptune

With the ascendant in a square to the planet Neptune, we have an extremely sensitive side within us, something that we can have difficulty handling in the meeting with the environment. We can be drawn to various forms of escape to cope with everyday life and other people. If Neptune is in the fourth house, it is possible that we grew up with one or two parents who themselves were absent or who had problems with some kind of addiction problem. Neptune represents spirituality, creativity, escape and our emotions. It could also be that we had parents who were into something spiritual or had an artistic/creative side.

If Neptune is in the tenth house there is a connection with work, career and our imprint in this life. With Neptune here, we may have big dreams in this area but, due to the aspect to the ascendant, experience setbacks in achieving them.

With a square between the ascendant and Neptune, it is important that we work on understanding our great sensitivity and that we work on setting boundaries to maintain our integrity. We may also need to review what we learned from home and deal with feelings or behaviors related to escape of various kinds.

Pluto

With a square between the ascendant and the planet Pluto, we can struggle with various forms of control. It can be control in the form of a need for control or that we feel controlled by other people. With this aspect, we can experience that control is something outside of ourselves, which means that we easily become "controlling" of our surroundings rather than taking control of ourselves.

The aspect can also manifest itself in the form of own control needs in everyday life. We can also experience resistance when it comes to change and transformation in life.

If Pluto is in the fourth house, we can carry with us events or experiences from childhood where control was outside of ourselves. In the worst case, this placement could mean that we experienced some form of pure control or power takeover from a parent, but it could also be that we had a parent who had a lot of power in himself and who we perceived as very powerful.

With a square between the ascendant and Pluto, it is important that we become aware of the concept of control and how we handle this within ourselves. We may also need to work on inner healing where we dare to face uncomfortable and slightly more "dark" parts of ourselves, so that we become more integrated into our person.

An opposition from the Ascendant

If we have an opposition from the ascendant, it usually means that one of the planets involved is opposite the first house, that is, in the seventh house. This is because the distance in this aspect is 180° (opposite in the chart).

Since the parties involved in this aspect are always opposite each other, there is a challenging energy but also some similarities between the signs involved. In an opposition, both points and planets lie on the same axis (more about the axes of the birth chart can be found in our book Soul Astrology). So, in this case the ascendant is in the first house and the planet is in the seventh house, both of which are part of the relationship axis. The first house represents us and our personality, while the seventh house represents our relationships and themes related to relationships. So, when we have an opposition in between, it's a lot about creating a balance, where we take into account ourselves but also other people.

When we have an aspect in the form of an opposition somewhere in our chart, balance is always an important keyword. Many times, we have a tendency to put too much time and energy into one end, while the other gets forgotten or de-prioritized. So, in this case we might be putting too much focus in the first house or on our relationships in the seventh house.

If we have an opposition from the ascendant to any planet in the seventh house, it can mean that we find it easy to see these qualities in others or that we have a hard time integrating them into ourselves. So, with this aspect we need to look at the qualities and planets that are opposite our ascendant and see how we can work with them in ourselves but also in our relationships.

Depending on which planet we have in this aspect, the energy comes out a little differently. Now follows a review of all the planets and how they influence in an aspect to the ascendant.

The Moon

With an opposition between the ascendant and the Moon, it means
that we have the Moon in the seventh house. With the Moon in this
aspect, we often have a caring side in our relationships, and we can
also be drawn to relationships where we can "take care" of the other
or vice versa, that our partner "takes care" of us. The Moon here
makes us very receptive and sensitive in meeting other people and
here it can be important to have our integrity. We need to beware of
entering into adaptation or co-dependence in our relationships.
Since the Moon has a challenging aspect to the ascendant, there can
also be an imbalance when it comes to expressing our feelings. Maybe
we find it easy to express them in our close relationships but not
when meeting other people. Here it is valuable to review our
relationship to our inner emotional life and look at what we carry
with us from childhood or other events in life.

The Sun

If we have an opposition between the ascendant and the Sun, it
means that the Sun is in the seventh house and that relationships are
an important theme in this life. The Sun represents our inner core and
where we are meant to shine and manifest our energy in this life,
which means that we will very likely develop a lot through our
partnerships and relationships.

Due to the challenging aspect here between the Sun and our first
house, there may be some kind of imbalance in our relationships that
we need to review. Perhaps we put too much focus on relationships
and diminish ourselves, or we may find it difficult to be fully
ourselves in a relationship. We can also have a split part within us

where we find it easier to be in our Ascendant and its energy or on the contrary, the Sun Sign and its qualities. Here it is valuable to work on bringing both signs into our lives and what they represent.

This aspect can also mean that we find it easier to see the power in other people than in ourselves, that is, we exalt others and diminish our own strong power.

Mercury

With the planet Mercury in opposition to the ascendant, Mercury is in the seventh house. With Mercury in the seventh house, we may be drawn to partners who are intellectual and communicative, and we may also attract people around us who talk 'over us'.

As the aspect creates a challenging energy to our first house and ascendant, we may experience some form of limitation in our communicative expression, which may cause us to hold ourselves back in this area. Here it is valuable to look over this part within us and see if we carry something from, for example, childhood that limits our expression or our throat chakra.

In some cases, the aspect can also mean that we have an overactivity in our expression, i.e. that we have a need to talk because we feel insecure in ourselves.

Venus

When we have the planet Venus in opposition to our first house and to the ascendant, it means that Venus is in the seventh house. This means that we can be drawn to partners and relationships who are materially well off or who are good at creating money.

With an opposition between the ascendant and the planet Venus, we can find it easy to appreciate and value other people and their qualities but more difficult when it comes to our self-worth. So, the aspect can mean that we have some kind of blockage related to our self-worth and how we value ourselves.

With Venus in opposition to the ascendant we may also experience a limitation when it comes to creating abundance, money and material things in our life. This may mean that we need to work a little extra hard to build up these parts within us and in our life.

Mars

With the planet Mars in opposition to the ascendant, this means that Mars is in the seventh house, and we can be drawn to relationships with a lot of Mars energy. Mars represents power, willpower, anger and our ability to initiate things. When Mars is opposite the ascendant and in the seventh house, we may experience some difficulty in bringing out our own energy from Mars. Here we may have to work on integrating the energy of Mars and the qualities that the planet carries so that we have them available in everyday life.

When Mars is in the seventh house, we can meet partners who are strong-willed and even carry a lot of anger, as it is part of Mars' energy. Here we can pay attention to this and strive towards healing ourselves, so that we have a good connection with our own power and also with our anger. If we are not in touch with our own anger, we can meet partners who reflect this in our relationships.

Jupiter

If we have the planet Jupiter in opposition to the ascendant, it means that Jupiter is in the seventh house. With Jupiter in the seventh house, we can be drawn to people and partners with a lot of knowledge but also people who have a strong conviction (positive or negative).

With this aspect, we can experience that other people have more knowledge and influence, which means that we can easily look up excessively to people outside of ourselves. An example is if we meet a partner who has strong beliefs, something that we are drawn into and lose ourselves. Here we need to work on seeing possibilities and wisdom within ourselves, rather than putting it outside of ourselves. Based on that, it is valuable and important that we constantly strive to find our truth and what resonates with our inner self - our soul.

Saturn

If we have an opposition from the ascendant to the planet Saturn, it means that Saturn is in the seventh house. With Saturn in the house of relationships, we may be drawn to relationships where our partner has a lot of Saturn's energy. In its lower form, we may meet a partner who tries to limit us or hold us back in some way. In his higher energy, we can meet someone who is hardworking and has a lot of drive within him.

Since in this case we have a challenging aspect to the ascendant, we may experience precisely that other people are trying to control or stop us, something we need to heal and balance within ourselves. By building up our integrity, setting boundaries and creating an inner authority, we become secure in ourselves and the meeting with others.

This aspect can also mean that we experience a certain difficulty in building and manifesting what we strive for, something that often becomes easier with time - especially if we are prepared to put some effort into what we really want to invest in.

Uranus

With the planet Uranus in opposition to the ascendant, this means that Uranus is in the seventh house. When we have Uranus, the planet of chaos and innovation in the house of relationships, we can be drawn to relationships that are a little quirky and outside the box. We can also come across relationships that highlight and reflect the rebelliousness in us in a powerful way. With Uranus here, we can also enter relationships with a lot of chaos and unexpected events.

With this aspect, we may experience some difficulty in bringing out this rebellious side in ourselves, which means that we need to consciously integrate its energy within us. We can do that by looking at any limitations we have brought with us from home and daring to do things that break templates and norms. By challenging ourselves and daring to be innovative, we can take this quality with us in the meeting with the outside world and other people.

Neptune

When we have the ascendant in an opposition to the planet Neptune, it means that Neptune is in the seventh house. When we have Neptune here, we can experience a great sensitivity in ourselves but also in our relationships. Neptune carries an extremely sensitive, subtle and delicate energy and in a way, we can see the planet as an overtone to the Moon.

This aspect means that we can easily experience some kind of illusion or romanticized image of a partner, something that makes us a little "blind" to what actually is. We can also see a lot of potential and dreams through meeting a partner or that our partner carries these qualities, but not us.

When we have Neptune in a tough aspect to the ascendant and our first house, we can have difficulty setting boundaries and maintaining our energy and power. Based on that, we need to integrate the energy of Neptune more into ourselves, work with our sensitivity and become experts in our own energy.

Pluto

With the planet Pluto in opposition to the ascendant, this means that Pluto is in the seventh house. Pluto represents transformation and deep transformation but also themes of control and power. So, in the lower energy, this aspect can mean that we meet partners who are controlling or who are very "powerful" in their energy.

Pluto here can also mean that precisely through our closest relationships we will experience and undergo major transformation processes during this life. When Pluto is in opposition to the ascendant, we may experience that control is something that lies outside of ourselves, which means that we need to work on regaining control over our life and building it up within us. It may be that we had a childhood where we felt that someone was controlling or had a lot of influence over us and our life.

CHAPTER 17
YOUR CHART RULER
IN THE BIRTH CHART

In the last chapter we look at your Chart Ruler. Each zodiac sign is ruled by a specific planet. These planets are called ruling planets or Rulerships. By looking at which planet rules a sign, we can see that there is a connection between the planet and the sign.

Example: The planet Venus rules over the sign Libra, which means that both the planet and the sign have a strong connection with relationships, balance, etc. This is a slightly more advanced method in Astrology, but it is valuable in bringing out additional layers of important information for us.

By looking at the planet that rules a certain sign, we can get more information about what is going on, connected with that area of our life. We can use this method to look at all the signs around the chart but in this part, we are only going through the ruling planet of our ascendant sign. The planet that rules our ascendant sign is called chart ruler.

Our chart ruler is valuable as it, together with the ascendant sign, sets the tone and energy of our chart. By looking at our chart ruler we can see major life themes for this life and where this will play out. We can also see the underlying energy of our ascendant, i.e. what drives us in our encounter with the outside world.

So, the ascendant sign itself shows how we relate to our surroundings in the meeting with people while the Chart Ruler shows the underlying driving force.

We imagine that we have Cancer as the ascendant sign, which means that we generally have a feminine and empathetic appearance. Since Cancer is ruled by the planet Moon, the Moon becomes our Chart Ruler here. We look where the Moon is and see that it is in Sagittarius (Adventure, learning) in the sixth house (the house of service, health & work).

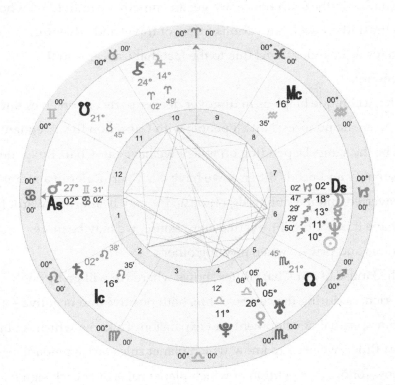

So how can we interpret this? With Cancer in the ascendant, we have a natural empathetic ability, and we can easily pick up and sense our surroundings.

There is a part of us that searches for security and family, whether it is our biological family or more in the form of our soul group. Since the Moon is in Sagittarius, we get a slightly different energy when we mix these two together. Here we can see that the sensitivity and characteristics from Cancer remain, but there is also a side of us that is exploratory and longs for adventure, a part of us that needs to bring a sense of freedom, expansion and mutability into our everyday life for to feel satisfied in life.

So, with Cancer in the ascendant and the Moon (the Chart Ruler) in Sagittarius in the sixth house, we get an empathetic individual who will most likely seek out various forms of travel and adventure, perhaps more inner travel due to the fact that Cancer is in the ascendant.

This technique helps us to discover deeper parts of ourselves but also to create nuances. Not all people with Cancer on the ascendant will be the same. Depending on where we have our Chart Ruler, our personality and needs differ. If we have our Chart Ruler in a more extroverted and masculine sign/house, we may be more forward. If we have it in a more introverted sign/house, we may be more cautious and private when meeting others.

The House of our Chart Ruler shows where we will go through experiences during the course of life, both positive and negative – all for our spiritual development and expansion. To know which is our Chart Ruler, we need to know which planet rules our ascendant sign. So now follows a repetition of which planet rules over each sign in the Zodiac.

The planet Mars *rules* over the sign Aries

The planet Venus *rules* over the signs Taurus & Libra

The planet Mercury *rules* over the signs Virgo & Gemini

The planet Moon *rules* over the Sign Cancer

The planet Sun *rules* over the sign Leo

The planet Jupiter *rules* over the sign Sagittarius

The planet Saturn *rules* over the sign Capricorn

The planet Uranus *rules* over the sign Aquarius

The planet Neptune *rules* over the sign Pisces

The planet Pluto *rules* over the sign Scorpio

Below is a short overview with selected keywords, which describe the location of your Chart Ruler.

So, start by looking at your ascendant sign and find out which planet rules that sign. Then look at what house the planet is in. Then you can look at the description to see important life themes for you and your soul in this life. Finally, look at the sign your Chart Ruler is in and blend its energy and qualities with your ascendant sign. It shows you what combined energy you carry strongly and what energy you radiate when meeting other people.

The Chart Ruler in the First House

Life themes: Leadership, independence, initiative, self-development.
With the Chart Ruler in the first house, you are meant to develop
your leadership and be the one to guide others, through
independence and pride. It is also a lifetime where you will face
challenges that more or less force you into situations where these
characteristics and qualities have the opportunity to develop.

The Chart Ruler in the Second House

Life themes: Material focus, inner & outer Resources, self-worth.
With the Chart Ruler in the second house, you are meant to build up
your inner resources and create a loving self-image. You are here to
build material security and learn to create abundance in the various
areas of life. So, security on a physical and material level becomes
important keys. Look at the current sign here in combination with the
ascendant sign to see what energies you carry strongly when meeting
others.

The Chart Ruler in the Third House

Life themes: Communication, ideas, learning, new perspectives.
With the Chart Ruler in the third house, you are meant to build your
communication skills and focus on your own learning. There is also a
strong connection to your voice and expression. Look at the current
sign here in combination with the ascendant sign to see what energies
you carry strongly when meeting others.

The Chart Ruler in the Fourth House

Life themes: Home, family, security, roots, your private sphere.
With the Chart Ruler in the fourth house, you are meant to grow
through family dynamics and free yourself from what does not
benefit you spiritually. You also have an important task that involves
creating a home and security within yourself, regardless of whether it
is through your family or some other context. Look at the current sign
here in combination with the ascendant sign to see what energies you
carry strongly when meeting others.

The Chart Ruler in the Fifth House

Life themes: Self-expression, creativity, playfulness, children.
With the Chart Ruler in the fifth house, you are meant to open up
your creative flow and reach out to people around you. By finding
your passion, joy and creative energy, you can create joy for yourself
and for others. Look at the current sign here in combination with the
ascendant sign to see what energies you carry strongly when meeting
others.

The Chart Ruler in the Sixth House

Life themes: Health, service, developing skills, good practices.
With the Chart Ruler in the sixth house, you are meant to delve into
your health and learn to understand and take care of your body.
You are also here to develop abilities within yourself, which you can
then give to others in the form of service. Look at the current sign
here in combination with the ascendant sign to see what energies you
carry strongly when meeting others.

The Chart Ruler in the Seventh House

Life themes: Relationships, balance, analysis, to relate.

With the Chart Ruler in the seventh house, you are meant to develop yourself through meeting other people. In relation to others, you create an understanding of yourself, both in terms of your inner darkness and your inner light. Learning to create balance in life's relationships is also a big focus. Look at the current sign here in combination with the ascendant sign to see what energies you carry strongly when meeting others.

The Chart Ruler in the Eighth House

Life themes: Shared resources, sexuality, transformation, crises.

With the Chart Ruler in the eighth house, you are meant to learn the art of sharing something with another human being, on a deep spiritual level. It can be about money, intimacy or sexuality. You also have a big development journey, where you grow through crises and transformation. Look at the current sign here in combination with the ascendant sign to see what energies you carry strongly when meeting others.

The Chart Ruler in the Ninth House

Life themes: Travel, expansion, adventure, higher learning, truth.

With the Chart Ruler in the ninth house, you are meant to discover yourself and life, through travel and adventure. Through inner and outer journeys, you will find what is important to you and your inner truth about who you are on a soul level. Look at the current sign here in combination with the ascendant sign to see what energies you carry strongly when meeting others.

The Chart Ruler in the Tenth House

Life themes: Career, life task, physical Manifestation, our imprint. With the Chart Ruler in the tenth house, you are meant to make a lasting impression here on earth, through your job or through life's mission. You are here to learn to overcome adversity and work hard for your dreams. When you do, you can create and manifest all that you long for. Look at the current sign here in combination with the ascendant sign to see what energies you carry strongly when meeting others.

The Chart Ruler in the Eleventh House

Life themes: Friends, Groups, Community, Purpose, Innovation. With the Chart Ruler in the eleventh house, you are meant to explore yourself through groups or larger contexts. You also have a mission that involves contributing something to society as a whole and working for a higher purpose. Look at the current sign here in combination with the ascendant sign to see what energies you carry strongly when meeting others.

The Chart Ruler in the Twelfth House

Life themes: Spirituality, healing, deep processes, karmic healing. With the Chart Ruler in the twelfth house, you are meant to explore your innermost self and find your connection with the Universe. You are also here to heal experiences from your past and thereby free yourself from old karma and things that limit your life. Look at the current sign here in combination with the ascendant sign to see what energies you carry strongly when meeting others.

Your Birth Chart carries Magical Keys,
keys that can unlock new doors on your life journey.

Interpreting nuances and energies in your chart gives you
endless possibilities for healing & expansion.

Want to learn more?
If you are interested in delving deeper and learning
the basics of Spiritual Astrology, we offer sessions and readings on:
www.hansmartinatwinflames.com

THANK YOU FOR YOUR TIME!

If you enjoyed this book and found it helpful, we would be so grateful if you could take a moment to share your experience by leaving a review. It can help us reach out to more people - thereby showing how we can use spiritual astrology to develop and reach our potential.

Follow our Newsletter and get your free spiritual Activation and E-Book.

56342166R00215